THE MAKING OF AMERICAN CATHOLICISM

The Making of American Catholicism

Regional Culture and the Catholic Experience

Michael J. Pfeifer

NEW YORK UNIVERSITY PRESS
New York

NEW YORK UNIVERSITY PRESS
New York
www.nyupress.org

References to Internet websites (URLs) were accurate at the time of writing. Neither the author nor New York University Press is responsible for URLs that may have expired or changed since the manuscript was prepared.

Library of Congress Cataloging-in-Publication Data
Names: Pfeifer, Michael J. (Michael James), 1968–   author.
Title: The making of American Catholicism : regional culture and the Catholic experience / Michael J. Pfeifer.
Description: New York : New York University Press, 2021. |
Includes bibliographical references and index.
Identifiers: LCCN 2020015829 (print) | LCCN 2020015830 (ebook) |
ISBN 9781479829453 (cloth) | ISBN 9781479889426 (paperback) |
ISBN 9781479801824 (ebook) | ISBN 9781479804184 (ebook)
Subjects: LCSH: Catholic Church—United States —Influence.
Classification: LCC BX1406.3 .P44 2021 (print) | LCC BX1406.3 (ebook) | DDC 282/.73—dc23
LC record available at https://lccn.loc.gov/2020015829

LC ebook record available at https://lccn.loc.gov/2020015830
New York University Press books are printed on acid-free paper, and their binding materials are chosen for strength and durability. We strive to use environmentally responsible suppliers and materials to the greatest extent possible in publishing our books.

Manufactured in the United States of America

10 9 8 7 6 5 4 3 2 1

Also available as an ebook

In memoriam, Daniel Golebiewski

CONTENTS

Introduction

This book argues that regional and transnational relationships have been central to the making of American Catholicism. It makes this case by analyzing the development of Catholic cultures in the South, the Midwest, the West, and the Northeast and their contribution to larger patterns of Catholicism in the United States. Exploring the history of Catholic cultures in New Orleans, Iowa, Wisconsin, Los Angeles, and New York City, the book examines the interaction of religiosity, national and cultural origin, race, gender, class, and region in the varied and uneasy synthesis of Catholicism and American identity over time.

In recent decades a lively scholarly literature has sought to determine the nature of the American Catholic experience and the historical factors that have shaped it, showing that American Catholic institutions developed from a delicate interplay of a hierarchical international religious culture centered in Rome with a American republican culture strongly influenced by Protestant and secular critiques of Catholicism.[1] Historians of American Catholicism have also begun to more fully understand that U.S. Catholic history, like that of many American religious groups, did not begin and end at water's edge. Catholics perhaps especially (although hardly exclusively) among U.S. religious groups long sustained strong transnational connections, not only with Rome but well into the twentieth century as well with coreligionists in centers of European Catholic culture including Ireland, France, Belgium, Spain, the Austro-Hungarian Empire, and Bavaria as well as in western hemispheric centers of Catholic culture such as Mexico City.[2]

The study of the history of American Catholicism has been a robust field of inquiry in recent decades, producing conceptually rich social, cultural, and intellectual histories that have broken free from the limitations of traditional Church history with its sometimes narrow institutional and ecclesiastical focus. Yet at times the macro focus of recent American Catholic scholarship has almost looked past the local, the level of the parish and the diocese at which most American Catholics have actually experienced their religious culture(s) since the early nineteenth century. Moreover, American Catholic studies continues to evince comparatively little attention to region, with the weight of scholarship still focused on the Northeast and Mid-Atlantic and little attention paid to the varied regions of the United States west of Buffalo. Yet the American Catholic experience diverged significantly among regions with, for instance, the northeastern pattern of Irish Catholic predominance having less salience in other areas of significant Catholic population such as Louisiana, the Upper Midwest, and Southern California. While histories of American Catholicism have hardly ignored the distinctive geographies of U.S. Catholic historical experience, region has not typically been a central frame of analysis in American Catholic studies, which has tended to emphasize the development of a larger U.S. Catholic consciousness composed of relatively inconsequential regional variations. While, for example, John Tracy Ellis, in his foundational survey *American Catholicism*, acknowledged difference in region and noted that "Catholicism [in the Midwest] has been, perhaps, more progressive and venturesome than in any other region," his pathbreaking analysis focused only intermittently on southern, Midwestern, and western developments. Region is not key to Ellis's analysis, yet it has been a pivotal context for the development of American Catholic cultures.[3] More recent accomplished and valuable surveys of American Catholic history have also certainly been cognizant of region but arguably have not made it integral to their analysis, to an extent understandably so given their goals of synthesis, yet in the process they have underemphasized an important aspect of the spatial and temporal development of American Catholicism.[4]

Immigrant Catholic cultures also have hardly been ignored in the literature, yet the lengthy significance of transnational ties for Catholic cultures in the United States has not been extensively pursued, with many Americanist scholars evincing a water's-edge approach after migration that was never actually experienced by Catholics in the United States. Catholic immigrants in many cases long sustained extracontinental ties with believers in their Catholic homelands through transoceanic and transborder transfers of devotional practices, literatures, and religious objects and through cross-fertilization by clergy and lay travels to and from Rome as well as particular Catholic homelands, including Ireland, Germany and Austria, France and Belgium, Spain and Mexico.

Eschewing a national or nationalistic focus that might elide or neglect global connections or local complexity, this book offers an interpretation of the American Catholic experience that encompasses local, national, and transnational histories by emphasizing the diverse origins of Catholic immigrants to the United States, their long-standing ties to transnational communities of Catholic believers, and the role of region in shaping the contours of American Catholic religiosity. The book carefully charts the development of particular local cultures that embody significant aspects of the social history of Catholicism as it evolved in the regions of the South, the Midwest, the West, and the Northeast, and in turn contributed to the making of a larger American Catholicism. I argue that regional American Catholic cultures and a larger American Catholicism developed as transnational Catholic laity and clergy (including French, French Canadian, Belgian, West African, Haitian, German, Czech, Irish, Polish, Spanish, Indigenous, Mexican, Latin American, and Italian) ecclesiastically linked to and by Rome in a hierarchical, authoritarian, and communalistic "universal Church" creatively adapted their devotional and ideological practices in particular American regional contexts that emphasized notions of republicanism, religious liberty, individualistic capitalism, race, gender, and class.

The larger frame is shown in the book through interwoven parish and regional histories. Chapter 1 explores race and Catholicism over time in the American South through a deep case study of a parish in the South's most Catholic city. Our Lady of Lourdes Parish was founded in 1905 as New Orleans expanded in the early twentieth century from its historic concentration along the Mississippi River northward to Lake Pontchartrain, draining swampland and constructing streetcar lines. Lourdes was dedicated to the 1858 French Marian apparition central to fin de siècle European and American Catholic popular devotions. In the early to mid-twentieth century, as the Catholic Church in New Orleans belatedly "Americanized" with the end of the dominance of French-speaking clergy and a shift from Creole patterns of religiosity that emphasized independence and anticlericalism to American Catholic ones that emphasized obedience and respect for clerical authority, Lourdes emerged as a prestigious, growing parish pastored by monsignors and attended by working-class and middle-class white residents of the Uptown Freret neighborhood. In line with the racial segregation of New Orleans Catholicism in the early twentieth century, pastors discouraged worship by the sizable numbers of black Catholics in the neighborhood, telling them they should worship at a nearby "Catholic Negro" territorial parish instead. Blacks who attended Lourdes were relegated to back and side pews and compelled to take communion after whites. However in the 1950s and 1960s, in response to the racial integration of public and parochial schools and the spatial mobility afforded by the automobile, whites increasingly departed the neighborhood for the growing suburbs and the parish uneasily integrated. In the several decades before the church was flooded and damaged in Hurricane Katrina in 2005 and then closed in 2006, African Americans (some were "cradle Catholics" of Creole of Color ancestry, some were converts from black Protestantism) became a majority of parishioners, several African American and West African priests served as pastors, West African nuns served at the parish school, and the worship at Lourdes came to emphasize a synthesis of traditional American Catholic devotional styles with African American and West African music, dance, and oratory. Thus, in the decades prior to its closing in 2006, Lourdes dramatically transitioned from a segregated Jim Crow white parish into a Catholic congregation where African Americans took pride in the centrality of black culture and leadership. This analytical microhistory of Lourdes Parish in the context of the lengthy history of New Orleans Catholicism argues that racism and racial identity divided New Orleans Catholics through segregation, desegregation, and integration, even as a common Catholic culture posited a shared religious identity that transcended racial divisions.

While New Orleans Catholicism is merely one distinctive variant of southern Catholicism, it is an important one, as New Orleans was the nineteenth- and early twentieth-century South's second largest (after Baltimore) and most Catholic city by population, while more than a third of all black Catholics in the early to mid-twentieth-century United States lived in Louisiana. Historian Randall M. Miller's notion of "cultural captivity"—in which minority southern Catholics fit uneasily within a majority Protestant southern culture—works poorly for New Orleans and southwest Louisiana, areas in which Catholics were historically a majority or near majority. The south Louisiana historical experience, involving a culturally predominant Catholic population derived from French and Spanish colonialism, differs meaningfully from the patterns of historically Protestant areas of the Upper and Lower South with a Catholic minority rooted in early modern English Catholicism and the Maryland tradition and then in nineteenth-century Irish immigration. Yet New Orleans Catholicism's major themes of a late Americanization from Gallic roots and an early twentieth-century transition to Jim Crow racial separation has much to tell us about the transnational forging of American Catholic cultures and the tragically significant American Catholic encounter with racism. The experience of African American and French-descended Catholics in New Orleans, whose history dates to colonial Louisiana and in the case of black Catholics involved a shift from inclusion to segregation to integration, also diverges meaningfully from American Catholic histories rooted in mid-nineteenth-century and later European Catholic immigration and adjustment to American conditions in an "Immigrant Church."[5]

The book then shifts to the small-town and rural Midwest, an important but relatively neglected setting in the formation of American Catholic cultures. Chapter 2 charts ethnicity, transnational identities, and parish formation in the nineteenth-century Catholic Midwest. In the antebellum and early postbellum periods, Iowa City was somewhat unique for its relatively modest size in encompassing the diverse, heterogenous character of nineteenth-century Midwestern Catholicism, including significant numbers of Irish, German, and Bohemian (Czech) Catholics. Amid the centrifugal pressures initially exerted by their diversity, the second chapter argues, Iowa City's Catholics experienced in miniature larger processes that would play out across the Midwest and among American Catholics more generally. Uneasily integrated for several decades in a single parish housing the town's three significant ethnic Catholic communities, St. Mary's Parish would fracture in favor of ethnic separatism, the formation of distinct ethnic parishes, in the latter decades of the nineteenth century. Yet in the early to mid-twentieth century, assimilative and Americanization pressures exerted by both the larger society and Church leaders would cut the other way, undermining older particularistic ethnic identities, eventually rendering ethnic Catholicism a quaint memory.

Chapter 3 explores Marian apparitions, gender, ethnicity, and transnational connections in the Upper Midwest. Wisconsin's Catholic culture was fashioned from a multiplicity of ethnic and devotional backgrounds, including strong and evolving notions of Catholic femininity and Marian piety with significant transnational influences. In the latter decades of the nineteenth century, for example, a "cultus" that included a shrine and devoted followers developed around the claims of Adèle Brise, a French-speaking Belgian immigrant and lay "sister" (tertiary), asserting that "Our Lady of Good Help" had appeared to her in Robinsonville (later called Champion) in northeastern Wisconsin in 1858 or 1859. Nearly 150 years later, in December 2010, the bishop of Green Bay, David Ricken, pronounced the apparitions to Adèle Brise valid, making these the only American apparitions to be officially recognized by the Catholic Church. By contrast, in 1955, the bishop of La Crosse, John P. Treacy, found Mary Ann Van Hoof's claim of receiving apparitions from "the Queen of the Holy Rosary, Mediatrix of Peace" in Necedah in central Wisconsin to be inauthentic, and he prohibited Catholics from worshipping with Van Hoof and her followers. Lacing her reports of Mary's appearances with apocalyptic Cold War rhetoric that sought the conversion of Americans to devotion to Mary to avert atomic mass destruction at the hands of the atheistic Soviets, Van Hoof's claims briefly attracted thousands of Midwestern Catholics, including significant numbers of Polish Americans, seeking mystical experiences of Mary during the height of the Cold War in 1949–50. The history of Wisconsin's Marian apparitions suggests the crucial role of transnational and ethnic Catholic identities in the forging of an American Catholic culture. It also suggests the neglected but meaningful role of the Upper Midwest as a site in the perpetuation of a Marian Revival that stretched from Catholic Europe to far-flung global outposts of Catholic immigration and evangelization. Catholic Wisconsinites, along with French, Portuguese, Poles, Germans, Mexicans, and others, have inventively deployed the Marian image as they have contended with rising nation-states and social change that sometimes has impinged on Catholic identity and the primacy of local interests. Seers of Mary, many of them women such as Adèle Brise and Mary Ann Van Hoof, have claimed prophetic power and social status, leading communities of Marian believers and challenging hierarchical male and clerical authority. More particularly, the persistent appeal of

Adèle Brise's visions of Mary on the Green Bay Peninsula in the 1850s, even as they have been strategically redirected in the early twenty-first century into America's first official Marian apparition cult, indicates the long-term resonance of her refashioning of Catholic femininity and Marian piety within Upper Midwestern Catholic culture.

Chapter 4 moves westward beyond the plains, the Rockies, and the Sierras, tracing the evolving significance of colonialism, national origin, ethnicity, and Catholic culture in Southern California. In 1814, a Franciscan priest, Fray Luis Gil y Taboada, laid the cornerstone for a church at the founding plaza of Los Angeles, at the site of the original "submission" chapel established by the Spanish in 1784. Originally intended to serve mixed-race settlers, La Iglesia de Nuestra Señora la Reina de los Ángeles (the Church of Our Lady Queen of Angels), nicknamed La Placita, became the focal point of Catholic culture in Los Angeles—and of the mediation of cultural relationships between Hispano-descended Catholics and the largely Protestant Americans who migrated into Southern California after American annexation in 1846. As Los Angeles rapidly urbanized in the late nineteenth and twentieth centuries and Mexican Catholics lost their majority status, the Plaza Church came to represent to Anglo-Americans the region's purportedly quaint and anachronistic Spanish past. With significant migration from Mexico to Los Angeles in the early twentieth century, the Plaza Church remained a key locale for Mexican American Catholic religiosity, but it also became a central site for white Angelenos' fashioning of a usable past and reconstruction of a vivid historical tableaux amid Los Angeles's rapid growth, effacement of much of the historical landscape, and vilification of Mexican Americans. However, as Latin Americans migrated to Los Angeles in large numbers in the latter decades of the twentieth century, La Placita took on new, dynamic roles that put a new spin on its historical status as the spiritual beachhead of the Spanish colonization of indigenous peoples in what became Los Angeles. Since the 1970s, La Placita has become a key site for Mexican and Salvadoran immigrant religious devotions and community rituals, a center for activism on behalf of immigrants' rights, and a sanctuary for Latin American immigrants threatened with deportation by the U.S. government.

This chapter's close analysis of La Placita's history highlights the significance of Latinos in American Catholic history and the inadequacy of interpretations that have largely neglected the presence of Hispanic Catholics before the mid- to late twentieth century or inaccurately emphasized the fragility or collapse of Hispanic Catholic traditions after the American annexation of areas that had been under Spanish and Mexican control. There were many Catholic Wests, all shaped to an extent by the relatively transitory nature of migration and residence in the region. For example, San Francisco's and Sacramento's Northern California Catholicism was much more influenced by Irish clerics than Los Angeles's. La Placita's history indicates the distinctive trajectories of the formation of Catholic cultures in the American West, histories that do not comfortably fit a Catholic history model based upon European Catholic immigration and Americanization.[6]

Chapter 5 moves back east, exploring Irish American Catholicism and the shifting contours of urban northeastern Catholic identity from the nineteenth century through the twentieth. The Irish-born archbishop John Hughes created Manhattan's Holy Cross Parish in 1852 to serve the thousands of Irish Catholics moving north of Lower Manhattan into what became known as Longacre Square (later Times Square) and the developing neighborhood of Hell's Kitchen. Pastored by Irish, Irish American, and Irish Canadian priests, Holy Cross maintained a strong Irish American identity into the mid-twentieth century. Holy Cross's path charted the transformation of the disciplined folk piety created by the "devotional revolution" in Ireland in the nineteenth century into an American Catholicism dominated by Irish American clergy who sought to defend communalistic Catholic distinctiveness amid the rapid urban growth and burgeoning individualistic capitalism of a historically Protestant nation. Holy Cross experienced the complexities of this Irish American forging of an American Catholicism. Ulster-born Charles McCready, rector from 1877 until 1913 and an ardent Irish nationalist, was recruited to New York by Dr. Edward McGlynn, who would draw international attention as the fiery rector of the working-class Irish parish of St. Stephen's in Manhattan, where McCready initially served him as assistant. In 1887, Archbishop Michael A. Corrigan removed McGlynn as rector of St. Stephen when he refused to repudiate his endorsement of antimonopolist Henry George's single tax doctrine that sought to redress the inequalities created by Gilded Age capitalism. After McGlynn refused to report to Rome, Church authorities excommunicated him. In 1894, two years after the Vatican's apostolic delegate, Francesco Satolli, lifted McGlynn's excommunication, the radical Irish American priest celebrated Christmas Mass at Holy Cross, pastored by his longtime friend Charles McCready.

Fr. Francis Duffy, pastor at Holy Cross from 1920 to 1932, drew national fame as chaplain for the U.S. Army's 69th Regiment in World War I (including a cinematic treatment in the 1940 film *The Fighting 69th*, in which Pat O'Brien portrayed Duffy). Over the course of his career, Duffy strove to reconcile Americanism with Catholicism. Prior to his appointment at Holy Cross, Duffy edited an innovative and liberal theological journal, the *New York Review*, which was shuttered by the archdiocese after Pope Pius X's 1907 condemnation of the heresy of modernism. During his time at Holy Cross, Fr. Duffy helped author Catholic Democratic presidential candidate Al Smith's impassioned 1927 defense in the *Atlantic Monthly* of the ability of American Catholics to serve in public office against those who charged that fealty to Rome rendered Catholics incapable of good republican citizenship and responsible officeholding. Monsignor Joseph McCaffrey, who pastored Holy Cross in the tumultuous years of social change from 1932 until 1968, created a highly popular radio ministry around the Miraculous Medal Novena as New York Catholicism suburbanized from its roots in ethnic parishes in Manhattan. A longtime chaplain with the New York City Police Department, McCaffrey also articulated an outspoken reactionary stance on urban cultural change, including smut, juvenile delinquency, and the postwar urban crime wave. McCaffrey participated in a white ethnic Catholic reaction against the postwar city that would contribute to the reconfiguration of American conservativism in the latter decades of the twentieth century. From its historic Irish American identity with strong ties to Tammany Hall and the New York City Police Department, Holy Cross transitioned with dramatic shifts in the demographics of Hell's Kitchen in the mid- to late twentieth century into a parish serving a racially and economically diverse flock.

Holy Cross's story charts key themes and moments in the development of an Irish American Catholic and white ethnic Catholic identity, including the emergence of a reconfigured devotional culture in the wake of the Irish famine, the elaboration of ultramontane concepts of Church hierarchy, and the working out of notions of relations between Irish-descended Catholics and American culture, including in matters of politics and race. In sum, New York City's influential urban Irish American Catholicism, as with regional American Catholic cultures in the South, Midwest, and West, inventively drew from local, national, and transnational sources to achieve a difficult and uneven synthesis of Catholic and American cultures.

Clerical sexual abuse emerges at times in these pages, for example in the first chapter's discussion of Fr. Malcolm B. Strassel, the white pastor of Our Lady of Lourdes in New Orleans from 1968 to 1975, a pivotal period when the once segregated lilywhite parish achieved an African American majority as African Americans stayed in or joined the parish and white parishioners left. In 2009, two decades after his death in 1987, Strassel was credibly accused of fondling a boy's genitals in the early years of his pastorate at Lourdes. The archdiocese paid to settle a civil suit brought by Strassel's victim, which the archdiocese finally acknowledged in 2018, when it released a list of fifty-seven credibly accused New Orleans clergy. Strassel's abuse also highlights how historical patterns of clerical sexual abuse have disproportionately harmed Catholics of color, African American, Latinx, and Native American young persons who, given their communities' lack of status and resources, have been less protected from predatory clergy than white children.[7] While the Church's secrecy surrounding such cases until recently and the limitations of the information that dioceses have released are significant handicaps, clerical sexual abuse is a major theme in American Catholic history (and in the history of other American religious denominations and nonreligious organizations). In the American Catholic context, key factors in the history of clerical sexual abuse are the highly patriarchal nature of the Church's organization; the "otherness" and countercultural nature of its sexual and gender norms (nonmarried, celibate clergy; nonmarried, celibate religious sisters); the traditional power and influence of priests within Catholic communities; and the gap between the Church's emphasis on celibate clergy and an American culture from the early twentieth century onward interested in expanding notions of sexual freedom. While statistics suggest a preponderance of clerical abusers underwent seminary formation between the 1950s and 1970s, scattered cases of credibly accused earlier abusers (for example in the early twentieth century) suggest clerical sexual abuse is hardly new but is profoundly historically constructed, with abuse and abusers shaped by historical trends and by a greater recognition of the problem in more recent decades and a greater ability of victims to come forward as well as most recently a greater willingness of the Church to acknowledge credible accusations. Catholic homophobia, which has informed the response of the Catholic right to the clerical abuse scandal in an effort to blame homosexuality and gay priests for clerical abuse, is also historically constructed, a conservative reaction against the emergence of gay identity and the notion of sexual orientation in the mid- to late twentieth century. Like all of the American Catholic history in this book, clerical sexual abuse partakes of a dynamic interaction of particular Catholic cultures and American society and culture, in ways that facilitated clerical sexual predation, its concealment by Church hierarchy, and, eventually in the early twenty-first century, efforts to redress this problem and its largely unacknowledged history.[8]

My approach in this book is admittedly heuristic. With simultaneous emphasis on the local, regional, national, and transnational, I revive parish history without its problematic antiquarian and overly pietistic rather than analytical tendencies. Rather than a top-down or bottom-up approach, I alternate looking at clergy and laity, as both were important in a hierarchical Church that depended not only on bishops, diocesan priests, and men and women in religious orders, but also on the faith and the support of laywomen and laymen.

The analysis throughout is guided by Leslie Woodcock Tentler's still relevant 1993 observation that Catholic studies lies on the margins of the study of American history. Despite some progress, Catholic history is still not sufficiently integrated into academic understandings of the American past. Catholicism seems to be particularly awkward for historians with its refusal to easily fit within prevailing political analyses, in light of the still lively intellectual legacy of nineteenth-century American anti-Catholicism, and due to the secular bent of most academic history that construes religiosity as more of a problem or an aberration than a meaningful cultural phenomenon.[9] Yet even within an era of rapidly declining formal religious affiliation, at 20 percent of the population, Catholics still make up the largest religious denomination in the United

States—a status they have held since the mid-nineteenth century—and Catholicism simply must be taken seriously to understand American cultural, social, and political history. Throughout this book, I have employed my skills as an American social historian to seek to understand the role of the complex Catholic experience in the development of particular American regional cultures and in the creation of a larger American social landscape.

1

The Strange Career of New Orleans Catholicism

Race and Our Lady of Lourdes Parish, 1905–2006

On a sunny, steamy morning in early August 2005, around a dozen worshippers gathered for nine o'clock Mass in a side chapel of Our Lady of
Lourdes Church, a mission-style edifice on Napoleon Avenue in Uptown
New Orleans's Freret neighborhood. As the air conditioning softly
rumbled, a young Nigerian priest, Fr. Raphael Ezeh, celebrated Mass,
assisted at the altar by the church's seventy-four-year-old deacon Everett
Williams, a former seminary student who had served as the first African American superintendent of public schools in New Orleans from
1985 until 1992. The mostly African American worshippers were joined
by several habit-wearing Nigerian nuns, sisters from the Daughters of
Divine Love who helped to run the parish's school. Hymns before and
after Mass and responses during the liturgy blended African American
and Igbo cadences and idioms. At the prayers of the faithful when the
priest asked what else should be prayed for, one parishioner requested
the intercession of Our Lady of Prompt Succor for protection against
hurricanes, making recourse to a Marian devotion that had originated
in French Creole New Orleans in the early nineteenth century, in the
wake of the anticlerical French Revolution and the Louisiana Purchase
that would bring an inundation of Protestant Americans. The interces-
sions ended that morning with a prayer for blessings for the upcoming
celebration of the parish's hundredth anniversary, which was scheduled
to be held in a month's time.[1]

Long-unfolding patterns of culture, religiosity, and social change that
spanned several continents and centuries helped to fashion the small
weekday gathering of the Catholic faithful in Uptown New Orleans a
few weeks before Hurricane Katrina devastated and transformed the
Crescent City. This chapter closely traces the history of Our Lady of
Lourdes Parish from its founding in 1905 through its closing after Ka-

trina in 2006 as a window into the evolution of the South's most Catholic city from the nineteenth century through the twentieth, with a particular focus on the evolving significance of race and the role of transnational identities. Lourdes's difficult and lengthy journey displays not merely the distinctiveness of Louisiana and New Orleans Catholicism, rooted in a French Catholic heritage rather than an Irish Catholic one, but also the vexatious encounter of southern Catholics with race and the complex adaptation and synthesis of particular transnational and ethnic Catholic cultures in the working out of a larger American Catholicism. An analytical microhistory of Lourdes Parish in the context of the lengthy history of New Orleans Catholicism reveals that racism and racial identity divided New Orleans Catholics through segregation, desegregation, and integration, even as a common Catholic culture posited a shared religious identity that transcended racial divisions. Throughout the experience of Lourdes Parish, and in New Orleans Catholicism more broadly in the twentieth century, the particularities of white supremacism and racial identity interacted in dynamic tension with the universalistic claims of a common Catholic culture embracing all believers even as the New Orleans Church belatedly Americanized from its Gallic roots. One product of this tension was the distinct black Catholic culture that emerged at black-majority Catholic parishes in the Crescent City as black Catholics struggled against racism in the Church, vividly so at Lourdes because the parish itself was transformed during the desegregation period from a Jim Crow white parish into an African American–majority parish. While white supremacy and segregated parishes shaped the experience of African American Catholics elsewhere in the country, as we will see when we look at New York City in this book's fifth chapter, the concentration of large numbers of black Catholics in the Crescent City and the South's full-scale adoption of Jim Crow eventually led to the creation of thoroughly (but never completely) separate white and black Catholic worlds. New Orleans then is a key locale for understanding the American Catholic encounter with race and racism and the ways in which African American Catholics have shaped a black Catholic culture as they have resisted white supremacy within the Church.[2]

I

In the spring of 1905, New Orleans archbishop Placide Louis Chapelle decided to establish a new Catholic parish to serve the Crescent City's expanding Uptown neighborhood after a committee of three priests surveyed the developing area intersected by Napoleon Avenue north of St. Charles Avenue and found eighty to ninety Catholic families living there. While press reports initially suggested that the church might be designated Our Lady of Mercy, Chapelle, perhaps after consulting with the thirty-eight-year-old English born priest Leslie J. Kavanagh, whom he would soon appoint as pastor, denominated the new church Notre Dame de Lourdes, dedicating it to arguably the most popular Marian apparition of the late nineteenth and early twentieth centuries, a particular devotion to Mary that had emerged in the decades since 1858 as central to French and transatlantic Catholic devotional cultures.[3] Responding to and anticipating Uptown expansion and population growth, Archbishop Chapelle determined that the parish's boundaries would encompass a wide swath of expanding (and as yet unbuilt) Uptown lying from east to west between Louisiana and Peters (now Jefferson) avenues and north to south between Claiborne and St. Charles avenues. Fr. Kavanagh, appointed pastor on April 20, 1905, soon purchased property on Napoleon Avenue bounded by Freret, Jena, and Howard (later renamed LaSalle) streets. In the following months, Kavanagh oversaw the construction of a building that housed a church (on the second floor), rectory (at the front of the first floor), and school (encompassing the rest of the ground level). The pastor invited nuns from the Province of the Sisters of Christian Charity, whose community already worked in nearby St. Henry Parish, to staff the school. The death of Archbishop Chapelle in a yellow fever epidemic delayed dedication of the church until Sunday, September 11, but Fr. Kavanagh celebrated the first Mass at Lourdes on August 15, the Feast of the Assumption.[4]

The early twentieth-century opening of Lourdes marked the spatial and Catholic expansion of Uptown New Orleans as the Crescent City and its Catholic institutions extended from their historical concentration on the natural levee of the Mississippi River north to the swamplands that abutted Lake Pontchartrain. Founded in 1718 by French colonizers, New Orleans remained a remote port through which the French and Spanish empires shipped tobacco and indigo until purchase by the United States in 1803 made the Crescent City central to the lucrative export of cotton and sugar and to the internal trade in slaves that labored in the expanding cotton and sugar hinterlands of the Mississippi River Delta and Gulf Plain. The Americans inherited an ethnic and religious landscape shaped by French and Spanish colonialism and strong ties to the French and Spanish Caribbean. French-speaking Catholic Creoles from a variety of French, Hispanic, and West African backgrounds lived near the river in neighborhoods comingling slaveholders, their slaves, and a third social caste, free persons of color (*gens de couleur libre*). Ten thousand refugees from the successful rebellion of slaves against French rule in Saint-Domingue nearly doubled the Crescent City's population and significantly augmented its share of Creoles of Color after Spain expelled them from Cuba in 1809–10. Incorporation by the United States also brought increasing numbers of Americans into the city, along with their Protestantism, binary notions of race that contrasted with the tripartite caste system that had prevailed under French and Spanish control, and Anglo-American understandings of commerce, law, and public culture. With some exceptions, white Americans and their slaves settled the upper blocks of the old city, where American commercial activity flourished in what came to be known as the American Quarter, today's Central Business District, in contrast to the lower blocks, the French Quarter (Vieux Carré), where white Creoles and Creoles of Color predominated. Affluent Americans built palatial residences in the Garden District along St. Charles Avenue stretching Uptown, conveniently located in an area at low risk from flooding and at equal distance from the environmental and social hazards of the Mississippi riverfront and the "back of town" swamplands where the city's poorest, many of them African American, lived. The city's ethnic composition acquired even further complexity in the 1840s as thousands of Irish and Germans, many of them Catholic, took passage to the South's leading port and joined the city's ranks of laborers, artisans, and entrepreneurs, many of them settling in semirural areas on the urban periphery, such as the Uptown riverfront district of wharves and warehouses that became known as the Irish Channel.[5]

New Orleans experienced an eventful Civil War, which included Union Army occupation in 1862 and a violent reconstruction, as white conservatives contested black Creoles', freed persons', and white Republicans' quest for racially egalitarian governance in a deadly 1866 race riot. The Crescent City saw further transformation in the postbellum years, even as it lost its antebellum prominence as a transportation hub to northern ports and railroads and its business life suffered a stagnation that made it relatively unattractive to immigrants compared to burgeoning northern cities. Following the Civil War, large numbers of freed people flocked to the city from outlying plantations, doubling the African American population from 25,423 (14,484 enslaved) in 1860 to 50,456 in 1870. Thousands of Sicilians added a Southern European dimension to the historically Creole French Quarter in the late nineteenth century. The construction of streetcar lines along St. Charles Avenue further uptown and along Esplanade Avenue northeast of the French Quarter in the late nineteenth century enabled elites to leave the inner city for fashionable suburbs on what had been the semirural periphery. The exodus of the gentry for streetcar suburbs enabled immigrants such as Sicilian Catholics and Eastern European Jews to convert many inner-city residences into tenement housing as they secured livelihoods as vendors in municipal markets. At the same time, Creoles of Color, many of them Catholics still resident in the historically Creole lower districts of the city, lost standing as their traditional intermediate status between whites and enslaved blacks within a tripartite racial order collapsed with the ongoing Americanization of New Orleans and the rise of Jim Crow racial proscription after Reconstruction. In *Plessy v. Ferguson* (1896), the U.S. Supreme Court validated Jim Crow and the doctrine of separate but equal, rejecting black Creole (and Catholic) Homer Plessy's claim to equal accommodation on the New Orleans streetcars. Although older identities retained some salience and Creoles of Color such as Homer Plessy resisted the drawing of the color line in public accommodations and, as we shall see, within Crescent City Catholicism, the rise of Jim Crow drew a line between whites and blacks that in the twentieth century erased the older and more intricate set of racial relationships that had developed under the influence of French and Spanish colonialism and Caribbean immigration in the city's formative years.[6]

New Orleans's significant population growth and spatial expansion out to Lake Pontchartrain created the Freret neighborhood that would develop around Our Lady of Lourdes in the early twentieth century. In

the nineteenth century the "back of town" areas that became Freret con-
sisted of flood-prone wetlands of the Bouligny and Avart plantations.
Clearing and settlement of the swamp began in the mid-nineteenth century with the establishment of Catholic and municipal cemeteries on
Soniat and Valence streets, and by the 1880s residential building had
begun gingerly "back of town," with Victorian houses lining several
blocks from the Lake Pontchartrain side of St. Charles Avenue to Dry-
ades Street. At this point, Freret Street, an artery named after an antebellum New Orleans mayor and cotton press operator who would give the
district around Lourdes its name, stopped only a few blocks out of the
Central Business District. But substantial port and rail improvements,
the growth of small manufactures, the construction of a ship lane out to
Lake Pontchartrain, and continuing European immigration, especially
from Italy, overwhelmed older residential districts and laid the ground-
work for further Uptown expansion.[7]

The draining of "back of town" swampland with new hydraulic tech-
nology and the establishment of electric and then street rail service on
St. Charles and Napoleon avenues led to the construction of more than
two thousand houses in Freret by 1919. As the neighborhood around
Lourdes filled in, the wealthy moved into mansions lining Napoleon
and Peters avenues, while lower-middle-class and working-class whites
and African Americans rented shotgun houses and bungalows on interior streets. The 1920 census documented Freret as a neighborhood of
considerable racial diversity, 53 percent white, 42 percent black, with
the rest listed as mixed race. A representative 1920 census district included "many who worked as laborer, cook, porter, or laundress" but
also "longshoremen, stenographers, teachers, salesmen, machinists, and
merchants."[8] Most residents were native-born, but many had recent ties
to Italy, Germany, and other European countries; the neighborhood's
preponderance of working-class voters would be supportive of Governor
Huey Long's populism in the Great Depression in the 1930s. Although
Freret encompassed New Orleans's Catholic majority in 1920, the area
was also characterized by religious diversity. African American Protestants worshipped at two Baptist churches, white Protestants formed
Methodist Episcopal and Baptist congregations, and New Orleans's Jewish population also had a meaningful presence in the recently formed
neighborhood. The Southern Baptist Convention funded the construc-

tion of Baptist Hospital up the street from Lourdes in 1924; priests from Lourdes would minister to Catholic patients at Baptist Hospital, which did not admit black patients until 1968. Small businesses and shops, many established by Italian and Jewish merchants in the years that followed the opening of Lourdes in 1905, clustered on Freret Street near the growing Our Lady of Lourdes plant, and in 1924 the New Orleans Public Service established a streetcar line down Freret linking downtown with Tulane and Loyola universities further uptown.[9]

The journalist and historian Coleman Warner describes Freret in the first decades of the twentieth century as a late example of "the 'old walking city' model, with homes built close together, sidewalks and streets used as public gathering spaces, and residences located a short walk away from shops and churches."[10] Warner notes that Freret replicated the biracial residential pattern evident in New Orleans's American section in which "wide boulevards with grassy divides (known as 'neutral grounds') served as corridors of residence for affluent white families and as boundaries for a 'superblock' that grew more and more black—and working class—as one neared the neighborhood's center."[11] Proximity did not mean the integration of blacks and whites, however, as Jim Crow barred African Americans from eating and drinking with whites at Freret's restaurants and bars, receiving care at the same hospital as whites, or attending the same schools or worshipping at the same churches, including Our Lady of Lourdes, as whites.[12]

II

The opening of Lourdes in 1905 extended and took meaning from the lengthy history of Catholicism in New Orleans. Unlike eastern cities such as Boston, Philadelphia, New York, Charleston, or even Baltimore, the South's largest city had possessed a Catholic majority for most of its formal history. New Orleans's Creole Catholic culture was thoroughly Gallic, shaped by evangelization by continental religious orders during French and Spanish colonial control and, for a century after the American purchase in 1803, the persistence of practices of importing priests and bishops from France and of using the French language in the vernacular portion of Masses. Only fitful efforts were made at recruiting native-born, English-speaking clergy, initiatives that many Francophone clergy opposed. Several elements distinguished New Orleans's French Creole Catholicism from American Catholic norms as they were developing elsewhere in the country. Strains of continental French piety, rationalism, and republicanism, such as Jansenism, Voltairianism, and Gallicanism, strongly influenced white and black Creole thought and behavior in an independent, skeptical, and at times anticlerical direction that resisted ecclesiastical control and simple submission to Church doctrine. The city's Francophone Catholicism entailed a universalistic ethos that welcomed the conversion and inclusion of persons of African descent within the Church's sacramental life. The city's black Creole Catholics in turn grasped the opportunity for dignity and elevation in status that participation in Church institutions conferred. The arrival in the city of thousands of Catholics from Ireland, Germany, and Sicily in the nineteenth century had meant the establishment of parishes with Irish, German, and Sicilian majorities but had done little to undercut the prevalence of French-speaking clergy and the leadership of French-born ecclesiastics. For example, in 1860, only eight out of thirty-two diocesan priests had Irish or Anglo-American surnames; in 1880, a mere twelve out of seventy-two clerics bore "Irish or Anglo-Saxon names"; in 1887, one hundred diocesan priests spoke French and only seven did not; and as late as 1914, nearly half of the 163 diocesan priests had been born in France or Alsace-Lorraine. The Irish American Catholic culture that came to dominate the urban Northeast, a blending of Irish folk piety and Victorian values of self-discipline and respect for authority forged in post-famine Ireland and in the Irish diaspora in northern U.S. cities, had comparatively little influence in New Orleans.[13] French-born Archbishop Chapelle thus established Lourdes Parish even as the Crescent City's Catholic culture remained profoundly Gallic but on the verge of a late Americanization that would undercut long-standing French control and Creole dominance by the first decades of the twentieth century.

Religious orders that arose amid the universalistic, evangelical thrust of early modern Catholic reform in the era of the Protestant Reformation shaped the early contours of New Orleans's Creole Catholicism. The work of Catholic religious orders in colonial Louisiana occurred in the context of French and Spanish imperial mandates that all inhabitants of the colony, whether indigenous, settlers, or slaves, should possess Catholic identity, a marked contrast to the ambivalence that the Protestant

English displayed toward conversion of Natives and slaves in their North American colonies. Angela Merici founded a community of religious women devoted to the teaching of girls and the care of the ill in Brescia, Italy, in 1535, and the Ursulines quickly spread throughout Western Europe, including France. Twelve Ursuline sisters arrived in Louisiana in 1727 and in the following decades educated women of European, African, and indigenous ancestry. The Ursulines made considerable effort at baptizing and catechizing West African slave women. The French halted direct importation of slaves into Louisiana in 1743, assisting the Ursulines' cultivation of a community of pious Afro-Creole Catholic women, including slaves and free women of color, who would play instrumental roles in catechizing West African women and slave women from Protestant areas of the American South with the resumption of the slave trade under Spanish control in 1776 and with the American purchase in 1803.[14] Emily Clark and Virginia Meacham Gould argue that "the practice of maternally administered religious initiation in Senegambia [in West Africa] harmonized with the mother-centered approach of the Ursulines."[15] Meanwhile the Capuchins, a preaching order of friars established in Italy in 1520 in an effort to revive Franciscan ideals of poverty and simplicity, served as parochial priests in colonial New Orleans, administering the sacraments to Catholics of European, African, and Native American descent, including the baptism of children born out of wedlock to interracial liaisons. The Capuchins apparently left catechesis of nonwhites to the Ursulines, whose efforts were directed at women. Evidence suggests that Afro-Creole women, not European religious, may have been the primary agents in converting men of African descent to Catholicism as colonial New Orleans's Creole religious order emerged in the mid- to late eighteenth century.[16]

Free women of color sustained Catholicism in New Orleans in the late eighteenth and early nineteenth centuries as the French Revolution severed French state support for Catholic institutions and as the American purchase brought an inundation of Protestant Anglophones. However, in 1812 Rome appointed the French missionary priest Louis William Doubourg bishop of New Orleans, renewing the Crescent City's ties to French Catholicism and initiating an influx of French clergy and religious participating in a postrevolutionary Catholic revivalism that sought to return French society to a universalistic organic Catholic order.[17] Even as incipient Americanization began to challenge Catholic Creole New Orleans's comparatively inclusive ethos and more intricate and flexible notions of race, Henriette Delille, a free woman of color descended from a slave woman baptized and catechized by the Ursulines, worked with several companions in 1842 in New Orleans to found the Soeurs de Sainte Famille, or Sisters of the Holy Family, "the first Catholic religious congregation created by and for African American women," in order to aid free women of color and enslaved persons of African descent. Crucially, free persons of color also organized and supported Catholic schools, most notably L'Institution Catholique des Orphelins Indigents (the Catholic Institute for Indigent Orphans), also known as the Couvent School after its Afro-Creole benefactor, Marie Couvent. Creoles of Color similarly contributed funds to the building of new parishes, most notably St. Augustine in 1842, which would become a key location for the development of Afro-Creole Catholic identity in the Crescent City. But there were limits to the inclusivity of New Orleans's antebellum Catholicism. Black Creoles sat in separate pews from whites (who were often their relatives), while slaves sat in galleries or on side benches. The diocese also mandated separate sacramental registers for whites, Creoles of Color, and slaves, and cemeteries with separate areas for deceased whites and blacks. Creoles of Color maintained complex relationships with slaves, whom they sometimes knew intimately and sought to manumit and catechize, but whom they sometimes owned and felt a keen sense of social distinction from.[18] Historian Stephen J. Ochs holds that the black Creoles' "Gallic Catholicism, with its tinge of anti-clericalism, tended to emphasize communal activity and celebration organized around holy days and patron saints rather than a rigid adherence to rules of conduct or to dogma."[19]

As the persistently Gallic church in New Orleans fell fitfully in the nineteenth century into the orbit of the proslavery, racially reactionary leadership of the American Catholic Church that aligned with northern urban Irish immigrants and southern slaveholders in the Democratic Party, black Creoles drew on old and new religious ideologies and practices to craft a strain of community organization and political radicalism that would challenge emerging trends of American racial proscription. Numbering nearly eleven thousand and representing 6 percent of the Crescent City's population in 1860, this "influential urban minority" uti-

lized Jansenism, Vincentian ideals, and spiritualism as well as continuing republican ideals shaped by the French revolutionary heritage, the
recent Revolutions of 1848, and the French Empire's abolition of slavery
and grant of suffrage to ex-slaves in 1850 to assert dignity, equality, and
inclusivity against the rising tide of racial subordination and separation.[20] Jansenism, an offshoot of seventeenth-century French Catholic
reform that was condemned and ineffectually suppressed by the papacy
and the French monarchy, stressed individual conscience and a return
to core Christian principles and charitable acts against the worldliness of
the institutional Church. To the scandal of English-speaking priests assigned to Louisiana by Baltimore bishop John Carroll after 1803, Jansenism's democratic millenarian perfectionism thrived in French-speaking
Louisiana with the toleration of the Capuchin friars who administered
the Crescent City's racially inclusionary sacramental life, most notably
Antonio de Sedella, the rector of St. Louis Cathedral for several decades
before and after the Louisiana Purchase. Sedella contended with Archbishop Carroll to preserve Creole control of the cathedral and championed fair treatment of free blacks and slaves. For decades after, the
cathedral's large, racially mixed congregation attested to the legacy of the
inclusive, if paternalistically protectionist, vision of the Capuchins and
the Ursulines.[21] Afro-Creoles found similar inspiration in the culture of
seventeenth-century French Catholic reform in St. Vincent de Paul, an
advocate of a humanitarian mystical piety that emphasized charitable
works and himself an erstwhile slave in Tunis who converted his Muslim master (a Frenchman who had converted to Islam) back to Catholicism. The pro-Unionist, antislavery Afro-Creole newspaper *L'Union* ran
a lengthy, heavily romanticized serialized account of St. Vincent's life as
federal troops occupied the Crescent City in 1862.[22] Many black Creoles
also joined white French-speaking Catholics after 1850 in participating
in the growing popularity of spiritualism, acting as mediums to channel otherworldly utopian messages of universal brotherhood and world
harmony. Spiritualism in New Orleans pulled together diffuse currents
of early modern Catholic reform spirituality (St. Vincent de Paul and St.
Teresa of Avila were leading figures), enlightenment, and democratic
revolutionary era thought and utopian communitarian thinkers such
as Charles Fourier to advocate an egalitarian, experiential alternative
to orthodox religion and the increasingly reactionary social currents of

mid-nineteenth-century Louisiana. Resonating with earlier tendencies in Afro-Creole religiosity, spiritualism may have appealed to disaffected black Catholics as an alternative to an increasingly proslavery and eventually pro-Confederate institutional Church in Louisiana.[23]

Black Creoles in the Crescent City organized to confront a rising tide of racial reaction. Creoles of Color joined myriad fraternal and occupational organizations, religious confraternities, and benevolent societies and in the Civil War participated in Confederate and then (after Union occupation) federal militia. Voicing their stance for emancipation and racial equality in the newspaper *L'Union* and its successor, the *New Orleans Tribune*, Afro-Creoles also backed French-born priest Claude Paschal Maistre in his dispute with French-born archbishop Jean-Marie Odin. Archbishop Odin, like most of the clergy who served him in New Orleans, staunchly supported the Confederacy. Fr. Maistre, by contrast, championed racial egalitarianism and emancipation, aided black refugees (some of whom were escaped slaves), and refused to segregate the sacramental registers at his integrated parish, St. Rose of Lima. Declaring that Maistre was "inciting Negroes,"[24] Archbishop Odin suspended the renegade abolitionist cleric and placed his parish under interdict in 1863. Despite his disagreements with Maistre, Odin also defended the unique arrangements that existed for black Catholics in New Orleans, perhaps in part due to the important contributions black Creoles made to church coffers. Odin strongly resisted efforts at implementing segregation and separate black parishes at the Second Plenary Council of American Bishops in Baltimore in 1866. Forced by Odin to vacate St. Rose of Lima in 1864, Fr. Maistre worked with black Creoles to establish a new church without archdiocesan approbation, Holy Name of Jesus, at Ursulines and Claiborne streets. Fr. Maistre led his schismatic parish and championed black empowerment with substantial black Catholic support, including from the radical press, until his submission to the ecclesiastical authority of a new archbishop, the French-born Napoleon J. Perché, in 1870. Two decades later, the Crescent City's tradition of black Catholic protest found further outlet when Homer Plessy, who had been married in St. Augustine Church in 1888, challenged the legal basis of the city's racial segregation of its streetcars.[25]

In the late nineteenth century, drawing on their heritage of inclusion, egalitarianism, and self-activity, black Catholics resisted the segregation of the Crescent City's churches. In 1888, the Vatican appointed Dutch-born Francis Janssens as archbishop. Janssens had served seven years as bishop of Natchez, Mississippi, developing ties to the liberal American-ist wing of the Church hierarchy (most notably Archbishop James Gib-bons of Baltimore). Before the Americanist tendency was condemned by Pope Leo XII in 1899, liberal Americanist clerics had sought to adapt the Church to American conditions and to link Catholicism with social action, eschewing the conservative Catholic "perfect society" model that had long advocated conversion of individual souls but accommodation with state and society on social and political matters. Janssens raised hackles among Francophone clergy because he lacked French nativity and sought to Americanize the Church in New Orleans by opening a seminary to train native-born priests (the seminary would be closed by Janssens's French-born successor, Placide Chapelle). Although they wel-comed Janssens's condemnation of the rising tide of racism in Louisiana, black Creoles strongly opposed the archbishop's desire to implement the racial segregation decrees that had been promulgated by the Third Ple-nary Council of Baltimore in 1884. Janssens's efforts were shaped in part by the archdiocese's dire financial situation, the legacy of the fiscal mis-management of his predecessor, Archbishop Napoleon Perché. In 1889, Janssens obtained the Louisiana legislature's approval for the incorpo-ration of each parish in the archdiocese, thus spreading out the debt and financially enabling parishes that lacked parochial schools to build them. Janssens wished to build parochial schools as part of his Ameri-canization campaign and to serve the unmet educational needs of the city's growing Catholic population, including black Catholic children. Janssens sought to bring New Orleans in line with the Third Baltimore Council by seeking to link each parish with a parochial school. Janssens's parochial school building campaign was complicated by the fact that many Catholic schools in New Orleans, especially those for black stu-dents, had long operated semi-independently of parishes. Furthermore, the segregation of public schools and defunding of black public educa-tion after Reconstruction in Louisiana had left Catholic schools as often the only resort for black students. These developments had strongly impacted the heavily Catholic black downtown neighborhoods. Black Catholics, including Homer Plessy, pressed for more Catholic schools; Janssens responded with some additional educational arrangements for black children. Janssens's initial attempt to create separate black parishes floundered in light of funding problems and strong opposition from black Catholics and French clergy, but Janssens tried again in 1895. Seeking to defuse criticism by locating the all-black parish some distance away from the historically black Catholic downtown stronghold, Janssens established St. Katherine Church in the old St. Joseph Church on Tulane Avenue. Seeking to deflect attention from the church's resort to racial segregation by designating St. Katherine a "national parish," that is, an ethnic parish akin to those enjoyed by Irish and German Catholics in the United States, Janssens funded the all-black parish with a gift from the Philadelphia heiress and religious foundress Katharine Drexel.[26]

Archbishop Janssens and black Creoles clashed over whether racial separation or inclusion would best serve the interests of the Crescent City's black Catholics. As he publicly condemned a rising tide of white hostility in the South, including lynching, Janssens argued that black Catholics would benefit from worship in their own parishes, where they would not be confronted by the animosity of whites and the poor treatment they often received in racially mixed congregations. Janssens asserted that segregated national African American parishes would keep black Catholics who might be tempted by the Crescent City's vibrant black Protestant churches within the fold by offering them their own black Catholic institutions such as altar boys, choir members, schools, and clergy. Creoles of Color who met with Janssens to express their opposition were not persuaded. The Comité des Citoyens, led by Rodolphe Desdunes, expressed its view in the *Daily Crusader*, asserting that the notion of a segregated black parish contradicted the Catholic Church's claims to a universal faith; the group vowed to protest the "un-Christian, un-Catholic institution—the Jim Crow Church."[27] Emphasizing the social distinctions between black Creoles and African American Catholics who were the descendants of slaves, Janssens asserted in a letter to Katharine Drexel that black Creoles who opposed the project misapprehended the interests of the larger black Catholic community: "Some of our colored people are up in arms against one of the proposed colored churches. The leaders are bright mulattoes who never set foot in the church, some of them Freemasons, who imagine it will bring about a greater social separation. I foresee nothing of the kind. The regular negroes are in favor, and they too are abused. It is the poor darkey who is led astray from the church to the Baptist and Methodist colored shouting houses; the mulatto would believe himself contaminated to go to such places."[28] The *Daily Crusader*, in an article titled "The Uncatholic Church," held by contrast that Janssen's real intention was to obtain Drexel's money in order to pay off the debt of the new St. Joseph Church.[29] Janssens's experiment with a separate black parish, which contradicted the racially inclusive tradition of New Orleans Catholicism, was largely a failure. Boycotted by many black Catholics, St. Katherine primarily attracted black Protestant converts from the surrounding neighborhood and failed to draw enough worshippers to justify the construction of a parochial school. Although Janssens had voiced support for black priests, by necessity he placed St. Katherine Church in the care of white priests from the Vincentian order. Despite rising calls by black Catholics in the late nineteenth century for the ordination of African American priests, little progress had been made. Augustus Tolton, born enslaved in Missouri in 1854 and the first American priest publicly known to be black, was ordained in Rome in 1886, after which he returned to the United States and served as a priest in Quincy, Illinois, where he encountered significant hostility from white Catholics. Before his death during a heat wave in 1897, Tolton would serve as a founding pastor for St. Monica's, an African American national parish on Chicago's South Side. In June 2019 Pope Francis declared Father Tolton Venerable, a step that precedes beatification in a canonization case. The first ordination of a black priest within the United States occurred in Baltimore in 1891, with the second black priest to receive holy orders only in 1902. Stung by African American criticism, Katharine Drexel refused to fund additional churches in New Orleans unless black Catholics invited her to do so. Following Janssens's death in 1897, the new archbishop, Placide Chapelle, withdrew support for segregation efforts as the archdiocesan approach to black Catholics shifted back to the neglectful stance that had characterized much of the nineteenth century, a laissez-faire approach that however left space for the continuation of the practice of interracial worship that had long existed in the city.[30]

Archbishop Chapelle died in a yellow fever epidemic on August 9, 1905, a week before the scheduled dedication of Our Lady of Lourdes Church. Influenced by the strengthening legal foundation and hardening cultural climate of Jim Crow in Louisiana, Chapelle's successors revived

Americanization and segregationist policies that finally brought New Orleans Catholicism into alignment with the Third Plenary Council of Baltimore; their efforts profoundly shaped the context in which the new Uptown parish of Lourdes took growth.[31] The shift toward racial separation began under Archbishop James Hubert Herbert Blenk (1906–17), who was born in Bavaria but raised in New Orleans, where he converted from Protestantism to Catholicism and acculturated as a white southerner convinced that Jim Crow separation was the appropriate response to the white hostility fostered by "the Negro problem." Forgoing theology for pragmatic arguments in favor of segregation, Blenk followed the conventional Catholic "perfect society" approach—the view articulated by popes Leo XIII in 1885 and Pius X in 1903 that Church and state constituted complete independent realms, one concerned with the divine, the other the human, thus obviating the need for Catholics to confront social problems—in accommodating rather than questioning growing white racism. Weakened by the collapse of New Orleans's tripartite racial order and their declining legal, social, and economic status, Creoles of Color were unable to mount the concerted resistance that they had offered to Archbishop Janssens's segregated St. Katherine a decade earlier. In line with the decrees of the Third Plenary Council, Blenk reorganized the city's parochial schools so that each parish supported and staffed its own school. As white parents would not send their children to the same school as black children and integrated parishes could not afford to operate separate white and black schools, parishes in the new arrangement tended to drop parochial education for blacks. Blenk used this problem to press for black parishes with their own parochial schools, beginning with a school at St. Katherine staffed by the Sisters of the Holy Family, the Afro-Creole religious order. By the early twentieth century, Rome frowned on national parishes as an affront to the Church's "universal theology," so Blenk turned instead to the notion of racially identified territorial parishes. Avoiding the use of archdiocesan resources for ministry to black Catholics, Blenk could instead fund black territorial parishes with Drexel and Church mission monies intended for black Catholics and staff them with Josephite priests, an order devoted to the "Negro apostolate" that had begun working in Baltimore in 1871. In 1909, when Mater Dolorosa, a hitherto integrated parish in the uptown suburb of Carrollton, moved to a larger building, the whites in the congregation voted to exclude the parish's African Americans, many of them Creole French-speaking migrants from rural upriver civil parishes such as St. Charles and St. John. To meet the pastoral needs of the abandoned blacks of the parish, Blenk established St. Dominic Church (later renamed St. Joan of Arc), which became the first black territorial parish in New Orleans. Fr. Peter O. LeBeau, a Creole-speaking white missionary Josephite priest who had been working in Louisiana since 1897, became pastor, and Blenk purchased St. Louis School of Carrollton, which the Sisters of the Holy Family had operated in the neighborhood since 1892, and attached it to St. Dominic. Appeasing white supremacist opposition to black Catholic ministry and education, Blenk refused to allow black Josephite priests to work in the archdiocese, but he initiated the construction of an extensive system of segregated black territorial parishes and parochial schools (often staffed by Katharine Drexel's religious order, the Sisters of the Blessed Sacrament) and a four-year high school for black youth that later became known as Xavier Preparatory School.[32]

As many French clergy who had traditionally defended integrated parishes returned to France in the World War I era, black Catholics' desperate need for parochial schools amid the tightening of Jim Crow eventually allowed Blenk and his Alabama-born successor, Archbishop John William Shaw (1918–34), to overcome the deep-seated resistance to segregation in the downtown historic stronghold of black Catholicism. Although downtown black Catholics continued to protest, boycott, and lament the Catholic Church's abandonment of the core principle of universality, the Josephites established five black downtown parishes and schools between 1916 and 1929, often in poor-quality church buildings that had been abandoned by white congregations. The expansion of black territorial parishes similarly encompassed Uptown black Catholicism, with segregated black parish plants established in the mid- to late 1910s at Blessed Sacrament and Holy Ghost (staffed by the Holy Ghost Fathers, a German order devoted, like the Josephites, to working with African Americans) near the geographical boundaries of Lourdes Parish. In Jim Crow's racial reconfiguration of New Orleans Catholicism, then, Our Lady of Lourdes would take identity as a white parish, even as segregation never completely separated white and black Catholics in a religious culture that had been traditionally racially inclusive. While many Catholic priests and white congregations insisted that black Catholics ought to worship in black territorial parishes, some black Catholics continued to attend the churches where their families had long worshipped or parishes that were more convenient to where they lived or worked. Individual black Catholic resistance to Jim Crow occurred within the lacunae created by the universal, inclusive implications of canon law. Despite emergent Jim Crow practices in Catholic dioceses around the United States, Church law still held that clerics could not require African Americans to worship in separate churches and that the obligation to attend Sunday Mass could be satisfied in any Catholic church.[33]

III

From its inception in 1905, Lourdes Church developed strong ties to the growing Freret neighborhood, while priests at Lourdes saw as their primary mission the cultivation of the faith of white Catholics living within parish boundaries. Like most Catholic clerics in fin de siècle New Orleans, the parish's first pastor, Fr. Leslie Kavanagh, was foreign-born and had studied in France, but his lack of French descent distinguished him from much of the city's clergy and pointed in the direction of how the city's Catholicism would de-gallicize in the years that followed. Born in 1866 in an outlying district of Liverpool, England, a city that had seen large-scale Irish Catholic post-famine immigration, Kavanagh served in the British Navy and then studied and taught at institutions run by the Marist Fathers in France, Maryland, and in Convent, Louisiana. Kavanagh was ordained in 1903 after studying theology for a year at the Archdiocese of New Orleans's Bouligny Seminary, next to St. Stephen Church on Napoleon Avenue. The former Royal Navy midshipman served brief assignments at historically Irish parishes St. Peter and St. Paul in the Marigny neighborhood and St. Michael Church in the Lower Garden District before Archbishop Chapelle assigned him to found Lourdes Parish. As he took up the construction of Lourdes's plant and the fostering of its sacramental life—the church enumerated an impressive sixty-eight hundred communicants in its first full year, and in its first decade averaged from fifteen to ninety-seven baptisms, from three to twenty-six marriages, and from four to thirty funerals per year—Fr. Kavanagh worked to develop good relationships with prominent neighbors and Freret business owners and to envelop the new parish in neighborhood activities and governance. Forging close ties with neighbors such as *Daily Picayune* sportswriter and advertising chief Harry McEnerny and the family of Peter J. Reilly, an Illinois Central Railroad employee who had built one of the first houses in the drained wetland that would become Freret, Kavanagh also participated energetically in the Sixth District Property Owners' Association, hosting association meetings on the parish plant. As the Freret property owners sought enhanced city services in the neighborhood, the Lourdes pastor strongly opposed requiring that Improvement Association members be registered voters, a measure that would have excluded African American participation in light of the disfranchisement of blacks in Louisiana. Kavanagh admonished that he would not permit the Improvement Association to use parish facilities if the racially discriminatory measure went through. In August 1910, the association similarly deflected the racially charged efforts that one member made to enlist property owners against the construction of Burke's Flats, a planned apartment house for "Negroes" between Valmont Street and Peters Avenue. Enmeshing his church in the Crescent City's machine politics, Kavanagh lined up politically with the Regular Democratic Organization (RDO), also known as the Choctaw Club, led by longtime New Orleans mayor Martin Behrman, hosting RDO candidates at the parish plant, including gubernatorial contender John T. Michel, the incumbent secretary of state, who would be defeated by "reform" Democrat Luther E. Hall in 1912.[34]

Even as he objected to the tightening of neighborhood racial segregation, Fr. Kavanagh segregated the pews of his own parish, closely oversaw the expansion of the archdiocese's segregated parochial school system, and simultaneously pressed for badly needed provision of parochial education for black children living within Lourdes Parish boundaries. In 1909 a Josephite visitor to Lourdes Church reported that the pastor had installed a sign "for colored only" over a small number of the back seats, conforming to a larger pattern in which uptown English-speaking parishes along with downtown Catholic churches (which had a much longer and more substantial tradition of interracial congregations) conceded to white racial animosity in the first decade of the twentieth century by segregating pews and drastically reducing the seating available for black Catholics.[35] In 1906, as he created a system of segregated parochial schools supported by parishes (along with an array of black territorial parishes that had long been resisted by black Catholics, as discussed above), Archbishop Blenk established a Catholic Board of Education and appointed Kavanagh superintendent of Catholic schools, a position that the Lourdes pastor would hold until 1919. As superintendent, Kavanagh sought to standardize and professionalize New Orleans Catholic education by instituting enhanced teacher training, uniform textbooks, and examinations across the elementary grades. As he developed Lourdes's school, which served only white children, as an archdiocesan model and coordinated the archdiocese's burgeoning segregated school system, Kavanagh convened numerous meetings from 1912 to 1916 in support of "Our Lady of Lourdes Colored School." A permanent parochial school for Freret blacks would not exist, however, until the opening of the parochial school of Holy Ghost Church, a territorial black parish on the far eastern edge of the neighborhood, in 1916. Kavanagh aided the Holy Ghost Fathers as they began operations on the boundary of his parish. From this point on Freret African Americans were encouraged to worship at Holy Ghost, not at Lourdes, despite the convenience of the latter church in the heart of their neighborhood. New Orleans diocesan priest and Church historian Henry Bezou, who grew up in Lourdes Parish during Kavanagh's pastorate, aptly characterized the limits of the Liverpudlian's racial paternalism, which coincided with the segregating of Catholic New Orleans: "While there is no proof that Father Kavanagh was a racial integrationist, he did have the welfare of negroes at heart."[36]

As the Freret neighborhood grew to more than two thousand houses by 1919, Lourdes Church under Fr. Kavanagh expanded in worshippers and in devotional and associational life within the contours of a now largely segregated Crescent City Catholicism. Kavanagh remained busy, even beyond his substantial responsibilities as pastor and educational administrator. In 1910 he collaborated with a Boston organist to compile and publish a collection of Latin and English hymns, the *Crown Hymnal*, that would be adopted by several American dioceses. In 1918, during World War I, the former Royal Navy midshipman served as Catholic vicar general for the Gulf Coast, coordinating Catholic chaplains and associational work in aid of the war effort across eight southern states, Haiti, and Panama.[37] Following his service in the war effort, Kavanagh was elevated to domestic prelate (monsignor) in 1919. Mayor Martin

Behrman spoke after the investiture Mass, as did *Times-Picayune* newspaperman and parish spokesman Harry McEnerny, who aligned Msgr. Kavanagh and Lourdes Parish with anticommunist, antiradical, and xenophobic sentiments sweeping the nation following World War I. In Red Scare tones, McEnerny declared that "great work still awaits our distinguished friend [Kavanagh]. From the pulpit of the Catholic Church disorder and crime must be put down, the red flag of rebellion must not be allowed to be hoisted in this country . . . aliens must be . . . made to understand that while the United States is the home of the free and the land of the brave, anarchy and disobedience to authority will not be tolerated here."[38] Kavanagh's parish continued to grow in the years that followed the war, peaking (for his pastorate) at 3,150 parishioners in 1922. By the mid-1920s the parish school enrolled more than 450 pupils, taught by six Dominican sisters and five lay teachers with the aid of the pastor and his assistant priests. In an era in which American Catholic and Protestant cultures, in sync with increasingly influential business and advertising mantras, equated success with ever-rising tallies, reported sacramental numbers at Lourdes surged. Most strikingly Holy Communions rose from 19,883 in 1913 to 35,000 in 1917 to an extraordinary 71,800 communicants in 1929, the local fruit of Pope Pius X's efforts to encourage more frequent reception of the Eucharist. Other sacraments saw substantial, if less dramatic, increases, from ninety-seven annual baptisms in 1911 to a hundred twenty-eight in 1921, and from eighteen marriages in 1908 to forty-eight in 1926. Sacramental yields mushroomed even as the parish shrunk modestly in territory, shedding areas north of Claiborne Avenue to a new parish, St. Matthias, founded in 1920 to serve increasing "back of town" residential development lakeside toward Lake Pontchartrain.[39]

While reception of the sacraments proliferated at Lourdes, other aspects of a devotional culture were elaborated, with an initial residual Gallic veneer that was eventually absorbed in a sea of rapid Americanization even as the church's pastor coordinated Catholic associational efforts across the region during the Great War. Reflecting the still thoroughly Gallic milieu in which the parish was founded in 1905, Archbishop Chapelle denominated the church Notre Dame de Lourdes, an appellation that it would officially retain throughout its history. The parish's first and only assistant priest until 1919 was a sixty-eight-year-old French cleric with much experience in parishes around southeast

Louisiana, the Rev. Joseph Jaxel, who succumbed to a stroke a mere five weeks after his appointment to Lourdes in October 1905.[40] From the parish's inception in 1905, lay participation and evangelization was cultivated in the full repertoire of transatlantic fin de siècle popular Catholicism, but now in an increasingly American idiom: an array of sodalities, confraternities, and other societies organized by age and gender; parish missions led by visiting friars; novenas, tridua, the Forty Hours' Devotions, Holy Week, and feast day observances, particularly that of the parish's patroness, Our Lady of Lourdes, on February 11.[41]

Unsurprisingly, the Lourdes devotion received a great deal of attention in a parish dedicated to what was probably the most popular Marian apparition of late nineteenth- and early twentieth-century transatlantic Catholicism. One source with personal knowledge of Fr. Kavanagh asserts that the first pastor of Lourdes displayed a "fervid" devotion to "the Blessed Mother who had appeared to Bernadette Soubirous" in 1858.[42] The Lourdes cultus had a lengthy history in New Orleans, with its profound nineteenth-century ties to French Catholicism. Translations of accounts of the Lourdes apparitions appeared in New Orleans (and New York) newspapers by October 1858, less than two months after the events first received attention in France. In 1873, French-born New Orleans archbishop Napoleon J. Perché, declaring that he had long been "deeply moved" by Bernadette's experiences of the Blessed Mother, dedicated an altar to Our Lady of Lourdes at the diocesan cathedral in front of twenty thousand worshippers. Three years later, Perché made a pilgrimage to Lourdes, where he participated in a large-scale ceremony with several dozen bishops before a crowd of a hundred thousand. Intervening in a cultural debate in which secularizing American intellectuals sometimes mocked the alleged Catholic propensity for superstitious naïveté, the symptom they argued of a larger inability of American Catholics to think for themselves in a democratic, republican political culture, Perché argued that the proliferation of Lourdes books was a positive good in an era when "impious and immoral" publications were "disorganizing our modern societies."[43] The founding of Notre Dame de Lourdes in Uptown New Orleans in 1905 occurred in the middle of a decades-long Lourdes enthusiasm across the United States. Historian John T. McGreevy notes that by the 1950s one hundred twenty-seven churches in the United States had been named in honor of Our Lady of Lourdes, with countless more grottoes and altars dedicated to her.[44]

Within a few years of its construction the church on New Orleans's Napoleon Avenue designated sacred space that sought to strikingly evoke the Marian devotion to which the parish was dedicated. The fiftieth anniversary of the apparitions at Lourdes in February 1908 were marked at their namesake parish in the Crescent City with a triduum of High Masses and benedictions. At the opening High Mass, which the pastor celebrated, Archbishop Blenk preached and James Cardinal Gibbons of Baltimore, the foremost American in the Church hierarchy, made the closing remarks. A few months later the church installed a full-scale replica of the Lourdes grotto that sought to faithfully duplicate the physical setting of the apparitions reported by Bernadette Soubirous. A *Daily Picayune* reporter found the grotto, a donation from prominent lawyer and parishioner W .J. Waguespack, "a thing of wondrous beauty, the towering rocks forming an impressive picture, while in a niche the beautiful white-clad picture of the Blessed Virgin looks down upon the kneeling figure of the little peasant at the base of the rock." Particular care was taken to realistically evoke the rustic French landscape in which the Blessed Mother appeared, with "a tiny rivulet of water falling down the side of the mountain . . . [adding] a touch of realism to the beautiful scene." Central to the fidelity with which the grotto sought to evoke the Lourdes setting was the statue of Mary, which had been donated by parishioner Lawrence Fabacher, a well-known New Orleans brewer and restauranteur. Fabacher had purchased the full-size statue of Our Lady of Lourdes in Paris and had taken it to Lourdes, where he had the statue blessed and then received permission to touch it briefly to the spot where Mary first appeared to Bernadette.[45]

The Lourdes devotion remained a particular focus in the mid-1920s as the now-sizable parish erased its debt of $25,757.84 and erected a new church building to replace the overcrowded old church-school-rectory combination, which had been damaged in a 1915 hurricane. The large new church entailed a mission exterior and a Romanesque interior. But the structure's capacious dome imitated the Rosary Church at Lourdes and once again a Lourdes grotto replica would be a central feature of the sacral space, which contained pews that could seat 750 persons.

Well aware of the subsidence problems of what was drained swampland, builders working with a largely African American crew laid "257
reinforced concrete piles" as the foundation after they moved the old
multipurpose building to the side of the lot for future use as a school
and parish hall.[46] The statues of Bernadette Soubirous and Our Lady
of Lourdes were transferred from the old church, but in suggestion of
the parish's aura of growing prestige, most of the furnishings in the new
church, including the Lourdes grotto, were newly acquired or donated
by parishioners. Replicating the by now familiar pattern in which black
parishes received the castoffs of white parishes, Fr. Kavanagh donated
the former pews and high altar of the previous church to Holy Ghost
Church, the nearby African American territorial parish that would dedi-
cate its church a year later.[47] New York cardinal and archbishop Patrick
Hayes (whom Kavanagh had served under as Catholic vicar general for
the Gulf Coast in the recent war) dedicated the new church on May 17,
1925. A prominent young litigation attorney, William J. Guste, spoke for
the parish at the dedicatory events.[48] Waxing eloquent, Guste expressed
a confident corporatist ideology that situated the Catholic parish at the
center of American civilization, articulating not only the consistency
of Catholic belief with American citizenship but also the supremacy of
Catholic institutions to purely civic ones: "Who can comprehend the
importance of a parish church? As one strong link in a mighty chain, it
contributes its strength and power in ministering to the spiritual needs
of untold thousands. The parish church has done more in its simple,
constant and positive way to tranquilize the world than all the legislative
assemblies and diplomatic conventions of history. The dedication of this
church today is therefore a contribution not only to our spiritual, but
also to our civic and patriotic interests."[49]

A similar confidence marked the celebration of Pastor Kavanagh's
Silver Jubilee as priest in June 1928. At a reception marking the cleric's
silver anniversary, New Orleans mayor Arthur O'Keefe, successor to
Martin Behrman as leader of the RDO's Choctaw Club, praised Kavanagh's accomplishment in building such a prominent parish on what
had been merely "barren marsh land" when he arrived in 1905. The
Lourdes devotion remained a key focus in the parish with the onset of
the Great Depression, expressed in an idiom exhorting Catholic confes-
sionalism and family and gender ideology in response to a Protestant,

secularizing American mass culture embracing new understandings of femininity that were neither confined nor defined by the household and familial roles. A parish novena to Our Lady of Lourdes around her feast day in February 1933 arrayed a number of masses and sermons inculcating an assertive Catholic stance on American culture through Marian devotion. At the Lourdes grotto, visiting New York City priest John E. Wickham preached on topics such as "Mary the Spouse: Marriage in America," "Mary: The Rights of Woman," "Mary at the Foot of the Cross: The Meaning and the Value of the Mass," and "Mary and the Child: Why Parochial Schools."[50]

Yet the parish faced significant counterwinds as the Depression years began. Construction of the new church and a new rectory adjoining the church on La Salle Street had arrayed a bonded debt of $185,000 that would constrain parish coffers in ensuing years.[51] More crucially, the pastor's health was in decline, he began to depend more on assistant priests, and the attendance of parishioners began slipping away to nearby churches such as St. Matthias, St. Stephen, and the Church of the Holy Name of Jesus, a Jesuit edifice on St. Charles Avenue. Henry Bezou, Lourdes parishioner, priest, and parish historian, recalled that Kavanagh's "administrative abilities began to wane and even his usually debonair disposition began to change. He tended to be a bit testy at times and sharp in dealing with others. His Sunday sermons seemed repetitive and verbose."[52] Fr. Carl J. Schutten, an assistant priest who arrived in 1933, recalled that Kavanagh by this time was quite ill and often spent sleepless nights in bed reading from the books in his extensive library. Reminiscing a few months before his own death in 1979, Msgr. Schutten remembered that each night Kavanagh had the church sexton draw up the sixty-eight-year-old pastor's cold water bath, ice cubes chilling cold piped water, a ritual that may have combined Catholic asceticism with relief from the Louisiana heat in an era before air conditioning. As the assistant priest feared that he would, the founding pastor collapsed in the pulpit while celebrating Sunday Mass. Shortly after Schutten anointed him in his sick bed in the rectory, Kavanagh suffered a lethal hemorrhage of the liver and passed away on July 24, 1934. More than one hundred diocesan priests and members of religious orders and large numbers of parishioners filled Lourdes Church for Kavanagh's funeral two days later.[53] The archdiocesan newspaper,

the *Catholic Action of the South*, lauded Kavanagh's work in organizing and standardizing New Orleans's parochial schools and eulogized
him as an exemplar of pastoral clericalism. "Truly God's priest in every
respect, zealous to scrupulousness for the welfare of the souls entrusted
to his care, dilligent [*sic*] in his visits to the sick of his flock, solicitous
of the faith of those within his supervision, devoted to the service of
the Church of God, industrious in the teaching of the little ones, and
charitable to the very limit of his means."[54] The Liverpudlian cleric was
buried a few blocks away but still within the boundaries of the parish
at St. Vincent Cemetery on Soniat Street. Eventually, after the parish
took up a collection, a granite monument bearing a Celtic cross and the
priest's favorite prayer, the Memorare, which beseeches Mary's aid, was
erected at Kavanagh's grave.[55]

Archbishop Joseph F. Rummel appointed Dutch-born Msgr. Peter
M. H. Wynhoven pastor of Lourdes in November 1935.[56] Wynhoven was
a prominent advocate for labor and the poor and had founded the diocesan newspaper, *Catholic Action of the South*, in 1932. Speculation had
held that Wynhoven might be appointed John William Shaw's successor
as archbishop, but the hierarchy instead chose the safely ultramontane
Rummel, perhaps wary of Wynhoven's alignment with the progressive "Americanist" school of Catholic thought. Like many New Orleans
priests in his era, Wynhoven was recruited to Louisiana from Europe.
Having studied with Franciscans in his native city of Venray, Holland,
Wynhoven entered the Bouligny Seminary on Napoleon Avenue in
1904 and finished his seminary studies in St. Louis. After ordination, he
served as assistant priest at St. Francis of Assisi in Uptown New Orleans
and in 1910 took up position as vice chancellor of the archdiocese and
then as pastor at St. Joseph's in Gretna, just beyond city boundaries. Particularly concerned with the needs of the growing population of Sicilian
immigrants on the West Bank of the Mississippi River across from New
Orleans, Wynhoven soon embarked on "the Catholic social apostolate"
for which he became well known, championing and founding ministries
for the homeless, orphaned boys, and impoverished children and youth
and raising awareness regarding the social conditions that he argued
fostered criminality. Probably having been made aware of the important
role the "labor priest" played in mediating a protracted streetcar strike in
New Orleans in 1929, President Franklin D. Roosevelt appointed Wyn-

hoven chairman of a U.S. Regional Labor Board in October 1933. The "militant priest and citizen" also served on Mayor T. Semmes Walmsley's Public Welfare Board. Walmsley, aligned with the Old Regulars' Choctaw Club, was an ardent rival of governor and U.S. senator Huey Long, who sought to strip the New Orleans mayoralty of its powers.[57]

The outspoken activist priest Wynhoven seemed in some respects a Catholic counterpoint to Huey Long, a north Louisiana Baptist who had strong appeal in working-class white and black neighborhoods such as Freret, even as his sometimes vindictive policies did relatively little for African Americans and impoverished New Orleanians. Catholic intellectuals disliked what they regarded as Long's vacuous populism, which they saw as contradicting the Church's tradition of advocating "orderly social reform in accordance with divine law," as historian Justin D. Poché argues. For instance, the Jesuit periodical *America* invidiously compared Long's populism to that of Mexican president Lázaro Cárdenas, whose agrarian radicalism had degenerated into a violent anticlericalism that threatened the Mexican Catholic Church.[58] As he edited the *Catholic Action of the South* and managed the preceding diocesan newspaper, the *Morning Star*, Wynhoven pressed for activism to redress social inequities and denounced rising anti-Semitism in Europe but also expressed conventional Catholic sensibilities seeking "the improvement of the moral standards of motion pictures" and the protection of the rights of Mexican Catholics against an aggressively secularist Mexican state. Wynhoven's approach embodied, along with the name of the diocesan journal he edited, the "Catholic Action" impulse of 1930s and 1940s American Catholicism, an effort to stir the laity into collective efforts to engage the world by redressing deep-seated social issues through the lens of Catholic teaching.[59]

Msgr. Wynhoven's pronounced talents as a charismatic speaker and organizer shaped the nine years of his pastorate at Lourdes, which saw significant growth and elaboration of the parish's organizational life, albeit within the constraints of a now profoundly racially segregated New Orleans Catholic culture, which the activist pastor made little effort to challenge. Parish historian Henry Bezou characterized Wynhoven as "witty and pithy in his sermons, comfortable in his rapport with youth, genial in his greetings, and impressive in bearing, people flocked to his Sunday Masses."[60] Organizing the parish into ten fund-

raising districts, the pastor reduced the church's outstanding debt from
$176,000 to $76,000. Parish and sacramental participation increased,
perhaps under the influence of the social fluctuations precipitated by
the American entry into World War II. Parishioners rose from 4,186 in
1938 to 5,600 in 1943, baptisms went from 70 in 1936 to 172 in 1944, and
school enrollment wavered between 380 and 420 in the latter years of
Wynhoven's pastorate. Beyond fund-raising, the pastor was especially
active in organizing parish clubs, councils, and athletic activities, typically arranged by gender, generation, and marital status, to take best
advantage of peer dynamics but also to accord with and effectively pros-
elytize Catholic devotional, family, and gender ideologies. On top of his
pastoral responsibilities and his efforts coordinating social organizations
for the archdiocese, Wynhoven authored numerous motivational pamphlets and continued to edit the diocesan newspaper.[61]

As he edited the diocesan organ, the Lourdes pastor revealed the
constraints of his Catholic Action social vision for African Americans
in a 1943 opinion piece, "Rising Shadow," which pointed to an alleged
increase in black delinquency in the months after Pearl Harbor. Wynhoven warned that communists were ready to manipulate African
American discontent and that blacks should instead turn to Catholic
Church leaders for guidance. In an exchange of letters with the Lourdes
pastor, a local branch of the Knights of Peter Claver, writing in the tradition of black Creole Catholic activism, rebuffed Wynhoven's racial paternalism as not in keeping with "the Catholic spirit" and susceptible
to being cynically misread by racially conservative white southerners.
Wynhoven responded in turn that blacks had long turned a blind eye
to the warnings of clergy who worked for their "social betterment" and
again sought "to warn your people against the riotous and rebellious
spirit of the day." But a Josephite priest also complained in writing to
Wynhoven, asserting that his words risked alienating African American
Catholics and giving comfort to southern white supremacists in their
"undiluted paganism" (in which they converted white skin privilege into
an idol that supplanted Christ). The Josephite wondered why Wynhoven
had not developed more enlightened racial views in his thirty years of
social activism.[62] The Lourdes pastor remained busy with parish and
archdiocesan responsibilities even as black Catholics and progressive
white Catholics questioned the judgment of the Crescent City's most

prominent advocate of Catholic Action as the war's social flux augured the loosening of Jim Crow's boundaries. On a speaking tour on behalf of the Youth Progress Program, an archdiocesan effort to raise funds for segregated Catholic high schools for young white and black men, Wynhoven suffered a stroke and died in Massachusetts in September 1944. The pastor's remains were brought back to Lourdes Church, where an overflowing crowd, including a number of civic and religious leaders, attended the activist priest's funeral.[63]

Archbishop Rummel appointed Msgr. Lucien Joseph Caillouet as pastor of Lourdes in May 1946. Caillouet was born in Thibodaux in Louisiana's sugarland in 1894, the son of Lafourche Parish judge and journalist Louis Philip Caillouet.[64] Caillouet would serve as pastor at Lourdes until 1968, a twenty-two-year period that would encompass the highly consequential ecclesiological shifts of the Second Vatican Council along with dramatic demographic shifts in the Freret neighborhood and in Lourdes Parish and its school.

Lourdes Parish flourished in the late 1940s and 1950s as the post–World War II years marked a halcyon period for American Catholicism in terms of the status of the Church in American culture and in the number of vocations of American Catholics to the priesthood and religious life.[65] A committed fund-raiser, Msgr. Caillouet oversaw plant repairs to the old school and the convent in 1947 and erased the church's long-standing debt by 1950. In a technological innovation that transformed cultural life in the summer months in warm and humid Louisiana (as it did throughout the American South), air conditioning was installed in the church and in the rectory in 1953. In 1957 archdiocesan historian Roger Baudier tallied thirty-five vocations from the parish to the priesthood and religious orders in the previous eleven years (including twenty-one Dominican sisters; the school was in the charge of Dominican nuns), with another twenty-six seminarians, postulants, and novices who had been raised in the parish preparing for holy orders and consecrated life.[66] As the parish's fiftieth anniversary approached in 1955, the pastor redoubled efforts to build a new complex to replace the parish's aging, overcrowded school. Given the long problems with buckling floors and chronic subsidence in the 1924 church and periodic neighborhood flooding during heavy rains, "675 sixty-creosoted pilings" were driven as support as construction began on the million-dollar project.

Dedicated in 1957, the new school building could accommodate 650 or more students, an enrollment that the parish school would never reach in the succeeding fifty years of its operation. The new school complex also included a state-of-the-art auditorium-gymnasium and a convent for the Dominican women.[67]

In a 1959 archdiocesan parochial visitation report, Msgr. Caillouet meticulously and confidently assessed the state of his parish on the eve of the transformations of racial succession and the Second Vatican Council. A total of 571 students attended the new school—294 boys and 277 girls. The pastor estimated that 134 young people in the parish attended public grammar and high schools, forgoing a Catholic education due to their parents' poverty, "indifference . . . towards their children's welfare" or inability to gain admission to Catholic schools.[68] The pastor noted that 4,049 Catholics lived within parish boundaries. He thought that 70 percent of parishioners regularly attended Mass on Sunday and held that 99,000 had received communion in his church in the last year, a 10 percent increase over the previous year.[69]

IV

Even as the Civil Rights Movement and court-ordered desegregation challenged the foundations of Jim Crow and demographic shifts began to reshape the racial composition of the Freret neighborhood and the larger city of New Orleans, Msgr. Caillouet apparently dissembled in the 1959 visitation report as he denied that his parish continued to practice the racial segregation that had long been its custom. Reflecting efforts Archbishop Rummel had begun in 1949 to curtail Jim Crow practices in worship, the archdiocesan visitation questionnaire queried whether segregation was still implemented at Mass. Noting that 490 "Negroes" lived within parish boundaries and that "approximately 275" blacks regularly attended Sunday Mass, the pastor denied that ushers seated "Negroes" in segregated pews or that blacks were compelled "to wait until after the white parishioners to receive communion." However more than fifty years later, longtime African American parishioners at Lourdes remembered that in the early 1960s, more than a decade after the archdiocese had mandated integrated liturgies, ushers still seated African Americans in the back of the church, from where they would be the last to come forward to receive the Eucharist. African Americans also recalled that some black Catholics at Lourdes routinely defied Jim Crow's rigid boundaries, remembering that some light-complected African Americans would routinely sit in "white" areas and that "one black friend always sat where he wanted."[70]

Lourdes Parish in 1959 was at the center of a neighborhood and city undergoing significant demographic changes. Census takers counted 11,000 residents in overcrowded Freret's two census districts in 1940, as New Orleans expanded by 110,000 between 1930 and 1950 and would peak in population at 627,525 in 1960, part of larger trends toward dramatic Sunbelt industrialization, in-migration, and urban growth during World War II and in the postwar years. However, by 1960 Freret and the larger Crescent City were starting to experience the effects of long-term tendencies toward suburbanization, white flight amid desegregation, and the exodus of retail to the urban periphery—all facilitated by the increasing emphasis on the automobile—that would hollow out the urban core, diminishing the city's population, wealth, and racial diversity. Middle-class African Americans, some of them Catholic, including school teachers, plumbers, city employees, and Pullman porters, moved in to the neighborhood in the late 1940s and 1950s, seeking home ownership in what was regarded as a quiet and safe area. Among them were Harold and Olympia Boucree, cradle Catholics of black Creole descent and teachers in New Orleans's Catholic and public schools who bought a house in Freret in 1959 and began attending Lourdes. Harold had served as an organist at St. Monica, a segregated black parish in New Orleans's Central City. Remembering the rapid racial transition of portions of Freret, the Boucrees recalled that they were "the third black family on the block but all the whites were gone by the next year."[71] In 1952, the Orleans school board, responding to pressure from black parents seeking schools that actually were separate but equal, as the nearly six-decade-old *Plessy* decision mandated, converted Merrick Elementary, a segregated school for white children on Valence Street in the heart of the neighborhood, into a school for black children that would be named after an African American educator, Samuel J. Green. White parents responded by moving out of a historically racially mixed district now anchored by a black grammar school. During the 1950s, Freret's white population fell from 6,455 to 5,307, while its number of black residents rose from 3,995 to 4,680. Meanwhile, the GI Bill funded the construction of around fifty thousand homes by 1953, most of them restricted to ownership by whites, in subdivisions on New Orleans's periphery. In yet another symptom of the automobile's ascendancy, the Freret streetcar had ended operations in 1946.[72]

New Orleans's parochial schools, including Lourdes School, integrated in 1962. Archbishop Rummel had publicly supported integration since 1949, when he refused to attend a segregated service and had removed "white" and "Colored" designations from the pews. While de facto segregation persisted in many archdiocesan parishes in the 1950s, including Lourdes, churches were now supposed to be integrated even as archdiocesan hospitals and schools remained segregated. The 1954 *Brown v. Board of Education* decision—applying only to public schools— had particular implications for parochial schools in New Orleans, a city whose population included 11 percent of all black Catholics in the United States, many of whom attended Catholic schools but whose white political leadership opposed integration. In February 1956, Rummel had declared segregation "morally wrong and sinful" but, perhaps fearing white Catholic resistance and political and economic repercussions, did not offer a timetable for integration. In March 1956, Rummel threatened to excommunicate a pro-segregation group, the Association of Catholic Laymen, but the Vatican failed to publicly support Rummel's integrationist stance. In July 1956, Rummel announced that "certain difficulties" meant that integration of parochial schools would be delayed until at least the following year. Several years later, in 1959, responding to a segregationist Catholic leader, Emile Wagner, the archdiocese released a statement that "integration in education must come . . . at the earliest possible opportunity." The Citizen's Council in turn burned a cross on the archbishop's lawn. Yet the archdiocese still did not take steps to integrate its schools, perhaps because Rummel was by this time seriously ill, legally blind and unable to walk without assistance. Meanwhile, New Orleans public schools began to slowly desegregate in 1960, encountering much public resistance from white segregationists, including efforts to intimidate the parents of black and white students who participated.[73]

In May 1961 Rummel appointed the Catholic Council of Human Relations (CCHR), an organization with a board of directors of thirty-three whites and blacks mandated to assist the archdiocese with promoting "racial justice." The CCHR crafted an integration plan that sought to avoid the problems plaguing gradual public school integration in New Orleans. Working with Archbishop John Patrick Cody, who had been appointed Rummel's coadjutor in 1961, the CCHR pressed for the integration of all eight parochial elementary grades in fall 1962. Archdiocesan school superintendent Henry Bezou publicly announced the school desegregation plan on March 27, 1962, commenting that as a lifelong New Orleanian, he expected Catholics in the region to loyally follow Catholic Church policy. Archbishop Rummel excommunicated three white Catholic segregationist leaders, among them Leander Perez, the political boss of the nearby civil parishes of Plaquemines and Bernard, in response to their efforts to intimidate the parents of parochial school students and their denunciation of the local Catholic Church hierarchy. In contrast to the desegregation of Catholic high schools in northern cities such as Chicago and Philadelphia, integration proceeded largely without protest or violence in the Crescent City's parochial schools that fall, while New Orleans's suburbs saw greater disruption. But the state legislature retaliated by effectively cutting funding for Catholic schools and voting for grants in aid that supported students attending the segregated Protestant "Christian" academies that would enroll many of the white students removed by their parents from desegregating parochial and public schools.[74]

Demographic trends that began in the 1950s—even as Monsignor Caillouet raised money to build Lourdes's impressive new school and authored his optimistic, even complacent, visitation report that downplayed the persistence of Jim Crow in his pews—only continued in the decades that followed, largely eliminating the social bases of what had been one of the more prominent segregated white Catholic parishes in the city. As journalist and historian Coleman Warner notes, Freret's character as a late manifestation of the "walking city" eroded after 1960 as its historic racial diversity diminished and its retail district dwindled due to competition from outlying shopping centers. Efforts in the 1970s by New Orleans's first African American mayor, Ernest "Dutch" Morial, to revive the Freret business district met with only limited success. After Lourdes School integrated in 1962, most white parents withdrew their students and few white parents enrolled their children in the neighborhood's now integrated public schools, including Samuel J. Green, opting instead for private academies that promised a homogeneous white enrollment. Under integrationist mayor Moon Landrieu, elected with black support in 1969–70, an older "white paternalistic" pattern of city politics collapsed. Warner notes that as African Americans acquired increasing influence in the governance of New Orleans in the 1960s, their share of the Freret population increased from 47 percent to 61 percent. A rise in violent crime in the 1970s and 1980s, along with the continued stagnation of the neighborhood's business district and the decline of its housing stock, precipitated fears for safety in Freret and an exodus of blacks and whites. Even as the proportion of African Americans in the neighborhood increased from 1970 to 1990 to nearly two-thirds of its residents, the total number of blacks slipped from 5,372 to 3,829 and the number of whites fell from 3,398 to 2,005.[75]

Desegregation and the Second Vatican Council profoundly altered Lourdes Parish in the 1960s, with change most evident in the new and capacious school. The school built in the late 1950s for an enrollment of at least 650 saw a steady and significant decline in students over the course of the decade, tallying just 260 at the end of the 1970–71 academic year. White flight after integration explained much of the attrition. As parish historian (and archdiocesan superintendent of schools during desegregation) Henry Bezou explained, even white families that remained in the parish enrolled their children in private academies opened to avoid integration, or alternately in other Catholic schools that did not see meaningful integration. By the time Monsignor Caillouet retired as pastor in 1968, several classrooms were left empty, and only five nuns lived in cells in the convent built for thirteen sisters.[76] Bezou's assessment of Caillouet's pastoral role in the integration period was judicious, noting that the priest "was one of the first to sign the resolution drafted by Archbishop Rummel approving the *Brown vs. Kansas Board of Education* decision of the U.S. Supreme Court in 1954."[77] A longtime African American Lourdes parishioner was less charitable, explaining that "the story was that the white pastor encouraged the white students to leave. That was the Caillouet brothers."[78] Erosion in church attendance and parish membership was slower but nonetheless steady, particularly among white families, "who cut their parochial ties by moving elsewhere," in Henry Bezou's words, even as Caillouet adjusted liturgy and church "furnishments" to conform to the changes of Vatican II. Over the course of the 1960s parishioners declined from four thousand to around two thousand, with a proportionate decline in reception of the sacraments (partially offset by more frequent Communion, probably an effect of Vatican II's renewed emphasis on the centrality of the personal experience of the Eucharist).[79]

By the end of the 1960s the once segregated white parish may have approached an African American majority in terms of active parishioners and Mass attendance, but the pastor, Msgr. Caillouet, was slow to adjust to these changes. With Caillouet's retirement in 1968, Fr. Malcolm B. Strassel was appointed pastor and led the parish until 1975. Henry Bezou reported that Strassel, who was born in 1908 and ordained in 1934, volunteered for the Lourdes assignment because he "was aware of the need for priests in city parishes with substantial racial and demographic changes." Bezou explained that Strassel had a particular desire to work with black Catholics, stemming from his experience as an altar boy at Holy Name of Mary Church in the New Orleans neighborhood of Algiers, where he was "puzzled and repulsed" by Jim Crow practices at Mass that compelled blacks to receive Communion last and to sit in "Colored" areas. Assuming duties as Lourdes pastor, Strassel found the parish debt free and had repairs made to the church, including having a new foundation laid for the chronically buckling floor. Under Strassel, parish organizations, including the ushers and altar boys and the parish's Boy Scout troop, became racially integrated. Concerned about the underutilization of the school's substantial plant, the archdiocese for a few years converted it into a Community Model School, but converted it back to parochial status in 1976. With the Dominican sisters no longer working in the parish, Cynthia Smith, an African American teacher and laywoman, became principal. Laypersons and religious sisters would lead the struggling school in the years that followed.[80] In 2007, two decades after his death in 1987, Strassel was credibly accused of "fondling the genitals of a boy" while he was pastor at Lourdes during the period from 1969 to 1971. In 2009, the archdiocese paid to settle a civil suit brought by Strassel's victim, a fact that the archdiocese acknowledged publicly only in 2018 as it released a list of fifty-seven credibly accused New Orleans clerics.[81]

In 1975, Fr. Strassel was succeeded by Bishop Harold Perry, who would become Lourdes's first black pastor. Perry was born in Lake

Charles, Louisiana, in 1916; his father was a French-speaking rice mill laborer, his mother a domestic cook. After studying with the Divine Word Missionary Order in Mississippi, Illinois, and Wisconsin, he was ordained in Bay St. Louis, Mississippi, in 1944, becoming the twenty-sixth African American priest to be ordained in the United States. After assignments in Arkansas, Mississippi, and Louisiana, Perry was named auxiliary bishop of New Orleans in 1965, making him the first African American bishop in the twentieth century (twelve more black American bishops would follow by 1990). Following his consecration as bishop, Perry served several pastorates in New Orleans even as he remained active in civil rights work and in fostering ministry for black Catholics.[82]

Parishioners remembered that Bishop Perry make significant contributions as pastor at Lourdes in easing the lingering tensions of a "rough" period of racial transition and in overseeing the pivotal development of an African American cultural style in liturgies. Olympia and Harold Boucree recalled that the soft-spoken Perry engendered respect from whites because he held the office of bishop, while blacks at Lourdes took pride in the fact that he was the first black pastor and bishop. The Boucrees remembered that Perry integrated African American music into services, even while he insisted that the music must be "liturgically correct." Drums replaced the organ, and liturgical dance was introduced. The Boucrees explained that many black Catholics at Lourdes were converts from black Protestant churches, the fruit of Catholic evangelization efforts, "Negro Apostolates," that converted thousands of black Protestants between 1940 and 1965 who "brought their music" with them.[83] In 1978, a newly ordained African American priest, Fr. Fernand Cheri, was appointed to Lourdes, where he worked with local youth to organize the parish's first gospel choir. The gospel choir and Fr. Cheri's "liturgical innovations" attracted the largest attendance to the twelve fifteen Sunday Mass "in years."[84] Bishop Perry had long been interested in finding appropriate ways to synthesize Catholicism with African American culture, but he was wary of approaches influenced by black nationalism that might veer significantly from the main currents of American Catholic culture. In 1971 the National Black Catholic Clergy Caucus (NBCCC) announced that it intended to study the formation of a separate African American rite within the Catholic Church. In a joint statement with Ugandan prelate Emmanuel K. Nsubuga, who was visiting the United States at the time, Perry (then the only African American bishop) declared the notion of a separate black Catholic rite "divisive and harmful."[85]

Parish historian Henry Bezou described the 1960s and 1970s as a period of "financial as well as social travail" for Lourdes as the parish was no longer supported by the contributions of wealthy and middle-class parishioners and increasingly fell into debt, dependent on archdiocesan support. Evening services during the week were curtailed due to fears for security amid rising crime in the Freret neighborhood. Despite the problems, Bishop Perry optimistically addressed the parish at Christmas 1979 as the church's seventy-fifth anniversary approached. Perry offered thanks for myriad "spiritual benefits" and guidance from "our Blessed Mother . . . in the service of Jesus, her son" over the life of the parish. Perry also announced plans to renovate the church "to make it physically more beautiful and liturgically more meaningful in the Post–Vatican II period," including moving the confessional, introducing a "consultation room," dedicating an outdoor shrine, and restoring the baptismal font.[86] A Texas Jesuit, Rev. J. H. McCown, who spent a month working at Lourdes in 1979, described the parish's strengths and weaknesses in a letter to the *New Orleans Times-Picayune*: "Once a posh parish, it is now poor and half black (with some of the best Catholic singing in the city). Its nearly all-black parochial school is struggling by dint of staff's dedication, begging, and bingo to stay alive. Half the students are not Catholics. Their parents pay what they can for an education that they deem superior and more conducive to goodness in their children."[87]

Between 1982, when Bishop Perry stepped down, and 2006, when the church closed after Katrina, eight priests served as pastor or administrator at Lourdes as the parish dealt with declining membership, challenging finances, and persistent rumors that the archdiocese was interested in closing the church or school. As New Orleans Catholicism further diversified with the arrival of Catholic immigrants from Vietnam and Latin America, the now predominantly African American parish struggled on.[88]

As it approached the celebration of its centenary, Lourdes, a segregated white parish for its first half century and then an integrated parish with an African American majority in the decades that followed, took on a West African inflection. The new synthesis of African American and West African culture at Lourdes reflected the comparative strength of Catholicism in the Global South relative to the United States or Europe at the turn of the twenty-first century. But in another sense the new African accent at Lourdes also brought black Catholicism in New Orleans, which had originated with French Ursuline nuns and Afro-Creole Catholic women working to effect conversions within the matrifocal culture of Senegambian slaves in Louisiana, full circle. Fr. Raphael Ezeh, ordained in his native Nigeria in 1996, became pastor at Lourdes in 2002. Ezeh was an Igbo born into a Catholic family who had attended a government-run Catholic school at the cathedral in his home city in Nigeria. The Catholic culture of southeast Nigeria that Ezeh grew up in was the fruit of missionary work by the Holy Ghost Fathers, also known as the Spiritans, a religious order founded in Paris in the early eighteenth century that became heavily involved in African missions in the nineteenth century. Discerning a religious vocation and against the initial wishes of his family who wanted him to instead pursue marriage and a family in accord with the values of "the tribe," Ezeh joined the Missionary Society of St. Paul, a religious order of priests and deacons founded in Nigeria in 1978 and dedicated, among other things, to work among inner-city African Americans in the United States. After coming to America in 1999, Fr. Ezeh served as parochial vicar at Lourdes under Fr. John Cisewski. In 2010, Ezeh recalled that he had heard that Lourdes would have been closed if the Missionary Society of St. Paul had not assumed its pastoral care in 2002. At the same time sisters from the Daughters of Divine Love, an order of Nigerian nuns, were invited to assist with Lourdes School. The Daughters of Divine Love were founded in 1969 during the Biafran War, the devastating conflict that followed the effort of largely Igbo and Christian states in the southeast to secede from Nigeria, encountering staunch resistance from northern states that were predominantly Hausa and Muslim.[89]

Recalling his time at Lourdes, Fr. Ezeh remembered a "vibrant" and "active" parish, with ministries expanding from fifteen to thirty-five, and "liturgically rich celebrations," including "elaborate" Holy Week services, all with "an added African perspective/dimension." Ezeh believed that the school, while expensive for the parish to maintain, laid a "solid" academic, spiritual, and social foundation for its students. Asked what might have been distinctive about Lourdes Parish, Ezeh replied that "in a way, Lourdes had a fine balance in its liturgy and worship. We had parishioners who were traditional and conservative and a younger population that wanted some, but not too much, gospel music. I remember one senior who leaned towards traditional music but preferred the upbeat Mass and then complained when the choir sang louder than she's used to. But she kept coming to the later Mass." Ezeh recollected financial struggles as the parish made renovations to the church as its planned centennial celebration in September 2005 approached, along with the frustration of parishioners that archdiocesan support could have been greater "for these good things happening at Lourdes."[90]

V

On August 29, 2005, a few weeks short of the hundredth anniversary of the dedication of Lourdes Parish, the storm surges of Hurricane Katrina overwhelmed the levees protecting New Orleans, eventually flooding 80 percent of the city, killing nearly fifteen hundred, and destroying or badly damaging scores of buildings. African Americans, who constituted 67 percent of New Orleans's pre-Katrina population, made up 76 percent of the flood victims. Low-lying areas, including predominantly African American neighborhoods such as the Lower Ninth Ward and Gentilly, were especially badly affected, taking more than ten feet of water, as did the wealthier, mostly white neighborhood of Lakeview. Racially mixed and somewhat higher elevation Freret was less severely impacted, taking four to six feet of water, but with significant damage to many structures.[91] At the time of the storm Fr. Ezeh, the Lourdes pastor, was visiting family in Nigeria. In his stead, another Nigerian Missionary Society of St. Paul priest, Fr. Casimir, was saying the parish's schedule of daily and Sunday Masses. As the Katrina flood waters inundated the former cypress swamp of Freret on September 1, Memorial Medical Center, two blocks up Napoleon Avenue from Lourdes, was marooned without electricity and running water. In the sweltering crisis at the former Southern Baptist Hospital, which had been long under the pastoral care of Lourdes priests, medical staff may have administered lethal doses of painkillers to at least seventeen patients. A doctor and two nurses were eventually arrested for their alleged actions in the chaotic aftermath of Katrina, but a grand jury did not indict them.[92] Down the street from the hospital at Lourdes, Fr. Casimir and the Daughters of Divine Love sisters were trapped at the flooded Lourdes rectory and convent. After they were rescued by boat, the Nigerian religious made their way to the New Orleans Convention Center, one of the locations in the Central Business District where those who had been unable to evacuate from the now deluged city had gathered. After two harrowing days at the convention center, which lacked supplies such as food and water, the priest and nuns who had held out at Lourdes Parish during the storm were evacuated to another Missionary Society of St. Paul parish in Napoleonville, Louisiana, and then conveyed to Houston, where the Nigerian religious order had its American headquarters. In the meantime, Fr. Ezeh had also arrived in Houston, where he was reunited with the Nigerian religious who helped him to run Lourdes Parish.[93]

Collecting information from Fr. Casimir, the DDL sisters, the parish secretary, the school principal, and several of the parish's youth coordinators, Fr. Ezeh assessed the state of the parish in the immediate days that followed the storm. The church was probably the least impacted, taking around four feet of flood water, damaging the pews and the already old carpet. But the church's stained-glass windows, with their indelible saints' images, were unaffected. The three-story rectory sustained window damages and its basement, used by archdiocesan Catholic Charities, had been thoroughly flooded. The three-story Lourdes school, with the convent on its top floor, sustained greater damage, with perhaps five feet of flooding on the ground floor, a portion of the roof torn off, precipitating leaking into the gym, windows broken, and documents, books, and equipment destroyed. Hearing from parishioners who had evacuated to New Iberia, Louisiana, Dallas, and New York, the pastor walked around the Houston Astrodome, where thousands of evacuees from New Orleans had been sheltered, but did not encounter any parishioners there.[94]

In October, as parishioners began to trickle back into the neighborhood and to decide whether or not they would permanently return to New Orleans, Fr. Ezeh oversaw the process of cleaning the parish plant and met with archdiocesan officials to discuss the future of the church and school. By mid-October 93 children from the school had returned to the city (283 had been enrolled before the storm), but their parents were advised to enroll them in other schools as considerable cleaning and repair would be required before Lourdes School would be ready to reopen. In the weeks that followed, as the pastor called parishioners to ascertain their well-being and to ask them whether they intended to return, he celebrated Mass on parish grounds, in the convent chapel and in a tent in the schoolyard. Twenty attended Mass on Sunday, November 6. A deanery meeting in early November laid out criteria for the future of inner-city parishes based upon the archdiocese's Catholic Life 2000 document, which in its findings had held that if an Uptown parish should close, it would be Lourdes. The Catholic Life 2000 criteria stipulated that parishes must have seven hundred families and should have been self-sustaining for three consecutive years, requirements that Lourdes Parish clearly could not meet. At an Uptown deanery meeting in mid-November, parish representatives argued that no Uptown parish ought to be closed, as theirs was the area of the city least affected by the storm and the most likely to rebound in population. Archdiocesan officials responded that any parish that wished to remain open would have to be financially self-sustaining, as the archdiocese was uninsured for losses over eighty million dollars. From these meetings, Ezeh gathered that the archdiocese would probably not offer much help and that in order to survive Lourdes would need much external assistance, perhaps donations from parishes elsewhere in the country that sought to help with the rebuilding after Katrina. The pastor also surmised that it would probably be easier to find funds for cleaning and restoring the school than for the church. Some suggested handing over the school to the archdiocese, thus freeing the parish of financial responsibility for it, but this also left the decision of the fate of the school—up in the air because it, unlike some parochial schools, had sustained storm damages—in the hands of the archdiocese. By late November eighty out of around four hundred parishioner families had either returned to the neighborhood or said they would as soon as their home was rebuilt. Forty-five attended Sunday Mass at the parish plant in late November. Drawing on the week's reading from Ezekiel, Ezeh urged his parishioners to place their faith in Christ, their shepherd, who unlike flawed and inadequate state and federal governments and insurance companies, would hear their "cries and groans" and shepherd them to "safety and greener pastures." By Christmas, with the help of volunteers and FEMA, the school and the parish center had been repaired and cleaned, but due to church-state separation, FEMA could not work on the church. With the church still unusable four months after the storm, Christmas and New Year's Day Masses were held in the convent chapel.[95]

A month into the new year, in February 2006, Archbishop Alfred Hughes announced that from March 12 Lourdes would be temporarily closed and clustered with St. Matthias Parish, some fifteen blocks north, originally a satellite of Lourdes and like it long a segregated white parish that had developed an African American majority in the decades after integration. The archdiocese terminated its contract with Fr. Ezeh's religious order, the Missionary Society of St. Paul, and Lourdes parishioners were instructed to now attend St. Matthias. The rationale was that, with many still damaged and closed parishes in New Orleans, diocesan priests should be given preference in staffing. In the archdiocese's restructuring plan, which Hughes justified as a response to the population losses and property damages wrought by Katrina, Lourdes was one of twenty parishes of tenuous status that would be clustered with more viable parishes until further review, while eight parishes and missions would be permanently closed. Sharing the news with his parishioners, Ezeh stressed that Lourdes was fortunate in that it had not been permanently closed, but that parishioners returning to the city must do their best to attend Mass at Lourdes (or St. Matthias) so that they would be counted as current parishioners and, to the extent that they could, that they should donate funds to Lourdes so that the repair of the parish plant could continue. Ezeh also announced continuing efforts to seek external aid, cash donations from congregations elsewhere in the United States with ties to Lourdes parishioners or interest in helping New Orleans recover from Katrina. Ninety attended a final Mass at Lourdes on March 5 before the clustering with St. Matthias under a new pastor, John Asare-Dankwah, a diocesan priest from Ghana. As he stepped down as pastor, Ezeh noted the suffering and pain caused by Katrina, including the storm's preemption of the parish's long-awaited centennial celebration and now the closure of the church. But he urged Lourdes parishioners to stand up and fight for the survival of their church, as the congregants of other shuttered parishes in the city were doing. And parishioners took up the struggle, developing long-range plans that they sought to share with the archdiocese. Although electricity had not yet been restored to the parish plant, Lourdes parishioners nevertheless organized a delayed centennial celebration that took place in the schoolyard, with a full Mass celebrated by New Orleans auxiliary bishop Roger Morin.[96]

Yet the efforts of Lourdes parishioners to save their church were ultimately of little avail. In April 2008, Archbishop Hughes announced that Lourdes Parish would be suppressed—that is, permanently closed—and that the parish would be merged with St. Matthias and a Central City African American parish, St. Monica, into a new parish called Blessed Trinity at the site of St. Matthias Church. Citing losses to Katrina—20 percent of the archdiocese's 491,000 Catholics had not returned after the storm, which had exposed the archdiocese to $120 million in uninsured property losses—Hughes closed and merged twenty-five parishes, nineteen of which had been shuttered since Katrina. As he announced the additional closures, Hughes argued that the decision made with "responsible pastoral sense" but stated that "my heart reaches out to all people who are hurt, wounded, fearful of the future, perhaps even angry."[97] In the wake of the archbishop's decision to permanently close so many churches, strong resistance mounted at some parishes. Citing a lack of consultation by the archdiocese, which they argued had ignored their considerable efforts to demonstrate their viability and plan for the future, parishioners at uptown parishes St. Henry and Our Lady of Good Counsel borrowed tactics from the "vigiling" movement that had resisted parish closures in Boston in 2004–5. Parishioners at St. Henry and Our Lady of Good Counsel occupied their church buildings for ten weeks, until the archdiocese brought in police to evict them in January 2009.[98] One New Orleans parish successfully resisted Hughes's efforts to have it closed and merged. St. Augustine Church in Tremé, established in 1842 and a foundational church for the development of New Orleans's Afro-Creole Catholicism, was slated in 2006 for closure and merger with St. Peter Claver, a nearby African American parish. Drawing on the deep tradition of Crescent City black Catholic protest, St. Augustine parishioners organized a sit-in at the rectory and a protest at Mass that compelled Hughes to delay closure by eighteen months, albeit with the removal of the parish's longtime (since 1990) activist, Afrocentric pastor Fr. Jerome LeDoux, the originator of the parish's well-known "Jazz Mass." In March 2009, shortly before Hughes retired, the archdiocese finally lifted St. Augustine's probation and the font of black Catholicism in the Crescent City was permitted to remain open.[99]

All told, Lourdes was one of thirty-four parishes and twenty-four schools that were closed in the archdiocese's post-Katrina contraction. The closure of so many churches and schools in a process that few of the affected parishioners viewed as open or inclusive led several Mardi Gras krewes during the 2009 carnival season to parody Archbishop Hughes, a cleric raised and trained in Boston's authoritarian Irish American Catholic culture but the leader of New Orleans's multicultural, pluralistic Catholicism during a period of unprecedented, catastrophic change, as "a prelate closing churches to grab their money."[100] Although the losses of Katrina may have provided the immediate context for the New Orleans parish closures, in national terms the phenomenon was hardly unique. Many dioceses in the early twenty-first century responded to demographic shifts that shrank the number of parishioners, the rapid decline in the number of priests and religious sisters, and financial liability in the wake of the clergy sexual abuse scandal by shuttering and clustering significant proportions of their parishes. With declining and aging populations, the Northeast and Rust Belt were particularly affected. For example, between 2003 and 2008 Boston closed 63 of 257 parishes, while during the same period the diocese of Green Bay, Wisconsin, downsized from 212 to 160 parishes.[101]

Although the closing of Lourdes Parish occurred in a citywide and national context of Catholic Church contraction, the most poignant meanings occurred at the local level, in the experiences of the parish community and the individual worshipper. Interviewed several years later, Lourdes congregants expressed frustration with the archdiocesan decision to close. Jill Benoit, a key participant in efforts to save the church, believed that archdiocese officials had not listened to the voices of parishioners. "The bottomline is that the archdiocese closed down the church and school despite limited damage to the property and much opposition from the parishioners and the neighborhood associations. . . . We had developed long range plans. Lourdes parish/church and school were viable members of the community." Benoit, a lawyer, pointed out that the closure of the parish also meant the loss of distinctive sacral space, noting that the church's unique "altar dedicated to the Blessed Mother" was "a beautiful altar that is basically rotting since Katrina."[102] Longtime parishioners Harold and Olympia Boucree were more philosophical. Holding that "Lourdes closing and Katrina were coincidental," the Boucrees believed that Fr. Raphael Ezeh and his predecessors had effectively kept the parish alive despite lagging support from the archdiocese. "Fr. Raphael worked very hard on the hundredth anniversary—[there was] not much support from the archdiocese, the archdiocese was concerned about the maintenance of the physical plant, had to pull funds from other churches, declining membership, had long been thought that it would close." The Boucrees said that former Lourdes parishioners were "confused," though, as to why Lourdes had been shuttered while similarly struggling St. Matthias had stayed open. They speculated that this may have been because St. Matthias had closed its school and was thus able to rent out the property, leading the archdiocese to believe that St. Matthias was doing better than Lourdes.[103] Another longtime active Lourdes parishioner, Sadie White, spoke of the closure of the parish as akin to the painful death of a loved one. White said that the loss of the sacral space where the sacraments had been enacted over the life cycle was a dispossession keenly felt by a community of believers at Lourdes stretching generations. "The sacramental life of the family and ancestors, when they speak of the loss of the parish it's like they have lost a love one. They speak of family members who were baptized and received first communion and reconciliation and those who were confirmed and married from Lourdes and those who graduated from the school. And yes the pain of burying a love one. They speak of members they miss and the painful separation they experience."[104]

Asked what was distinctive and meaningful to them about their worship at Lourdes, former African American parishioners emphasized the church's distinctive racial history as a Jim Crow parish that integrated and then embraced an African American Catholic identity. Former congregants highlighted a complex sense of community fashioned from the integration struggle along with a shared sense of history in a particular sacral space that extended back to the pre-integration era and that also incorporated white parishioners whose families had worshipped at the church for decades but who had largely stopped attending. Sadie White stressed her powerful personal experience of the transformation from segregation to full inclusion, but also the ambiguities of devotional change in the post–Vatican II years. "In the years I attended I have seen African Americans move from sitting in the back and on side pews to full ministry in church. [The] old confessional removed, side pews removed, altar rail removed and ceiling art painted over and knowing how this affected older members. . . . I have seen the rejection and acceptance of African and African American priests in the parish."[105] Olympia and Harold Boucree said that they "experienced great comfort and satisfaction at the change" from segregated to integrated to predominantly African American. The Boucrees emphasized that the few whites who remained were quite integrated and participated fully in parish life. Asked for their favorite memories of worship at Lourdes, the Boucrees cited "wonderful holy days, [with the] integration of African American music into the liturgy—[and] dance added to [the] liturgy."[106] Noting that by the time she joined the parish in 2000 it was mostly attended by African Americans along with a few whites and Hispanics, Jill Benoit argued that Lourdes was notable for its "culturally diverse" approach to worship, for its prominence in the history of twentieth-century New Orleans Catholicism, and for its service to the Freret community. "It has been said on numerous occasions that the vast majority of religious in the archdiocese of New Orleans attended school and/or graduated from Lourdes school. This was when the school was predominantly white. . . . The church was often staffed by monsignors as pastor—more than any other church. . . . Bishop Perry had a tremendous impact on the growth and type of worship in the parish. With his presence, more African Americans came into the church and became parishioners. The Dominican Sisters were also instrumental in the education of the children who attended the school. . . . We had a parish center that catered to the larger community, predominantly the elderly and poor."[107]

Merger into the new parish of Blessed Trinity at the location of St. Matthias Parish did not come easily for some former Lourdes parishioners. The archdiocesan newspaper, the *Clarion Herald*, published a sanguine report suggesting a painless transition in which former Lourdes and St. Monica congregants quickly adapted to their new shared sacral space. The *Herald* noted that leading up to the merger the priest celebrating Mass would be certain to mention when he was using sacred items from the closed parishes, such as the processional cross from Lourdes and the Communion cup from St. Monica, but ended this practice after the merger at the suggestion of the parishioners from the shuttered churches.[108] The reality of the transition was more complicated. In 2010, Harold and Olympia Boucree said that they and "a good core" of former Lourdes parishioners now attended Blessed Trinity, while "many" other former Lourdes congregants attended St. Katharine Drexel (Holy Ghost), the once segregated African American parish where Lourdes priests had once shunted neighborhood African Americans who wanted to practice their Catholic faith at lilywhite Jim Crow Lourdes. Several years after the merger, priests at Blessed Trinity in their homilies and in reading the prayers of the faithful still ardently spoke of the need to overcome hard feelings from the closures and to accomplish unity as a congregation. Additional ironies emerged in the years that followed the closure of Lourdes church and school. In 2012, as the Freret neighborhood rebounded as a hipster haven, the archdiocese arranged for Blessed Trinity Parish to lease the revamped 1957 Lourdes School building—the school plant built by Monsignor Lucien Caillouet on the unforeseen eve of integration was still an impressive facility—to Holy Rosary Academy and High School, schools that enrolled considerably more white students than Lourdes School ever had in the post-integration era. Meaningful integration had finally come to Lourdes School, but only after Lourdes Parish had closed.[109]

For more than a decade after its closure in the wake of Katrina, the massive 1924 Spanish-mission-style Lourdes Church on Napoleon Avenue sat locked, boarded up, and unused, its once impressive interior decaying in the humid, swampy New Orleans climate. There was some echo, though, of Lourdes's joyous, African American and African-inflected post-integration worship fifteen blocks north at the merged parish of Blessed Trinity at the site of St. Matthias Church. In a Katrina-damaged and restored World War II–era art deco church building that once housed a segregated white parish born amid New Orleans's early twentieth-century geographic expansion and the extension of Jim Crow to the city's Catholic congregations, the mostly African American parishioners gathered at ten o'clock for a Mass that often stretched until noon. Although the priests in the first years after Katrina spoke with Ghanaian and Tanzanian accents and their homilies reflected the synthesis of Catholic and indigenous African religiosities dynamically under way since the mid-twentieth century in sub-Saharan Africa, much of the service was in the African American idiom forged during nearly three centuries of black Christianity in New Orleans. An amplified, energetic, soulful gospel choir melded the texts and melodies of

Catholic liturgy with the stirring rhythms of black Protestantism. Congregants responded kinetically with exclamations to key moments in the liturgy, homily, and music. Some worshippers stood and danced to the music of the gospel choir. A pervasive sense of community and an extroverted welcome—including an extended sign of peace at the beginning of Mass in which nearly every congregant embraced or shook the hand of everyone else present in the church—signaled a style of worship that contrasted significantly with the staid, formal, interior-directed manner of participation that prevailed in white-majority Catholic parishes elsewhere in the city. Homiletics also differed. A decidedly right-leaning Catholic cultural warrior focus on denouncing social change, contemporary immorality, abortion, and same-sex marriage often dominated the rhetoric from the pulpit elsewhere in the city. While such issues occasionally received attention in sermons here, the pastoral emphasis was more likely to be on taking personal responsibility for one's spiritual growth and the well-being of one's neighbor while participating in a community ravaged by structural inequities and violence. As at Lourdes in its post-integration decades, a culture of faith forged in a struggle to claim Christian dignity amid slavery and then Jim Crow claimed a communion of all souls here in a sacral space that once limited African Americans to the side and back pews and the end of the communion line.[110]

2

The Making of a Midwestern Catholicism

Transnational Identities, Ethnicity, and Catholic Culture in Iowa City, 1840–1940

Oral tradition holds that in the nineteenth century, Irish families at St. Mary's Catholic Church in Iowa City rented pews on the west side of the church, while German families preferred pews on the east side. This is because the high altar in Iowa City's oldest Catholic church is flanked on the left by a statue of St. Patrick, the patron saint of Ireland, and on the right by a statue of St. Boniface, the patron saint of German Catholicism.[1] Even though the story may oversimplify ethnic divisions and identity among Catholics in a developing Midwestern town in the nineteenth century, it does convey the important truth that national origin and subsequent diasporic identity formation played crucial roles in the first century of Catholic culture in the American Midwest. Indeed the story of contending altar statues of ethnic patron saints is all that remains within the parish's collective memory of what were highly contested battles among three Catholic ethnic groups—the Germans, Irish, and Bohemians (Czechs)—over space, clerical leadership, devotional styles, and the nature of layperson involvement in what was Iowa City's only Catholic parish for several decades in the mid-nineteenth century.[2]

This chapter uses Iowa City's history of transnational, multiethnic Catholic cultures to trace the complex and varied origins of a regional Midwestern Catholic culture. Iowa can in a sense be seen as indicative of the Catholic experience in the Lower Midwest, where diverse ethnic Catholic enclaves scattered across a largely rural landscape that also attracted large numbers of worshippers from various Protestant denominations, especially Methodists and Congregationalists. With the exception of more densely Catholic northeast Iowa, much of the Hawkeye State displays this Lower Midwestern pattern of Catholic enclaves within a majority-Protestant religious landscape.[3]

Located at the approximate juncture point of densely Catholic north-east Iowa and sparsely Catholic central and southern Iowa, Iowa City provides an excellent setting to trace the formation of a regional Catholic Midwestern culture rooted in plural ethnic diasporas and transnational connections. In the antebellum and early postbellum periods, the town was somewhat unique for its relatively modest size in encompassing the diverse, heterogenous character of nineteenth-century Midwestern Catholicism, including significant numbers of Irish, German, and Bohemian Catholics. Amid the centrifugal pressures initially exerted by their diversity, this chapter argues, Iowa City's Catholics experienced in miniature larger processes that would play out across the Midwest and among American Catholics more generally. Uneasily integrated for several decades in a single parish housing the town's three significant ethnic Catholic communities, St. Mary's Parish would fracture in favor of ethnic separatism, the formation of distinct ethnic parishes, in the latter decades of the nineteenth century. Yet in the early to mid-twentieth century, assimilative and Americanization pressures exerted by both the larger society and Church leaders would cut the other way, undermining older particularistic ethnic identities, eventually rendering ethnic Catholicism a quaint memory. Indeed, Iowa City's relatively cosmopolitan nature as a small and slowly growing university town may have hastened this process, at least after 1900 (in contrast, for example, with communities of German Catholics elsewhere in the rural and urban Upper Midwest that persisted in their distinctiveness until the 1930s and sometimes after). According to census data, Iowa City's population numbered 1,250 in 1850 and then mushroomed to 5,214 by 1860, but did not surpass 10,000 until 1910 and by 1940 had reached only 17,182. The city's relatively modest size and population stasis until the early twentieth century constrained the formation of Catholic parishes and the building of Catholic churches and gave relations between its multiethnic Catholics a certain intensity, while the university town's cosmopolitanism may have conversely served to hasten the decline of ethnic particularism after 1900.[4]

While Iowa City's multiethnic Catholics of European descent were hardly unique in pursuing ethnic separatism in the nineteenth century and in the attenuation of their ethnic particularism in the twentieth century, unlike Catholics in the Northeast and in the Upper Midwest but similar to Catholics in much of the South beyond southern Louisiana, they manifested their Catholic identities in the context of a Protestant-majority landscape. While Iowa City Catholics' pursuit of ethnic homogeneity in parishes as they sought to preserve the Catholic cultures they associated with their European homelands resembled in some respects what occurred in urban northeastern locales such as New York City, the relative paucity of Catholic presence amid a landscape of ever-fracturing Protestant congregations may have heightened the quest for Catholic ethnic separatism in the nineteenth-century Lower Midwest. In short, the shared and distinctive qualities of the Lower Midwest within American Catholicism serve to highlight the significance and the particularity of region within American Catholic history.[5]

A Catholic presence in Iowa City dates to its inception as territorial capital in 1841 and the labors of Fr. Samuel Mazzuchelli, an intrepid Dominican friar born in Milan in 1806 and assigned in 1828 by Cincinnati bishop Edward Fenwick to serve as a missionary priest for the vast Northwest Territory. Mazzuchelli professed vows to the Dominicans in Milan as the order was recovering from a period of suppression and internal disorder under Napoleonic and then Austrian rule. After the young Milanese friar arrived in the United States, he served far-flung Catholic communities around the Great Lakes, particularly Native Americans and French Canadian and mixed-ancestry Métis fur traders. Fr. Mazzuchelli, often anglicized as "Matthew Kelly," also administered the sacraments to lead miners, many of them Irish Catholics, as they arrived at Galena and Dubuque in the mid-1830s.[6] After the establishment of the diocese of Dubuque in 1837 and of Iowa Territory in 1838, Mazzuchelli assisted Mathias Loras, the first bishop of Dubuque, in rapidly organizing Catholic congregations and building churches in territorial settlements, including Davenport and Burlington. Perpetuating Catholic ties linking the Mississippi Valley to France that stemmed to the colonial era, Loras and other French émigré priests in territorial Iowa participated in a postrevolutionary Catholic revivalism that sought to restore French society to a universalistic organic Catholic order following the iconoclastic, anticlerical French Revolution. Loras had been born in Lyon in 1792 to a prominent family; seeking to purge the silk weaving city, France's third largest, of the ancien régime, revolutionaries had condemned and executed the future Dubuque prelate's father and several of his aunts and uncles.[7]

The European missionary priests Mazzuchelli and Loras played key roles in establishing a Catholic congregation in Iowa Territory's new capital city. Mazzuchelli, who like other Catholics in the early decades of the nineteenth century often spoke and wrote of the consonance of Catholicism with American republican ideology (even as anti-Catholic thinkers articulated the opposite), had cultivated ties to territorial legislators in Burlington, with the legislature meeting in the winter of 1840–41 in St. Paul the Apostle Church, which the Milanese friar had established. Mazzuchelli recalled in his memoirs, written and published in Italian as he visited Milan in 1843, that Iowa City arose in a matter of months on a site that "was in June of 1839 an uninhabited solitude covered with trees." Drawing on a legislative enactment reserving lots for churches in the new capital city, in December 1840, with a security of two thousand dollars, Mazzuchelli acquired two parcels for a Catholic church. The Italian priest noted that representatives of nascent Protestant congregations that included "the Primitive Methodists, the Methodist Episcopalians, the Presbyterians, [and] the Unitarians" eagerly did the same, creating a vibrant religious marketplace in the infant territorial capital. Mazzuchelli celebrated the first Mass in Iowa City on December 20 at the house of a "German mechanic," Ferdinand Habestroh, "not far from the State House," with twenty-eight of the town's thirty Catholic settlers attending; he then preached Iowa City's "first dogmatic sermon" in "the Hall of a small hotel." On July 12, 1841, Loras laid the cornerstone of St. Mary's Church, which was dedicated to the Assumption of the Blessed Mary; Mazzuchelli explained that "as she is the Patroness of the Diocese it was fitting that to her should be dedicated the first church of Iowa's Capital." At the dedication, Mazzuchelli preached on the consistency of Catholic worship with American republican government, addressing "the large gathering present on the subject of the Religious and even political advantages resulting from the practice of Divine worship, and that the truths of the Gospel are the basis of true liberty and true patriotism." The church was constructed by the spring of 1843, with a basement subdivided for a rudimentary dwelling for the priest and a schoolhouse. At the land sales in Dubuque, Loras purchased land on the outskirts of Iowa City to be used for a Catholic cemetery. Looking ahead, Mazzuchelli believed that five hundred German Catholics already lived in the environs of Iowa City and that they, along with Irish settlers and "converts," would within a few years "form a large parish, and one of some importance also, in the matter of the influence exerted by any city wherein reside the members of the Legislature, the Governor and State Officials."[8]

From the 1840s through the mid-1850s, as Bishop Loras published letters in Irish and German Catholic newspapers in eastern and Midwestern cities seeking to lure Catholic immigrants to Iowa, the predominantly Irish and German congregants of St. Mary's would be served by French and Irish priests. For much of the nineteenth century, the American Catholic Church would rely on clergy recruited from Europe, for whom the concrete realities of American life often existed in tension with their participation in an ultramontane revival centered in Europe that renewed emphasis on papal, Roman-centered authority, stressed the prestige and power of priests as religious specialists intermediating between the laity and the sacred, and rejuvenated an array of devotions such as the Sacred Heart of Jesus that emphasized identification with a suffering Christ.[9] Loras had recruited French priests and seminarians to Dubuque in his early years leading the diocese, and several of these priests, including Anthony Pelamourgues, Anthony Godfert, and B. M. Poyet, would serve at St. Mary's in the 1840s. Despite their shared nativity, Loras had contentious relations with his French clergy, with Pelamourgues (who was the founding and longtime pastor at St. Anthony's Church in Davenport, from 1839 until 1868) objecting that Loras was creating parishes and churches more rapidly than the Catholic population and the available clergy warranted. Like many footloose Catholic clerics in the nineteenth-century United States, Anthony Godfert, who in 1844 became the pastor resident in Iowa City, would seek better opportunities by departing Loras's authority in 1846 to serve in the new diocese of Milwaukee under Bishop John Martin Henni, a Swiss German.[10] J. P. McCormick and Mathias Hannon, Irish-born pastors at St. Mary's in the early 1850s, embodied the disciplined folk piety created by a "devotional revolution" that transformed Irish Catholicism in the years before and after the famine and large-scale Irish immigration to the United States. Decades later, in 1891, Hannon vividly recalled an intrepid cleric's existence in Iowa City, lodging at a boarding house "directly south from the old State House" (before a formal rectory was built in 1854) as well as saying Mass and attending sick calls at missions

and stations all around the Hawkeye State, filling in with white settlement west of the Cedar River, as far south as Mount Pleasant, and as
far to the north and west as Fort Dodge.[11] Like many Catholic priests
in the antebellum United States, Iowa City clerics contended against
the anti-Catholic, nativist backlash that followed significant Irish and
German Catholic immigration. In Iowa City, sectarian disputation over
school funding and the use of the Protestant Bible in common schools
spilled into the election for school funds commissioner, with Methodists publicly opposing a Catholic candidate and Catholics burning Bibles
distributed by Methodists. St. Mary's priest B. M. Poyet and Alexander Bushnell, a Methodist minister and Whig Party operative, engaged
in vitriolic exchanges in Iowa City newspapers, with Bushnell alleging
Catholic anti-republican designs on the county school fund and noting
the weakness of religious liberty in papal-dominated areas of Catholic
Europe. Poyet parried by denouncing what he perceived as Bushnell's
anti-Catholic bigotry and invoking the patriotism of French Catholic
American Revolutionary War hero Marquis de Lafayette.[12]

Over the next dozen years, St. Mary's slipped into crisis, as the parish's
sizable numbers of Irish and Germans and lesser but nonetheless significant numbers of Bohemians disputed over whether their ethnic communities were adequately and equitably served by the parish's polyglot
Catholicism. The seeds of ethnic factionalism developed as Iowa City's
Catholic population grew in size and complexity in the late antebellum
era; the 1850 census had tallied 152 German-born and 86 Irish-born residents in Johnson County, while the 1860 census enumerated 1,407 born
in Germany, 1,258 in Ireland, 820 in the Austrian Empire (including Bohemians) and 891 born in yet other countries.[13] In 1853 an Austrian Jesuit
priest, Franz Xavier Weninger, led a mission in Iowa City that yielded
six converts and culminated with the erection of a forty-foot cemetery
cross. For three decades beginning in 1848, Weninger conducted approximately eight hundred missions among Catholic communities
around the United States, inspiring the formation and construction of
many new parishes and churches, especially among Germans. In Iowa
City, his visit led German Catholics to begin organizing a German parish, designating land in the northeastern part of the city. Germans at St.
Mary's had organized a short-lived German school during Fr. Hannon's
pastorate, and the German language school revived in 1857 under his

successor, Fr. Mathias Michels, a priest born in Luxemburg and trained in France. Michels sought to serve Bohemian Catholics at St. Mary's by bringing in a Czech Redemptorist father, Francis Krubil, in 1856 to lead a mission for Bohemian parishioners. Yet Irish parishioners disputed Michels's efforts at managing the needs of the parish's three distinct ethnic communities, asserting that he favored the Germans, who by this time may have been outnumbered by the rapidly growing numbers of Irish Catholics in Iowa City.[14]

The contention between ethnic communities worshipping uncomfortably under the same roof at late antebellum St. Mary's reflected significant differences in traditions and styles of Catholicism carried from countries of origin and further transformed in diasporic communities evolving in response to American conditions while remaining in communication (through clergy traveling back and forth, devotional books and sacred objects such as statuary, the ethnic press, and newly arrived immigrants) with their national/religious homelands.

Practicing a recently forged "disciplined folk piety" refracting centuries of Celtic mysticism and shaping by searing experiences of the famine and English colonial oppression and bigotry, Irish Catholic immigrants (virtually all of them English speakers) readily assented to ultramontane clerical authority and the steady diminution of lay authority in the antebellum American Church as Irish bishops (such as New York's John Hughes) faced off against hostile, nativist Protestant Americans. In terms of liturgy and devotions, Irish Catholics preferred a relatively simple and austere form of worship and especially valued the sacramental act of confessing sins to a priest.[15]

For their part, German Catholics, shaped by a sense of their social disadvantage vis-à-vis Protestants within German society and by the embattled status of Catholicism in Prussia, strongly emphasized lay participation in church governance (*kirchenrat*), often coming into conflict with bishops (particularly Irish ones in the northeastern United States) and priests who sought to exert what lay Germans regarded as undue control over lay trustees and worshippers. Vienna's Leopoldine Society and Munich's Ludwig Missionverein supported German Catholic missions in the United States and facilitated German Catholic settlement, particularly in the Midwest. German Catholic immigrants strongly emphasized parochial schools, with particular stress on transmission of German Catholic culture through instruction in German. German Catholics also valued an elaborate baroque communalistic devotional style that included "processions and pilgrimages, confraternities, rich orchestral music and richly embellished churches" as well as a vernacular style stemming from Enlightenment Catholicism that emphasized robust congregational singing (*lustige Gesang*). German Catholic immigrant ideals were most fully realized in enclaves in Upper Midwestern states such as Wisconsin and Minnesota where they organized their own national parishes and through their votes controlled local polities, including public school systems.[16]

Czechs (along with German Bohemians), by contrast, immigrated from Bohemian lands ruled by the Austro-Hungarian Empire. Catholic churches in Bohemia reflected older feudal arrangements and were funded by noble patrons or from property held by the church, with fairly minimal lay support such as gifts for clergy or Mass stipends. As they sought to maintain a rich Baroque devotional style rooted in Bohemian Slavic traditions, Czech Catholic immigrants to the American Midwest struggled with unfamiliar expectations of lay funding for parishes as well as the lay initiative required to negotiate with parish and diocesan officials, especially in light of the paucity of Czech-speaking priests in the United States.[17]

Alleging that Irish and English-speaking worshippers were receiving favorable treatment to their detriment, even as the parish was led by a young German-born priest, William Emonds, who had become pastor in 1858, most of the Germans along with the Bohemians departed an overcrowded St. Mary's in 1862. Sacramental records at St. Mary's from this tumultuous period, written in Latin by Fr. Emonds, document the fluctuating ethnic mix at St. Mary's, with concentrations of baptisms of Irish, German, and Bohemian infants ebbing and flowing over time with the ethnic politics that engulfed the parish.[18] Fr. Franz Xavier Weninger led another mission in Iowa City in 1862 and encouraged Germans and Bohemians to form their own parish. Receiving permission from Clement Smyth, the Irish-born bishop who had succeeded Mathias Loras, the Germans and Bohemians who had left St. Mary's built a small church, dedicated to St. Francis Xavier, at Brown and Johnson streets in northern Iowa City, and a Bohemian priest, Adolph Spocek, served for a year as pastor. After Spocek left, the parish lacked a resident priest for a year, until April 1864 when Smyth assigned Capistran Zwinge, a Franciscan from Westphalia, Germany, who had arrived with other German Franciscans in central Illinois in the late 1850s to establish institutions to serve German Catholics in the Midwest. Soon the parish and its new pastor purchased a building for a rectory and made arrangements to bring in the Sisters of Charity of the Blessed Virgin Mary to run a school. Zwinge and parishioners then sought to raise funds to pay off the debt incurred in establishing a parish plant that now stretched a city block.[19]

In the year he administered the sacraments at St. Francis Xavier, Zwinge documented the travails of his congregation and a longer context of internecine struggles among Catholic ethnic groups in Iowa City in letters to his Franciscan superiors. A June 13, 1864, letter lamented general spiritual "indifference" among Catholics in Iowa City and bemoaned the small size of his church, "which in reality is the first story of a common dwelling," but he happily noted that many rural residents came to town for Sunday Mass, some from as far away as ten miles, and observed that the parish had conducted an open procession on the feast day of Corpus Christi, a favorite ritual of German Catholics.[20] A June 1, 1865, letter rehearsed the history of ethnic Catholic factionalism in Iowa City and recounted the quick falling out of Germans and Bohemians at St. Francis Xavier under his predecessor, due primarily to differences in how the two groups financially supported the parish, distinctions that stemmed to the contrasting Catholic cultures that Germans and Bohemians brought to Iowa from Europe. Zwinge's candid analysis indulged a German's condescending distaste for Czech culture but also a pastoral concern for both German and Bohemian Catholics.

Principally the Germans built the first Catholic Church in Iowa City. The Irish, however, increased more rapidly in number and the Germans formed the minority, until they became only an appendage to the parish. Father Michael [Michels] favored the Germans more than the Irish, and that displeased the latter. Father Emonds, (the present pastor, a Westphalian) sided with the English, and totally incurred the displeasure of the Germans, who never did harmonize well with the English. The Germans at the advice of Rev. Weninger, then separated from the original parish and built a new church. Their pastor, a Bohemian, united the German and Bohemian elements in one congregation. But since the Bohemians would neither contribute to the church, nor support the pastor, and since the Germans almost exclusively were obliged to maintain the priest, the latter, greatly disappointed in his own countrymen, inclined more to the German element. This, of course, provoked the Bohemians, and many unpleasant frictions arose. These circumstances may have induced the pastor to take his final sudden leave. I may remark, the Bohemians here, as is known fact, do pay very poorly for their church and the support of the priest. They want frequent dances even though they have not a shirt on their back. . . . Just the day before, a trial in court took place on account of some fighting-fray at their last dance for which they were heavily fined.[21]

Zwinge was not sanguine about reconciliation among the distinct ethnic Catholic communities in Iowa City. He noted that he had tried to get the Czech Catholics to come back to St. Francis Xavier, but with only limited success. He doubted that Germans and Bohemians could be successfully united in a parish in Iowa City.

After my arrival, I tried to win the Bohemians back to church. But they replied, that the Germans had declared, that they would throw the Bohemians out. I assured them that I would not tolerate that, and that they might come without fear. The Germans were not pleased; but I obliged them to give the Bohemians at least standing room. Since that time, some of the Bohemians come to our church. Up to date, however, they neither rented a seat, nor probably contributed a single quarter of a dollar. Some others frequent the English church. Most of them, I should judge, stay at home. These are our present conditions. An attempt to united the Germans and Bohemians, I consider a mere illusion. Perhaps a union with the Irish could be effected more easily. But also in this case, insurmountable difficulties will present themselves. For the Irish have their own church and, as long as Fr. Emonds is in charge, he would never permit it.[22]

On June 17, 1865, Zwinge's Franciscan superior in Teutopolis, Illinois, recalled him from Iowa City; in his time at St. Francis Xavier, Zwinge had enumerated 136 baptisms and seven conversions. Fr. Zwinge's departure imperiled the future of the German Catholic national parish on Iowa City's north side. Despite letters from parishioners pleading for the return of Zwinge or the assignment of another Franciscan, and even a visit from a delegation of parish representatives, John Sueppel and John Xanten, to Teutopolis, the German Franciscans in Illinois could spare no priests for Iowa City and the parish was only intermittently staffed by diocesan priests.[23] As one plaintive letter from parish trustees lamented, betraying a German Catholic sense of grievance at their purported second-class status (behind the privileged Irish) within American Catholicism, "We were so happy and contented and would no more believe that German Catholic parishes in America were treated by bishops as step-children. But all of a sudden we were plunged into this present sad and disconsolate condition so that, deprived of a pastor, we must look forward to a future that holds out to us little encouragement."[24] The parish closed in February 1867, with its congregation returning to St. Mary's. Much of St. Francis Xavier Church was destroyed in a fire in 1869.[25]

The compelled reunification of diverse ethnic Catholic communities at St. Mary's in the late 1860s was visually epitomized by the diorama of ethnic Catholic unity bringing together St. Patrick and St. Boniface, patrons of Irish and German Catholicism, respectively, astride the high altar at the new St. Mary's Church that was dedicated on August 15, 1869. Meanwhile on the east side of the new St. Mary's, gallery murals depicted four key Bohemian saints, Wenceslaus (Vaclav), his grandmother Ludmila, John of Nepomuk, and Adalbert. But unity at St. Mary's was short-lived. In the last decades of the nineteenth century, ethnic factionalism among Catholics in Iowa City led down the same pathway taken elsewhere by heterogeneous ethnic Catholic communities in the rural and urban United States, including the Midwest: the creation of separate national parishes predicated largely along ethnic lines. The difficult, fragile attempt to fashion a universal Catholic community in the university town, no longer the state's capital city (which had shifted to Des Moines in 1857), was abandoned in favor of congregations organized along lines of ethnic solidarity, a pattern that would hold until the early to mid-twentieth century.[26]

Seeking their own ethnic parish, free of the difficult, pluralistic compromises that the shared multiethnic devotional space at St. Mary's entailed after the return of the Germans and the Czechs, many Irish Americans departed from St. Mary's in 1873, forming St. Patrick's Church in southern Iowa City with Fr. Martin Rice as founding pastor. Originally housed in a structure at Dubuque and Burlington streets that had pre-

viously hosted a public library, lecture hall, and several Protestant congregations, St. Patrick's erected a new church at Linn and Court streets
with a first Mass celebrated there on February 2, 1879. The church's first
four pastors, through 1915, were Irish-born. The Irish parish operated a
school for boys, while girls from the parish were encouraged to attend St.
Agatha's Seminary at Jefferson and Dubuque streets. The Sisters of Charity BVM, an order that originated with Franciscan sisters who migrated
from Ireland to the United States in the 1830s, staffed Iowa City's Catholic
schools, including St. Mary's school. While Catholics of Irish heritage in
Iowa City lacked the numerical dominance that they enjoyed in much of
the urban northern United States, they participated in a larger American
Catholicism dominated by Irish American clergy that sought to defend
communalistic Catholic distinctiveness amid the rapid urban growth and
burgeoning individualistic capitalism of a historically Protestant nation.[27]

Long affected by their minority status among Iowa City Catholics behind Germans and Irish, Bohemians made their own departure from St.
Mary's at the end of the nineteenth century. Led by a Czech priest, Joseph Sinkmajer (born in Lysá, near Prague, in 1866), who had ministered
to them at St. Mary's, Bohemian Catholics departed in 1893 to form a
new parish named in honor of the Bohemian patron saint, the medieval
aristocrat and martyr St. Wenceslaus, in the Goosetown neighborhood
of northern Iowa City, a working-class Czech enclave since the 1850s.
When the cornerstone was laid on June 24, 1893, Sinkmajer preached in
Czech and Fr. John O'Farrell, pastor at St. Patrick's, preached in English,
stressing the new parish's identity as a national parish for Czechs: "To-day
my Bohemian brothers, you have raised a new Bethel. Here Bohemian
Catholics and others will come to worship God for this will be a holy
gate to heaven." The parish sustained strong sentimental ties to the home-
land, for instance raising six thousand kronen ($1,224) for the relief of
storm victims in Bohemia in September 1904. Inspired by the stirrings of
Czech and Slavic nationalism in the late nineteenth century and the creation of an independent Czechoslovakia after the collapse of the Austro-
Hungarian Empire following the Great War, Czech American Catholics
at St. Wenceslaus blended pride in a distinct ethnic heritage with the outward assimilation that post–World War I American culture demanded.[28]

Back at St. Mary's, following the exodus of many Irish and Czech parishioners, the latter nineteenth century would see the elaboration of a ten-

tative German Catholic sensibility, a diasporic devotional consciousness shaped by the Kulturkampf, the anti-Catholic policies of Prussian prime minister Otto von Bismarck.[29] But unlike many Midwestern urban and rural parishes with substantial German congregations, St. Mary's would never become a fully German national parish. This was because ethnic primacy had been contested there for decades, the congregation was always mixed and never exclusively German, English had long been the primary language of the parish, and Iowa City's Germans were comparatively assimilated by the time German Catholics became the dominant group in the parish in the late nineteenth century. In the thirty years of his pastorate, which had initially been strongly resisted by German Catholics in Iowa City, German-born pastor William Emonds traveled periodically to Austria-Hungary and Germany, where he purchased the Stations of the Cross that he installed on the walls at St. Mary's. In 1871 Emonds recruited nuns from his native German region of Westphalia, Prussia, Sisters of St. Francis fleeing Bismarck's repressive "May Laws," to Iowa City, where he found them a residence in the former rectory of St. Francis Xavier Church. Decades spent navigating the fraught ethnic politics of American Catholicism in the Midwest and Pacific Northwest did not erase Emonds's ties to German-speaking lands. Emonds returned to his native Germany for the last few years of his life and died in Cologne in 1903.[30]

During the lengthy pastorate at St. Mary's of A. J. Schulte, a German American priest born in Ft. Madison (to a father who had immigrated from Haselünne, Hanover) who served from 1891 until his death in 1940, the parish underwent substantial expansion of its plant and also displayed a defensive assimilation that eventually sought to deny the persistence of old world Teutonic traits, which in any case were more muted at St. Mary's than in many German-majority parishes across the Midwest. Yet the parish's German American identity was undeniable; in the early twentieth century, the surnames of many parishioners reflected German ancestry, traditional German songs were sung by old-timers at parish events, Schulte delivered a sermon in German at the Mass in 1907 marking the twenty-fifth anniversary of his ordination, and Schulte was an active leader in the St. Boniface League of Iowa, an association of German Catholic societies.[31]

In contrast to the uneasy Catholic pluralism of Iowa City and the Lower Midwest, German Catholics often held substantial majorities in the Upper Midwest—in Wisconsin and portions of Minnesota and the Dakotas—where they could sometimes control polities and dioceses, or at least compel a contentious pluralism with Irish American Catholics and other ethnic groups. In Minnesota, Saint Paul archbishop John Ireland (1888–1918) was one of the most prominent leaders of the Americanist wing of the Church arguing for adaptation to American conditions, including the advocacy of temperance (adamantly opposed by German bishops in Wisconsin) rather than the perpetuation of ethnic Catholic cultures and languages through national parishes and parochial schools. Ireland and his protégé, St. Cloud bishop Joseph Busch (1915–53), contended with dense populations of German Catholics in Minnesota and the Dakotas who by contrast saw Catholicism as a means to preserve German culture. German-speaking Benedictine monks from the mid-nineteenth century served the German Catholic heartland of Stearns County, Minnesota (seated at St. Cloud) and the largely Catholic German-Russians, stripped by Czar Alexander I in 1871 of the privileges that had attracted them to colonization of the lower Volga River steppes in the eighteenth century and unaccustomed to paying pew rents, who settled Dakota Territory, with the Fargo (originally Jamestown) and Sioux Falls dioceses established in 1889 and the Bismarck diocese created to serve German-Russians and Hungarians in 1910. Kathleen Neils Conzen describes a persistent strain of German American Catholicism permeating many aspects of society, culture, and politics in Stearns County, Minnesota, into the late twentieth century: "Less tangible evidence of local distinctiveness can be found in everything from the area's aggressive anti-abortion movement to the fiscal caution of its governmental bodies, the high persistence rates of its conservative farmers, the unusually large size of its families and the traces of traditional legalism, clericalism, and devotionalism that still mark its spirituality."[32]

The heavily German Catholic districts of northern Dane County, Wisconsin, provide another example of the evolution of German predominance in the Upper Midwest. In 1874, the archbishop of Milwaukee, John Martin Henni, granted permission for the establishment of St. John the Baptist Church in Waunakee. Archbishop Henni established St. John's at the request of nineteen German Catholic families who sought to worship exclusively among Germans instead of in a nearby mixed congregation with Irish Catholics. St. John's, serving a rich agricultural hinterland north of the state capital of Madison, retained its German American identity into the mid-twentieth century. In 1919, the Federal Bureau of Investigation dispatched an agent to look into allegations that the pastor of St. John's, C. J. Hausner, had made statements supportive of Germany and disloyal to the United States during World War I. The agent, C. I. Rukes, initially reported that Fr. Hausner "has had considerable influence over his congregation, and has instilled a spirit of disloyalty in them in a general way." But after an interview in which Fr. Hausner attested his support for the United States and its allies in the war and his purchase of war bonds, as well as his German-born father's support for the United States in the war, Rukes admonished Hausner that he must in the future avoid "indiscreet" remarks that might call his loyalty to the United States into question and recommended that the FBI not pursue investigation. While Hausner did not face the prosecution, imprisonment, deportation, or vigilante violence that some German American clergy experienced in the World War I era, he and his parish with time participated in a larger German American tendency to suppress the German language and other aspects of lingering German distinctiveness in an era that demanded "100 percent Americanism." Hausner became well-known in southern Wisconsin in the remaining decades of his pastorate (he served until 1935) for leading successful campaigns seeking the closure of local businesses on Good Friday. Fr. Hausner's concern for the preservation of the ethnic solidarity of the German American Catholic enclave broadened over time into an effort to compel the larger Wisconsin community, Catholic and non-Catholic, to respect Catholic and Christian piety. German Catholic distinctiveness evolved into a larger effort to exert Catholic values amid the secularizing and commercializing trends of 1920s and 1930s American culture.[33]

In Iowa City, like many Midwestern German Catholics and Lutherans in the era of the First World War and its aftermath, Fr. Schulte and St. Mary's also participated in a larger German American tendency to sublimate or discard more distinctive aspects of German culture. For example, two years before Iowa governor William L. Harding issued a "Babel proclamation" that forbade speaking any language other than English in public, a 1916 parish history downplayed the use of German in the parish, somewhat contradicting its own description of a lengthy history of German sermons and oratory by "German resident priests" at St. Mary's. During the war, even as some questioned the allegiance of Catholics with ancestral ties to nations at war with the United States, such as Germany and Austria-Hungary, Schulte and other Catholic leaders across eastern Iowa stressed their loyalty and their commitment, financial and otherwise, to the success of the American war effort. In the postwar period, Schulte expressed a traditional German American Catholic distaste for socialism that aligned well with the era's antiradicalism but fit less comfortably with the period's celebration of business culture and wealth creation. Speaking at the Iowa City Kiwanis Club in 1923 in a talk titled "Perils to Our Democracy," the longtime pastor of St. Mary's decried left-wing ideologies but also argued that the "lavish and extravagant display of great wealth does much to fan the flames of socialism."[34]

Further consequential shifts in the multiethnic cultures of Iowa City and Midwestern Catholicism occurred in the following decades. By the mid-twentieth century in Iowa City, assimilative and Americanization pressures (hastened by a new emphasis by the Church hierarchy on parishes organized along territorial rather than ethnic lines) eroded older ethnic separatism to the extent that participation as an individual believer in a larger American Catholicism influenced by ascendant advertising techniques and rising notions of consumerism in American society eclipsed participation in worship as a member of an ethnic community of believers tied strongly to the place of ethnic origin or, eventually, even to a territorial parish. By the late twentieth century, even as Iowa Catholicism's multiculturalism deepened significantly with the in-migration of Catholics from Latin America and Asia bringing their own transnational Catholic cultures with distinct pastoral needs, the older cultural battles among ethnic Catholics that had so shaped the nineteenth-century texture of Iowa City Catholicism had faded to a distant, quaint memory. In 1991, as St. Mary's Church celebrated it sesquicentennial, parishioners held a series of ethnic-themed dinners in the parish hall, including German, Irish, French, Bohemian, Austrian, Italian, Korean, Chinese, and Mexican dinners. The ethnic dinners enacted an appreciation for the parish's diversity, past and present, even as the notion of parish as ethnic enclave for particular European immigrant groups had long since lost relevance for many participants.[35]

3

Wisconsin Marianism and Upper Midwestern Catholic Culture, 1858–2010

Wisconsin's Catholic culture was fashioned from a multiplicity of ethnic and devotional backgrounds, including strong and evolving notions of Catholic femininity and Marian piety with significant transnational influences. In the latter decades of the nineteenth century, for example, a cultus that included a shrine and devoted followers developed around the claims of Adèle Brise, a French-speaking Belgian immigrant and lay "sister" (tertiary), asserting that "Our Lady of Good Help" (Notre Dame de Bon Secours) had appeared to her in Robinsonville (later called Champion) in the uncleared timberland frontier of northeastern Wisconsin in the late 1850s. Nearly a hundred fifty years later, in December 2010, the bishop of Green Bay, David Ricken, pronounced the apparitions to Adèle Brise valid, making these the only American apparitions to be officially recognized by the Catholic Church.[1]

By contrast, in 1955 the bishop of La Crosse, John P. Treacy, found Mary Ann Van Hoof's claim of receiving apparitions from the Queen of the Holy Rosary, Mediatrix of Peace, in Necedah in the marginal farmland of Juneau County in central Wisconsin, to be inauthentic and prohibited Catholics from worshipping with Van Hoof and her followers. Lacing her reports of Mary's appearances with apocalyptic Cold War rhetoric that sought the conversion of Americans to devotion to Mary to avert atomic mass destruction at the hands of the atheistic Soviets with the warning "Russia is more powerful than America," Van Hoof's claims briefly attracted thousands of Midwestern Catholics, including significant numbers of Polish Americans, seeking mystical experiences of Mary in an American nationalist idiom during the height of the Cold War in 1949–50.[2] A reported hundred thousand pilgrims had gathered in a Necedah farm field to await an expected apparition to Mrs. Van Hoof on the morning of the Feast of the Assumption, August 15, 1950, quite possibly the "largest assembly in rural Wisconsin's history" as well as "the single largest religious gathering in Wisconsin history."[3] While the mainstream appeal of the Necedah apparitions to mainstream Catholics faded after the condemnation by the La Crosse diocese, diocesan interdicts flowed in 1970 and 1975 as a small cult endured at Necedah. Mrs. Van Hoof reported continued apparitions and messages from Mary until her death in 1984. An elaborate shrine mixing Marian and spiritualist imagery enjoys Old Catholic (Ultrajectine) affiliation and continues to function at Necedah, operating a visitor center and a private primary school. Necedah, a village of fewer than a thousand far from Wisconsin's urban centers, remains a magnet for traditionalist and alternative Catholicism, indicating a continuing resonance of Van Hoof's decades-long extremist Marianist rejection of diocesan authority. In 2018, beyond the Old Catholic–affiliated Our Lady of Necedah shrine, a Society of Pius X–affiliated Our Lady of Victory Chapel and a Rosa Mystica Russian Orthodox Catholic Church of America both offered weekly Latin Tridentine Masses without Roman approbation, while the La Crosse diocese countered in its St. Francis Parish with weekly Sunday Latin and Polish Masses.[4]

The mid-twentieth-century Necedah apparitions offer an interesting counterpoint to the 1850s Robinsonville apparitions. Despite their different outcomes, both the Robinsonville and Necedah apparitions marked stages of a transnational Marian Revival originating in continental Europe in the decades after the French Revolution as European Catholics and their diasporas responded to anticlerical and anti-Catholic aspects of European and American liberal nationalism and its advocacy of an expansive modern state that undercut clerical authority and parochial communalism. After the turn of the twentieth century, practitioners of Marian piety in Europe and in the United States, including the Midwest, responded to the irreligious ideologies of socialism and communism and to the specter of the Cold War and possibility of atomic destruction following World War II. The appearances of Mary at Robinsonville and Necedah, while separated by a century, illustrate how the Upper Midwestern United States was as potent a setting for the Marian Revival as were more celebrated Southern European locales such as Lourdes, France, in 1858 and Fatima, Portugal, in 1917. Indeed, the Robinsonville apparitions, besides being the only Marian visions in the United States to receive official, if belated, Church approval, were apparently among the first significant Marian apparitions to occur in the country, highlighting the central, if somewhat neglected, role of the Upper Midwest in shaping the contours of American Catholic culture.[5]

Unlike in the northeastern United States and in portions of the American West, Germans rather than Irish predominated in the Upper Midwest's Catholicism. But Wisconsin's polyglot Catholicism drew from myriad sources including Catholics of French Canadian, Native American, Belgian, Irish, and eventually Eastern and Southern European backgrounds. The state's rural landscape seemed particularly amenable to the flowering of Catholic devotions, including Marian apparitions, that transplanted and transposed European Catholic beliefs and practices in Upper Midwestern soil, taking on new meaning in American contexts. Multifarious Catholic homelands combined with Teutonic dominance of Church offices that resisted Americanism and a largely rural landscape beyond the metropolis of Milwaukee to lend Wisconsin's Catholicism a creative quality. Catholic women who saw Mary and their followers in Wisconsin blended Old World notions of the sacred and Catholic communal identity with efforts to resist a dismissive male Church hierarchy, American liberal nationalism, the modern state, and Soviet communism. While all American regions have given rise to Marian cults, as we will see in this chapter the largely rural and densely but diversely Catholic Upper Midwest has proven particularly fertile soil for Marian seers and their followers.[6]

The Robinsonville apparitions occurred in October during a year in the late 1850s when Mary appeared to Adèle Brise. The actual year is unclear. The local press from the late nineteenth century through the early twentieth consistently reported the year as 1858, as did at least one associate of Brise. Yet another associate, Sister Pauline LaPlant, believed the year to be 1857, while Sister M. Dominica's well-researched 1955 book on the apparitions and the chapel they inspired held the year to be 1859. Bishop Ricken of Green Bay's decrees in 2010 used 1859 as the year.[7]

Brise told Sister Pauline that in early October she first saw the Virgin as she walked along a densely wooded Indian trail to a grist mill four miles from Robinsonville. Brise said that she "saw a lady all in white standing between two trees, one a maple and the other a hemlock." The apparition then "slowly disappeared, leaving a white cloud" in its wake. The frightened Brise then went on her way to the grist mill and returned home, where she told her parents what she had seen.[8] Brise related that a second apparition occurred the next Sunday at the same location as she walked to Sunday Mass at Bay Settlement, some eleven miles from her home. Brise once again saw a woman dressed in white eventually fading into "a little mist or white cloud." Brise's companions, her sister and a neighbor, saw nothing but noticed Brise's distress. Like her parents, Brise's companions wondered if the apparition was "a poor soul that needed prayers."[9] Following Mass, Brise spoke in the confessional of her fright at the woman in white that she had seen. Her confessor, Father William Verhoef, OSC, told her to not be afraid and asked her to tell him more about the experience outside the confessional. Fr. Verhoef then "told her that if it were a heavenly messenger she would see it again and it would not harm her, but to ask in God's name who it was and what it desired of her."[10] Returning home the same way with her two companions and "a man who was clearing land for the Holy Cross Fathers at Bay Settlement," Brise experienced the third and final apparition, a more fully described vision of a "beautiful lady" all in white with "a crown of stars around her head." Falling to her knees, Brise asked the lady whom she was and what she wanted of her. Mary replied, "I am the Queen of Heaven who prays for the conversion of sinners, and I wish you to do the same. You received Holy Communion this morning and that is well. But you must do more. Make a general confession and offer Communion for the conversion of sinners. If they do not convert and do penance, my son will be obliged to punish them. I can hardly hold his arm." Mary further admonished Brise, "What are you doing here in idleness while your companions are working in the vineyard of my son?" Mary instructed Brise to "gather the children in this wild country and teach them what they should know for salvation."[11] Adèle's father, Lambert Brise, soon constructed a small wooden chapel near the site of the reported apparitions, marking the origin of a shrine commemorating the event.[12]

The apparitions to Adèle Brise took meaning in the French-speaking Walloon Catholic culture Brise and her parents and their neighbors had transplanted to the Green Bay Peninsula. Adèle Brise had been born in Dion-le-Val, Brabant, a village southeast of Brussels in January 1831, shortly after the Belgian Revolution in 1830 severed Belgium from the Netherlands following a period of French control after the French Revolution and shortly before the newly independent Belgian state adopted a Laicist (secular) constitution modeled after the Napoleonic Code under Leopold I. Departing an intensively industrializing Wallonia, Adèle, her parents, and her three siblings immigrated to the United States in 1855, with Adèle's parents, Lambert and Marie, purchasing acreage in the town of Red River, Wisconsin, in August 1855. The Brises joined a rapidly growing Belgian colony transplanted to the hardscrabble, uncleared forest land of the Green Bay Peninsula, founded at Aux premier Belges in 1853 by Brabantian homesteaders seeking farms that would better support their families than was possible in Wallonia. Yet the Brises and thousands of other Belgians who arrived in Wisconsin in the mid-1850s faced difficult circumstances in clearing "virgin forest" for cultivation amid hunger, disease, and relative linguistic and social isolation from neighboring settlements.[13] The Belgian diaspora joined a long-standing French Canadian, Native American, and mixed-race (Métis) Catholic community at Green Bay as well significant numbers of German and Irish Catholics, German Protestants and secular German radicals, Scandinavian Protestants, and Protestant Yankees (from New England) and Yorkers (from New York State) migrating into the Badger State in the late antebellum years. Over the next several decades, the Belgian and Belgian-descended population of Brown, Kewaunee, and Door counties would mushroom to an estimated thirty thousand, providing an ethnic constituency receptive to Adèle Brise's Gallic visions of Mary and the development of the cult of Notre Dame de Bon Secours.[14]

In polyglot Wisconsin, the traditions of Belgian popular Catholicism would be observed in how the apparitions to Adèle Brise and the shrine that developed around them accorded with the forms and understandings of Marian visions stemming from early modern continental Europe yet remade in modern contexts. The chapel that was soon constructed and then would be subsequently rebuilt at the apparitions site—over the "stumps of the two trees that were sanctified by the apparent touch of the blessed virgin"—were in the Belgian manner of "a little house of devotion . . . [with] a simple altar and a statue or picture of the blessed virgin."[15] Within a few years, miraculously healed pilgrims would leave crutches at the chapel (including a larger 1861 structure with "Bon Secours"—Good Help—written above the entrance), transplanting Low Country and continental European beliefs in the thaumatological (healing) powers of sacred sites associated with saints, Christ, or the Virgin Mary even in an era that stressed scientific explanations, the questioning of religious belief, and the rejection of the privileges of Catholic clerical authority. Along the same lines, the shrine at Robinsonville emerged miraculously unscathed and unburned from the catastrophic Peshtigo fire that scorched large swaths of eastern Wisconsin in October 1871, supplication to Mary's powers by those who fled to St. Mary's Boarding Academy and processed through the night praying the Rosary with Adèle Brise reportedly providing effective protection even as the flames completely consumed nearby acres and killed more than a thousand.[16]

Continental European Catholic traditions refashioned in the American Midwestern context also included immensely popular annual processions at the shrine on August 15, the Feast of the Assumption, that attracted thousands by the 1870s, especially after the miraculous deliverance from the Peshtigo fire, and reaching a reported fifteen thousand by the 1920s. In 1928, the shrine's chaplain, Rev. Smits, purchased an adjoining property to end the practice of commercial amusements, including illicit alcohol consumption during Prohibition, that had long served as an unsavory sidebar to the collective observation of Marian piety at the shrine during the Assumption Feast Day.[17] While the Green Bay Peninsula's Belgian-descended community, some of whom had violently resisted Union Army conscription during the Civil War, would contend with Green Bay's Catholic bishops (who were Germans) over the Belgians' reluctance to support Catholic schools, "the socialistic leanings among the emigrants from the mining regions of Belgium,"[18] and the challenges posed by a local anticlerical, Jansenist sect as well as spiritualism (all contenders against the claims of orthodox Catholicism stemming from Europe), Marian piety in the shrine at Robinsonville over time proved a unifying mainstay of Belgian Catholic identity in the region, even as it rested uneasily at times with the prerogatives of the German Church hierarchy in the Green Bay diocese.[19]

In more particular ways, Adèle Brise's visions of Mary in the eastern Wisconsin woods of the late 1850s accorded well with traditions of Marian piety flowing from Gallic and continental European traditions. Historians Thomas A. Kselman and Steven Avella argue that "in the medieval era church officials already saw in [Mary] a universal symbol capable of replacing the local saints whose cults served as a basis for regional political and religious power."[20] Historian David Blackbourn notes that the modern type of apparition arose after 1400, most typically with a lay child as visionary. In the nineteenth century, under French influence, the focus shifted from the medieval emphasis on a sacred object to a vision of Mary. Blackbourn describes a nineteenth-century Shepherd's Cycle, with many visionaries being lowly cowherds, shepherds, and farm servants, with "dependent or outsider status" as well as an "emotional vulnerability" from difficult family circumstances. Mary would emerge as a surrogate mother for seers, with apparitions providing subversive potential for lowly, dependent seers who through reporting their visions could turn the world upside down. Nineteenth-century political, social, cultural upheaval also provided a crucial context, with popular receptiveness to visionaries arising from the "emotional consolation" of the apparition's apocalyptic message amid the "hard times" created by political and social change and fears of anticlerical liberalism and the expansive modern state. While many apparitions occurred across Catholic Europe in the nineteenth century, only a few would become more than locally known, and the Church would officially approve even fewer, with those small number of cases, such as Lourdes in 1858, becoming a "formidable official cult, often with a clear political purpose," such as the way in which the apparitions at Lourdes seemingly conferred divine approval upon Pope Pius IX's recent (in 1854) proclamation of the dogma of the Immaculate Conception.[21]

In important respects, even if not in others, the apparitions to Adèle Brise accorded with the larger patterns described by Blackbourn and other scholars of Marian piety in modern Europe. In her mid- to late twenties at the time of the apparitions, Adèle was older than the typical Marian seer, but she was similarly lowly and dependent, having been disabled by losing an eye in an accident as a girl. While biographies stress her personal piety—extremely important if the validity of the apparitions was to eventually be confirmed—sources also suggest an undercurrent of tension with her parents, whom she nonetheless obediently followed to America.[22] Immigrating to the United States meant abandoning, at least for the moment, Adèle's promise at her First Communion, made to "Our Lady" along with several of her friends, to join an Ursuline community in Brabant and to "devote their lives to the foreign missions." Even as Adèle's friends joined the religious community,

Adèle left for the comparative wilderness and intemperate climate of Wisconsin's Green Bay Peninsula. Brise's longtime associate, Sister Pauline LaPlant, notes that in this unfulfilled desire/promise lies the significance of Mary's reproachful statement to Adèle, "'What are you doing here in wilderness while your companions are working in the vineyard of my son.'"[23] Brise would devote the remaining thirty years of her life to heeding Mary's admonition to "gather the children in this wild country and teach them what they should know for salvation." One of Brise's biographers states that Adèle faithfully responded to Mary's instruction by "travel[ing] up and down the peninsula for seven years, not only catechizing the children but admonishing the sinner as well."[24] Eventually organizing a small group of unvowed lay (Secular Franciscan) third order tertiaries, Brise led the construction and operation of a school with instruction in French and English and a convent alongside successive chapels on the site of the apparitions.[25]

In another respect, Adèle Brise's experience resembled that of most if not all Marian seers, that of provoking a skeptical if not hostile response from the Church hierarchy, ever wary of popular religiosity outside of clerical control and skeptical of lay and feminine assertion and autonomy. In this case, cultural tensions between German-speaking bishops and French-speaking laity in the newly created Green Bay diocese (1868) played a key role, along with Brabantian Catholic traditions of lay religious leadership and skepticism of "arbitrary priest[s]."[26] The first bishop of Green Bay, the Austrian-born Joseph Melcher, reportedly placed an interdict on the Bon Secours chapel, refused Adèle Brise the sacraments, and threatened to excommunicate her if she persisted in speaking of the apparitions. Bishop Melcher demanded the keys for the chapel and school, which Brise gave him, pointedly noting "that he would be responsible for the souls lost due to the lack of instruction." Struck by Brise's "zeal and sincerity," Melcher returned the keys to her.[27] Brise and her sister companions ran into similar problems with Melcher's bishop successor, the Bavarian-born Francis Xavier Krautbauer. Krautbauer placed a ban on the chapel and school after he made an unannounced visit accompanied by the diocesan vicar general, Rev. Edward Daems, that apparently did not go well. Brise pleaded in an 1875 letter to Krautbauer that "the good pastors [local French-speaking priests] . . . could give better information" than Rev. Daems had and "in the name of our dear Mother, let us know the crime we have committed." Within a year or so, the diocese had lifted the ban and the school again operated and "pilgrimages were resumed."[28]

Adèle Brise's visions of Mary took form and meaning in a Gallic Marian culture that she and other Belgian immigrants had transplanted to the Wisconsin North Woods. While diocesan commentators have long linked Brise's apparitions to the contemporaneous and well-known apparitions to Bernadette Soubirous at Lourdes, France, in 1858, Karen E. Park persuasively argues that there is little evidence that Adèle Brise was familiar with the events at Lourdes and that it is more likely that she was aware of the apparition that occurred at La Salette, France, in September 19, 1846, accounts of which had circulated widely in the French-speaking world, including in Walloon Belgium during Brise's formative teenage years. Indeed, Brise's experience of Mary resembled the appearance of the Virgin to two shepherd children, Mélanie Calvat and Maximim Giraud, at La Salette much more so than it did the Lourdes apparitions. Park asserts that "Adèle's apparition, like the one at La Salette, contains no message of healing (though pilgrims were subsequently healed at both sites), but rather is a warning by Mary to a dechristianized people to either convert and repent or face the wrath of Jesus, a wrath constrained, just barely by Mary herself."[29] Likewise, Park notes that Mary's physical appearance at La Salette in the French Alps closely resembled her appearance on the Green Bay Peninsula: lacking a veil, garbed in yellow and white instead of blue, and adorned with a crown, whereas Bernadette had by contrast seen a "diminutive childlike figure."[30] Most significantly, Park argues, Mary delivered "nearly identical" messages at La Salette and on the Green Bay Peninsula, highlighting "the sin of neglecting the obligations of faith and the problem of poor catechesis," and warning that only Mary "holds her son's arm back," perpetuating a notion of Mary as mediator of divine mercy stemming to medieval Catholicism that would be discarded in Vatican II era theology stressing instead Christ's primacy, with Jesus's mediating power now surpassing that of Mary. Green Bay diocesan documents, including Bishop Ricken's 2010 decrees, omitted Adèle Brise's theologically problematic claim that Mary would hold back Christ's arm, and thus avert his punishment of the sinful, and ignored the likely connection to the now disfavored La Salette apparition.[31] Diocesan documents instead emphasized the supposed connection between Our Lady of Good Help and Our Lady of Lourdes, constructing an actually tenuous linkage to an apparition that Park suggests "operates securely within the boundaries of authority and dogma maintained by the Catholic hierarchy, and generally does not threaten the authority of the church, but amplifies and confirms it."[32]

Eventually diocesan authorities, recognizing the strength of local support for the apparitions and the work at the shrine, and seeking to counter schismatic and anticlerical elements that threatened loyalty to the Church among Belgians on the Green Bay Peninsula, settled into a long-standing pattern of toleration and at times cooperation with the Bon Secours / Good Help shrine, even absorbing the shrine's facilities and arranging for them to be taken over by a formal religious community, the Franciscan Sisters at nearby Bay Settlement, after Adèle Brise's death in 1896. Subsequent bishops laid the cornerstone for a new chapel in 1941 and appointed a resident chaplain in 1954, while for decades the Franciscan Sisters operated a Home for Crippled Children and later a Pre-Novitiate Franciscan High School at the site.[33] In this respect the Robinsonville apparitions differed markedly from the many local apparitions around Europe and the United States that never gained more than momentary or tacit clerical acceptance. This eventual local clerical sanction at what a Milwaukee newspaper in 1922 called the "most popular shrine for Catholics in the Middle West,"[34] paralleled in some respects the local processes that occurred with what became the official Marian cults of Lourdes and Fatima,[35] and also paved the way, many decades later, for official diocesan recognition of the validity of the apparitions to Adèle Brise, a unique recognition (so far) in American Catholic history.

In 2009, Green Bay bishop David Ricken initiated a formal investigation of the apparitions and appointed a commission to conduct the inquiry. On December 8, 2010—the Feast of the Immaculate Conception—Ricken "declar[ed] with moral certainty . . . that the events, apparitions, and locutions given to Adèle Brise in October of 1859 do exhibit the substance of supernatural character" and he approved "these apparitions as worthy of belief (although not obligatory) by the Christian faithful." The Green Bay bishop also canonically approved Our Lady of Good Help as a diocesan shrine and encouraged pilgrims to visit. As support for his decree, Ricken noted the judgment of three Marian experts that the accounts of the apparitions were found "to be free from doctrinal error and consistent with the Catholic faith," that Adèle Brise demonstrated upright character, that "oral and some documented sources" substantiated a lengthy tradition of conversions and healings at the shrine, and that all previous Green Bay bishops had supported the shrine in some fashion or other. Ricken noted that few documents survived from the shrine's early years but that this was because "Green Bay at the time of the apparition was frontier country."[36] As Park notes, Ricken's official narrative made numerous selective elisions that had the effect of downplaying Adèle Brise's agency and challenge to clerical authority, instead recasting Brise as a "docile and obedient daughter of the church." For instance, the Green Bay diocese's official narrative omits Brise's contentious relationship with the diocesan hierarchy and the ultimately unsuccessful attempts of multiple bishops to suppress the apparitions and prohibit Adèle Brise and her followers' activities at the shrine. Contemporaneous Belgian immigrant and historian Xavier Martin reported by contrast practices that reflected the lay leadership role Brise assumed as well as informal practices of popular religiosity among rural Belgian Catholic immigrants ostracized by German diocesan leadership: "In spite of all opposition, the multitude would congregate on the spot, and with Adèle would worship on the spot, and with Adèle would worship and even say Mass on certain days, without a priest."[37] Park persuasively suggests that the official Green Bay diocesan narratives have effectively stripped Adèle Brise of her potentially destabilizing prophetic and pastoral role as Marian seer, a role in which Brise ultimately claimed the religious vocation she had been denied in leaving Belgium and in which for decades she would lead Belgian immigrants marginalized in Wisconsin Catholicism and in the Wisconsin political economy in a nurturing community of believers rooted in the Gallic Marian Revival.[38]

Bishop Ricken's decision to recognize the validity of the apparitions to Adèle Brise may have been influenced by the continued potency of the local Marian apparitions in his predominantly rural diocese even as the Catholic Church faced a variety of challenges in the early twenty-first century, including, among other things, allegations of clerical sexual abuse, declining religious vocations, demographic shifts, and a downsizing of the Green Bay diocese from 212 to 160 parishes between 2003 and 2008.[39] But Ricken also redirected the Champion apparitions into chan-

nels congenial to early twenty-first-century Church understandings of
Marian theology, obscuring, as we have seen, Notre Dame de Bon Secours / Our Lady of Good Help's connections to mid-nineteenth-century
prophetic Gallic Marianism. In so doing, Ricken also subverted the apparitions' potential overlap with a "Marian apocalyptic" of new Marian
apparition cults inspired after 1945 by an "extremist conspiracy" reading
of the 1917 Fatima apparitions networked through pilgrimages to Marian
apparition sites (including Necedah). Sandra L. Zimdars-Swartz has use-
fully traced how "personal and cultural anxieties" have engaged Marian
energies on the fringe of the American Catholic right during and since
the Cold War, including at Necedah (especially after its condemnation
by the La Crosse diocese) and other unofficial American Marian sites,
and focused particularly on Medjugorje, Bosnia-Herzegovina, beginning in the early 1980s.[40] Yet in validating Our Lady of Good Help as the
first officially approved American Marian cult, Bishop Ricken rendered
the cult a benign and fully orthodox manifestation of post–Vatican II
Marianism, emptying it of its original function as a vessel of subversive Gallic immigrant power and depleting the Wisconsin apparition of
its potential connection with a sometimes threatening post–Vatican II
apocalyptic Catholic countercultural fringe. In short, even as veneration
of Mary became less integral within a secularizing Wisconsin culture in
which many Catholics focused less upon Mary after World War II and
Vatican II, the Catholic left sometimes rejected the efficacy of Marian
veneration for a progressive vision of society, and some rightist Catholics took energy from a reactionary, apocalyptic vision of Mary, Bishop
Ricken helped fashion an official Marian apparition cult rooted in Wisconsin's immigrant history but safely channeled into a notion of Marianism depleted of any meaningful subversive or destabilizing potential.

The respective Marian cults at Robinsonville and Necedah, established nearly a century apart, involved important similarities and differences. As with many reports of "public serial apparitions," the initial
encounter with the Virgin Mary was "ambiguous," with the seer alone,
and the apparition not revealing its identity until later appearances and
after the apparition became publicly known. Adèle Brise reported that
she first saw the Virgin garbed all in white as she walked by herself to
a grist mill, with Mary revealing her identity only a week later as Adèle
walked the same path with several companions. Mary Ann Van Hoof

reported that her first encounters with the Virgin occurred in her bedroom on November 12, 1949, and Good Friday, April 7, 1950, while Mary would not reveal her identity until an apparition as a "beautiful lady" in a blue mist over trees in a farmyard on May 28, 1950. As at Robinsonville a century earlier, the Virgin warned at Necedah that divine punishment was impending unless persons repented for their sins and modified their ways.[41]

Both at Robinsonville and at Necedah, the Marian apparitions in a sense ultimately became a way for the seer to resolve personal conflicts, with Mary emerging in a sense as a surrogate mother figure enabling the seer to claim status and prophetic power with a community of Marian believers. For Adèle Brise, visions of Mary salved her loss of a religious vocation in Belgium and her lowly status as a disabled, unmarried, immigrant Belgian woman. For Mary Ann Van Hoof, seeing Mary helped to redress trauma from a scarred childhood at the hands of a physically and psychologically abusive father and conflicts between her husband's Catholicism and her mother's spiritualism. Van Hoof had been baptized Catholic as an infant, but her parents were not practicing Catholics and she apparently returned to the Catholic Church when she married Godfred Van Hoof, a devout Catholic born in Buchanan, Outagamie County, who was sixteen years older than her. Her mother, Elizabeth Bieber, who had periodically lived with the couple on farmsteads in Wisconsin and in the Southwest, had served as the vice president of the Kenosha Assembly of Spiritualists from 1946 to 1948.[42] Ultimately this religious conflict would be resolved in the fusing of Catholic and spiritualist beliefs and iconography in the Necedah cult, with Marian apparitions combined with messages involving American Founding Fathers such as George Washington. In one example of fusion of Catholic and spiritualist beliefs, in 1956 Van Hoof stated that the Virgin Mary had told her that she had appeared to George Washington and had told him that the United States would endure "five sieges."[43]

In a pattern familiar to many Marian apparitions, both seers faced skepticism and even persecution from the Church hierarchy, although ultimately this resolved to a tacit acceptance and cooperation and eventual official recognition at Robinsonville while a cult endured at Necedah despite repeated official condemnation. Both seers were particularly suspect to the male Church hierarchy as laywomen making striking claims of divine presence; for example, La Crosse diocesan officials characterized Van Hoof as a twice-married nominal Catholic making a pathetic attempt to imitate the apparitions at Fatima. Both Brise and Van Hoof suffered and benefited as well from the complex, fractious religious landscape of polyglot Wisconsin Catholicism as they reported apparitions and collected believers. Both seers found receptive ethnic Catholic communities for their visions of Mary (for Brise, marginalized Belgian Catholics; for Van Hoof, Wisconsin Catholics, perhaps especially Polish Americans, particularly worried about the atheistic Soviet Union, which had recently absorbed Poland into its communist sphere of influence, and the atomic bomb) as well as diocesan hierarchies unsympathetic or at least inconversant with the milieus of ethnic Catholic minorities. La Crosse diocesan officials argued that anticlerical Catholic elements from Milwaukee—a stronghold of Polish Catholics who had long contested official Church authority—had played a key role in promoting and popularizing Van Hoof's claims, effectively and in their view dangerously severing the laity from clerical authority. The chancery similarly dismissed the reports of some of the crowd at Necedah of supernatural phenomena associated with Van Hoof's visions of Mary—potentially experiences of divine presence outside the purview or authorization of diocesan authority—as instances of mass hysteria. While Van Hoof's claims attracted Wisconsin and Midwestern Catholics from a wide range of ethnic backgrounds in 1950, a period when ethnic identities were losing much of their previous salience in American Catholicism, evidence suggests that Polish clergy may have been particularly sympathetic to Van Hoof, while German and Irish-descended clergy in the La Crosse diocese were more skeptical. Many pilgrims as well as some financial supporters of the apparitions in their early stages were apparently from Milwaukee, which contained a large Polish Catholic community that had often clashed with the Milwaukee Archdiocese, whose leadership had been historically German.[44]

In other respects, though, the Robinsonville and Necedah cults differed markedly. The apparitions to Brise were expressed in a prophetic frame shaped by the nineteenth-century Gallic Marian Revival that would eventually be purged from official diocesan narratives, while Van Hoof's visions were articulated in a Marian (and spiritualist) apocalyptic reflecting their post-Fatima, Cold War, anticommunist milieu. Most crucially, Robinsonville evolved from a regional Midwestern cult that eventually won (in modified, benign form) clerical toleration and official recognition. By contrast, Necedah initially enjoyed tremendous popular interest among Midwestern Catholics in an era of mass media and mass culture but after official condemnation rapidly declined into a small if persistent local Marian sect nevertheless drawing continuing interest from a national network of extremist Marianists and traditionalist Catholics on the post–Vatican II American Catholic fringe.[45]

In sum, the history of Wisconsin's Marian apparitions suggests the crucial role of transnational and ethnic Catholic identities in the forging of an American Catholic culture. It also suggests the neglected but meaningful role of the Upper Midwest as a site in the perpetuation of a Marian Revival that stretched from Catholic Europe to far-flung global outposts of Catholic immigration and evangelization. Catholic Wisconsinites, along with French, Portuguese, Poles, Germans, Mexicans, and others, have inventively deployed the Marian image as they have contended with rising nation-states and social change that sometimes has impinged on Catholic identity and the primacy of local interests. Seers of Mary, many of them women such as Adèle Brise and Mary Ann Van Hoof, have claimed prophetic power and social status leading communities of Marian believers and challenging hierarchical male and clerical authority. More particularly, the persistent appeal of Brise's visions of Mary on the Green Bay Peninsula in the 1850s, even as they have been strategically redirected in the early twenty-first century into America's first official Marian apparition cult, indicates the long-term resonance of her refashioning of Catholic femininity and Marian piety within Upper Midwestern Catholic culture.

4

La Placita and the Evolution of Catholic Religiosity in Los Angeles

C1784

The history of Los Angeles's oldest Catholic church, La Iglesia de Nuestra Señora la Reina de los Ángeles (Reina was added to the title in 1861), founded in the late eighteenth century, reveals continuities of Mexican American Catholicism in the American West despite adversities and discontinuities such as Spanish colonialism, Mexican independence and the Mexican church-state conflict, American conquest and absorption into a U.S. Catholic Church initially hostile or indifferent to Mexican Catholic religiosity, English-speaking Protestant and Catholic immigrations, and subsequent Mexican and Latin American immigrations and nativist backlashes.[1] Through this all, worshippers at La Placita have made and remade an essentially Mexican American and eventually Latino American Catholic identity in conversation with Spanish, Mexican, and American Catholic cultures yet ultimately unabsorbed by and at times resistant to the larger Catholic cultures with which the parish has interacted. Similar to the histories of the oldest Catholic churches elsewhere in the Spanish-colonized American Southwest in cities such as Santa Fe and San Antonio, La Placita experienced, for example, few of the Irish Catholic influences important elsewhere in California and the West. Even amid the profound transience that characterizes Los Angeles and Southern California's history, with its enduring Mexican Catholic character La Placita in a sense displays a remarkable dynamic stability.[2]

Yet La Placita's story also indicates the significance and complexity of the American Southwest's Hispanic Catholic heritage and the continuous role of transnational (in this case Mexican, continental European, and eventually Central American) communities of believers in shaping and reshaping local Catholic cultures. While Los Angeles shifted in the nineteenth century from a Spanish colonial outpost into a Mexican Catholic frontier town and then into an American Protestant city and arguably in the late twentieth century into a Mexican (and Central American) Catholic and Pentecostal and Evangelical Protestant metropolis (as secularizing Anglophones moved away from institutional churches and some Latinx believers moved from Catholicism to Protestant congregations), the evolving social and cultural matrix of worship at La Placita has charted all of these shifts amid the creative persistence of Mexican Catholic religiosity. La Placita's history is only one aspect of the history of Catholicism in the American West, the United States' least "churched" region, but it suggests both significant variation around the West in the development of Catholic cultures and the ways in which the American West diverges dramatically from a model of American Catholic history predicated on nineteenth-century European Catholic immigration and institution building. Far more than in any other region, transience and the difficulty of constructing Catholic institutions and Catholic visibility amid mobility and social change across a vast physical landscape have marked the experience of Catholics in the American West. While La Placita has been shaped by many migrations and political and cultural shifts, its Mexican-inflected Catholicism has been continually reconstructed by its parishioners and clergy. At the same time, the cultural symbols of La Placita and its Hispano-descended religiosity have been used by Latinx and Anglo Angelenos as a means to craft usable pasts in a metropolis defined by its limited historical consciousness.[3]

I

La Iglesia de Nuestra Señora de los Ángeles had its first manifestation as an adobe *capilla* constructed in the *pueblo* of Los Angeles around 1784 near the present intersection of West César Estrada Chávez Avenue and North Broadway. The church was an *asistencia*, that is, an assistant mission, subsidiary to and staffed from the Mission at San Gabriel, founded by the Spanish in 1771. The pueblo and its church, originating in 1781 with forty-four mixed-race settlers of African, indigenous, and Spanish descent, took their name from Our Lady of Angels of the Porciúncula, a Franciscan Marian devotion. Fray Juan Crespí had bestowed the name on the Los Angeles River Valley while passing through on the Gaspar de Portolá Expedition in August 1769. The Los Angeles pueblo, laid out in a grid plan adjoining a Gabrielino-Tongva Indian village, Yaanga, and centered in a plaza, involved the recruitment of entire families of lower class *mestizo* farmers and artisans from northwest Mexico to the northern frontier, with the hope that a mixed population of men and women would avoid the violent, disruptive predation of Spanish soldiers upon Native women that had occurred in the early years of the missions and presidios of Alta California. A source indicates that the chapel stood around six feet in height, seventy feet in length, and twenty feet in width, while "on the southern side of this chapel was built a little room which served as a sacristy, and where the priest took his chocolate after mass."[4] In line with its status as an asistencia, San Gabriel priests served the pueblo's chapel out of "mere charity," with pueblo residents traveling ten miles to San Gabriel for reception of the sacraments and most liturgies. In 1810 pueblo residents made complaint through their *comisionado*, Sergeant Xavier Alvarado, to Governor José Joaquín de Arrillaga that the mission priests had twice refused to make sick calls at the pueblo. The padre presidente of the missions, Fr. Estevan Tapis, followed up with the two San Gabriel priests, who argued that the mission's needs took priority over the pueblo's. The pueblo would soon successfully petition for its own church.[5]

Yet the building of a new church for the growing community on New Spain's northwestern frontier would take more than a decade, even as Mexicans fought for and achieved independence from Spain. In 1813, Ex-Prefecto Vicente Sarría on a canonical visit found the old chapel small and ill suited for continued use. In 1814, Fr. Luis Gil y Taboada, a priest recently assigned to San Gabriel, requested license from the padre presidente, Fr. José Señán, to lay the cornerstone for the new church on the feast day of Our Lady of the Angels of Porciúncula. Accordingly the dedication of the cornerstone apparently occurred on August 15, 1815, yet progress on the construction site at Aliso Street and the Porciúncula (now the Los Angeles) River—currently where Alameda Street overpasses the San Bernardino and Santa Ana freeways—was sluggish and the modest beginnings of a church building were destroyed when the river flooded later in 1815. In 1818, Governor Pablo Vicente de Solá suggested a locale on a higher elevation a little east of the 1784 chapel. Pueblo residents donated fifty head of cattle to pay for the construction, but the governor sold the cattle and asserted that the funds could come from the following year's budget. Construction ensued over the next several years with the labor of Native neophytes from the San Gabriel,

San Luis Rey, and San Diego missions directed by master builder José Antonio Ramírez. Missions around California donated livestock and barrels of wine and brandy to pay for construction costs. Local tradition held that Joseph Chapman, an American who had once been arrested for participation in a privateer gang that preyed on the California coast, directed Native laborers in bringing timber from the upper canyons to the Porciúncula valley for the church's construction. Like other immigrant U.S. men in Alta California, Chapman had been integrated into elite Californio society after converting to Catholicism, marrying a Mexican Californian woman and swearing allegiance to Spain. The new church, La Iglesia de Nuestra Señora de los Ángeles, was at last dedicated on December 8, 1822.[6]

The new chapel fashioned from adobe had a width of twenty-seven feet and a length of one hundred thirty-five feet and, like the church at San Gabriel, lacked pews, with the altar rail located perhaps ninety feet from the back wall and the church's ceiling resting on substantial beams. In 1960 historian J. Thomas Owen described the architecture of the 1822 church. "At the crossing there was a sweep of forty-nine feet, with transepts extending outward about eleven feet, and the building's walls were four feet in thickness." "Four pilasters on the side walls" split "the nave . . . into bays." A baptistry just beyond and to the left of the front entrance held a "sizable copper vessel for the keeping of holy water." The exterior included "a gently curved *espadaña*, or gable, which rose to a pointed finial at its center." A *santo*, a carved representation of a saint, was nestled high in the *espadaña*, over which a cross loomed. A *campanario*, a bell tower, was recessed to the left of the church's façade. The San Gabriel Mission had donated a bell apparently of late eighteenth-century vintage.[7]

The Los Angeles Plaza and its church represented an example of *mestizaje*, the racial and cultural mixture key to the culture of northwest Mexico, combining Spanish, Indigenous, and African notions of town planning, urban space, and religiosity in the context of Spanish colonialism.[8] The California missions, presidios, and pueblos in which the first incarnations of La Iglesia de Nuestra Señora de los Ángeles took shape were a late episode in Spanish colonialism and Catholic expansion in North America. The Spanish had first explored and sought to conquer and colonize Florida in the 1520s, while St. Augustine, Florida, in September 1565 would become a Spanish settlement and the site of the first permanent Catholic settlement in what would become the United States, with Franciscans and Jesuits soon thereafter setting up missions in Florida. Álvar Núñez Cabeza de Vaca, the devoutly Catholic second in command of the ill-fated 1527–28 Narváez expedition that made landfall near Sarasota, Florida, would be shipwrecked off the coast of Texas, rescued by Natives, and after extensive travels in the Southwest and northern Mexico would eventually become an advocate for humane treatment of Native peoples in writings to the Spanish monarchy. Most Catholic activities in Florida ceased when the British took control after the Treaty of Paris in 1763, with the exception of Catholic communities in St. Augustine and Pensacola. Spanish control of Florida would resume after the American Revolution in 1783 until cession to the United States in 1821.[9]

Further west, in the eighteenth century, Spanish soldiers and Franciscans colonized Texas, including a mission and military post at San Antonio established in 1718, but the European population remained small and conversions meager, with the Texas missions secularized (converted to diocesan control) in the late eighteenth century. Seeking seven cities of gold, Francisco Vázquez de Coronado led an expedition through the Southwest and southern plains that would reach the Zuni pueblos in New Mexico in 1540. Coronado was accompanied by four Franciscan friars, including Juan de Padilla, who would be martyred by the Wichita Indians in Kansas, becoming the first Catholic martyr in lands that would eventually become the United States. Spanish efforts in New Mexico intensified in the late sixteenth and early seventeenth centuries, with two dozen missions, ninety Franciscans, and fifty thousand Native baptisms reported in 1630. Natives revolted in 1680 when Popé's Rebellion destroyed the missions and drove the Spanish out of New Mexico. The Spanish returned in 1692 and revived the missions on a smaller scale, but in the eighteenth century Church and state in New Mexico quarreled and bishops of Durango asserted that the Franciscans had not learned Native languages and that the conversions they had effected had been superficial. Further west, Francisco Eusebio Kino, a Tyrolese Jesuit, would establish Spanish missions with Pima Indians throughout southern Arizona in the late seventeenth and early eighteenth centuries. Kino's approach in some ways may have displayed a greater respect for

Native cultures than many contemporaneous missions around frontier outposts of New Spain in Texas, New Mexico, and California, which typically treated Natives like children and sought to separate them from non-Christian populations as a means of effectuating their conversion to Catholicism within self-sustaining centers of Spanish civilization. In both New Mexico and Arizona, a modest Catholic institutional presence following Mexican independence in 1821 assisted the persistence and development of Native Catholic religious cultures blending Indigenous spiritual traditions with memories of early modern Spanish Franciscan and Jesuit missions.[10]

The construction of the new church in Los Angeles was deeply embedded in the colonial Spanish-Native relations that had characterized the Spanish missions in California from their inception in 1769. Even as the Spanish Empire secularized in the eighteenth century, Franciscan padres in the California Missions zealously sought the conversion of Indians to Catholicism, viewing the Natives as "spiritual children" but insisting on their conformity to adult obligations regarding sexual behavior, including marital fidelity and monogamy. A recent biographer, Steven W. Hackel, argues that Junípero Serra, the Mallorca-born founder of the California missions canonized by Pope Francis in 2015 amid much controversy over the treatment of Natives in the missions, was a complex figure. Seeking the conversion of the Natives for their spiritual welfare, Serra dismissed Indian religious practices as barbarous. Seeking souls for the Catholic Church and lands for the Spanish Crown, Serra clashed often with the expanding Spanish Bourbon state. Despite his strong personality, Hackel asserts, Serra had little identity beyond his religious order and his foremost concern was discerning what he viewed as the will of God.[11]

As their communities were decimated by diseases brought by Serra and the Spanish, Gabrielino-Tongva Indians in some contexts may have found Catholic spiritual cosmology compatible with a Native spiritual lens. Meanwhile, as elsewhere on the late frontier of New Spain including New Mexico, a consistent chasm split Spanish church and state. The mission friars feared that the pueblos would undermine Church authority, while Bourbon military and civil officials disdained religious orders and the missions and resented Franciscans' control of Native labor, with governors eventually in the 1820s disallowing Franciscans' ubiquitous use of corporal punishment with Indian neophytes. Although the expanding fields and livestock of pueblos such as Los Angeles and San José imperiled Native livelihoods, working in the settler economy, including in the construction of La Iglesia de Nuestra Señora de los Ángeles, may have been in some cases for neophytes a more attractive alternative than the harsh discipline and control exerted by the Franciscans within the missions. While Gabrielino-Tongva Natives experienced mistreatment and corporal punishment at the hands of settlers, pressures to convert to Catholicism were less intense in the pueblo and Natives adapted the Spanish language and sometimes formed families with *pobladores* (pueblo residents). Yet most Indians retained marginalized status as inferior *gente sin razón* (persons without reason).[12]

The construction of La Iglesia de Nuestra Señora de los Ángeles with significant Native labor would come to symbolize the decline of the spiritual and cultural authority of the San Gabriel Mission and the ascendancy of the Los Angeles pueblo and its plaza in Mexican California's public and religious cultures. The population of Los Angeles tripled during the Mexican period from 650 in 1820 to 1,680 in 1844.[13] After a decade-long debate, the Mexican government closed and secularized the California missions in the mid-1830s. While mission properties were supposed to be distributed to Natives, soldiers and settlers instead accumulated vast mission lands, becoming ranchers refashioning themselves as elite Californios who profited from a rising hide and tallow trade. While Gabrielino-Tongva neophytes became citizens with secularization, they lost their ancestral and mission lands, became dependent on labor on ranches, were subject to vagrancy laws, and were pulled even more into the orbit of the pueblo of Los Angeles. Californio landowners constructed new racial categories based not strictly on skin complexion but rather on ancestry, social class, culture, and status, distinguishing themselves from *indios* (Indians) but also from *vecinos* (small property holders) and *cholos* (persons of mixed-race heritage). While few priests served in Los Angeles either before or after the secularization of the missions, and California did not have a bishop until 1840 and only small numbers of Franciscan friars and secular priests, intermittent worship and clergy at La Iglesia de Nuestra Señora de los Ángeles helped to perpetuate Mexican Los Angeles's emergent stratified social order. The *ayuntamiento* (town council) insisted on segregation of Sunday Mass because "these Indians are a dirty class and on mixing prevent the people from hearing mass and dirty their clothes." In 1834 the Plaza Church provided the setting for the wedding of the governor of Alta California, Pío Pico, to Maria Ignacia Alvarado, and a three-day fiesta ensued in the Plaza, indicating, William David Estrada argues, that Los Angeles and its plaza had by the early 1830s become the center of Mexican California. Pico took his oaths of office in 1831 and 1835 in front of the Plaza Church. Miroslava Chávez-García argues that clerics in Mexican Los Angeles promoted reconciliation of marital partners rather than nullification of conflictual marriages as they assisted pueblo *alcaldes* and judges in seeking to bolster male authority and honor within families. However political conflict that pitted centralists versus federalists in Mexico City produced political instability in California in the 1830s and averted the full solidification of emerging social categories in Mexican Los Angeles. Church-state struggles in Mexico undermined the Church in California, particularly the abolition of compulsory tithing in the 1820s and the expropriation of the Pious Fund, which had funded the California missions. Bishop Francisco Garcia Diego y Moreno in the 1840s fruitlessly sought to restore tithing in his diocese and also failed to raise sufficient funds by insisting that parishioners pay *aranceles*, "stole fees," as they received the sacraments.[14]

Despite the bleak financial condition and sparse clergy of the Catholic Church in Mexican California, a result of an independent Mexico's rupture with Spain and the Vatican, evidence suggests all social classes participated meaningfully in the pueblo's Catholic religiosity. In his analysis of religion in nineteenth-century Los Angeles, Michael E. Engh notes that after 1832 most of the clergy at the Plaza Church were French priests associated with the Congregation of the Sacred Hearts of Jesus and Mary (the Picpus Fathers) who were quite tolerant of local Hispanic Catholic practices. Michael J. González's study of Los Angeles's Mexican period argues that while some Californios critiqued the wealth and luxury of the clergy even after secularization, longtime residents later recalled a vivid communal prayer life, including prayers before dawn, an Angelus at noon, and kneeling for an evening rosary. Wills of Mexican Angelenos similarly attested a sincere Catholic faith; for example, Don Vicente Ortega committed to his will that "he had long 'lived and professed' the teachings of 'Our Catholic, Apostolic Roman Mother Church.'"[15]

Following the American victory in the Mexican-American War, the United States annexed California, with Commodore Robert F. Stockton's troops marching onto the Los Angeles Plaza on August 13, 1846. Over the next several years, Angelenos experienced U.S. Army occupation, an uprising against American rule, the signing of the Treaty of Guadalupe Hidalgo, the arrival of increasing numbers of U.S. immigrants, and statehood in 1850. In 1849, Lieutenant Edward O. C. Ord surveyed Los Angeles, using the front of the Plaza Church as the focal point for compass calculations and a grid pattern that would accommodate ensuing American real estate speculation. During this period of transition, David Samuel Torres-Rouff argues, Mexican Californians and European American immigrants in the borderlands community of Los Angeles negotiated interculturally as they evinced respective views of race based on ascribed status versus a hierarchy predicated on skin color, and perspectives on urban space as communal versus as dependent upon the sanctity of private property. Yet familial and commercial ties and a shared commitment to controlling and disciplining Indians (for example, by subjecting Native vagrants to the chain gang) and mutual participation in legal executions and lynchings linked the Mexican and Yankee communities of Los Angeles amid the significant political, cultural, and social shifts of the 1840s and 1850s. During this transitional period, elite and middling Angelenos from both Mexican and U.S. backgrounds participated robustly in the pueblo's public culture, which centered on the Plaza and sometimes projected an ethos of intercultural harmony. The Plaza's public rituals included liturgies and other religious ceremonies at La Iglesia de Nuestra Señora de los Ángeles, staged animal fights (bullfights, cockfights, bull-and-bear fights), bilingual political meetings, fiestas, celebrations of national holidays, and legal and extralegal acts of collective violence. A Latter-Day Saint visitor, Henry Standage, captured in his diary the Corpus Christi procession on June 3, 1847, in which the New York Volunteers occupying the city participated. "As soon as mass was performed in the church the Priest with a long retinue came out into the Square, the Priest performing certain rites at each of the altars. The band belonging to the N.Y. Vols. playing while the procession was passing from corner to corner and the inhabitants showering roses all the time on the capital Priest's head and spreading costly garments on the ground for him to walk on."[16]

Benjamin Hayes, a Catholic Maryland-born lawyer who would soon be elected county attorney and then district judge, emphasized the polyglot, intercultural, and gender-imbalanced nature of worship at the Plaza Church in his description of the first Mass he attended there upon his arrival in Los Angeles in February 1850. Women predominated among the worshippers, an example of what Ana María Díaz-Stevens has termed the "matriarchal core of Latino Catholicism," women's carving out of autonomous space within male-dominated Catholic Church and Hispanic societies.

> The morning of the 3d, Sunday, brought crowds of people to the church from the neighboring ranchos. I went to Mass; after which witnessed the burial of an Indian who had died the day before. The corpse was interred beneath the floor of the Church. There is a graveyard adjoining the Church; for what reason the deceased was entitled to this distinction, I did not learn. Few men attended Mass; many women, many of them richly dressed, graceful and handsome. The whole scene, "American" by the side of "Mexican" (to adopt the language of the day), Indian and white, trader and penitent, gayety, bustle and confusion on the one side and religious solemnity on the other, was singular to me. A beggar at the door, as we sallied out at the conclusion of the service, struck my attention, although I did not understand the language in which he now chanted and again prayed, as many in passing placed their alms in his hand.[17]

In the 1850s and 1860s, elite and middle-class persons of Mexican descent in Los Angeles remained joint partners with U.S. immigrants such as Benjamin Hayes in Los Angeles's social and cultural life and politics, even as Californios and vecinos suffered a severe decline in status elsewhere in the state, for example in San José. The Plaza, including La Iglesia de Nuestra Señora de los Ángeles, remained the focal point for bicultural celebrations in the mid-nineteenth century, for instance in the Assumption fiesta in August 1857. The Assumption festivities, mixing Catholic devotionalism and popular amusements, were described in the *Los Angeles Star/La Estrella de Los Angeles*, a bilingual English-Spanish newspaper that began publishing in 1851:

At the conclusion of Mass the pupils of the female school headed by their instructresses, the Sisters of Charity, came out of the church in procession bearing the image of Our Lady under a canopy. They were joined by the Lancers and passing around the public square re-entered the Church. The appearance of the procession as it left the church and during its march was imposing. The canopy covering the representation of the angelic queen, tastefully ornamented, was borne by girls dressed in white. The girls of the school with their heads uncovered and in uniform white dresses followed; then came the Lancers, the rear of the company being brought up by a mounted group armed with lances. There was an evening procession on the Plaza. A bull-fight took place in the upper part of town in the afternoon, which was attended by a dense crowd. One hombre attempting to perform some exploits on foot which are usually at bullfights in Lima and Mexico, was caught and tossed high in the air a number of times by an infuriated bull and left for dead. A number of horses were badly gored and some killed outright.[18]

Yet rituals involving the Plaza Church elicited a range of responses after the American annexation, reflecting the ambiguities of intercultural dialogue amid social and cultural change. In 1855, a Christmas performance of Los Pastores, a procession of children and adults depicting the Three Magi and the shepherds in the manger scene, fascinated a German Jewish immigrant merchant, Harris Newmark, but repelled a rationalist Californio newspaper editor, Francisco P. Ramirez, who typically reported supportively on the activities of the Plaza Church in his newspaper, El Clamor Público. For Newmark, the Christmas procession pleasingly evoked his boyhood in Catholic Bavaria, but Ramirez found the performance embarrassing, labeled it "disgusting" and an "anachronism," and deemed the participants' chants "unintelligible and insulting." His memories refracted through Los Angeles's subsequent intense urban growth and Protestantization, Newmark would also sentimentally remember how in the 1850s, the Plaza Church's bells marked the day's passage in Los Angeles, "the bells ringing at six in the morning and at eight in the evening served as a curfew to regulate the daily activities of the town," an aural memory of the city's lost predominant Hispanic Catholic culture.[19]

Decades later, Newmark also fondly recalled the elaborate Corpus Christi processions of the mid-1850s that originated at the Plaza Church and involved stops at elaborate informal altars constructed in front of the homes of Los Angeles's Californio elite. Newmark's description highlighted the important role of the Californio elite but also widespread communal participation in the processions.

> Incidental to the ceremonial activity of the old Church on the Plaza, the *Corpus Christi* festival was one of the events of the year when not the least imposing feature was the opening procession around the Plaza. For all these occasions, the 102 square was thoroughly cleaned, and notable families, such as the Del Valles, the Olveras, the Lugos and the Picos erected before their residences temporary altars, decorated with silks, satins, laces and even costly jewelry. The procession would start from the Church after the four o'clock service and proceed around the Plaza from altar to altar. There the boys and girls, carrying banners and flowers, and robed or dressed in white, paused for formal worship, the progress through the square, small as the Plaza was, thus taking a couple of hours. Each succeeding year the procession became more resplendent and inclusive, and I have a distinct recollection of a feature incidental to one of them when twelve men, with twelve great burning candles, represented the Apostles.[20]

Despite Harris Newmark's avid memory of the Corpus Christi procession in the mid-1850s, Americanization and population growth in the mid-nineteenth century brought growing social differentiation. As Los Angeles's population tripled from 1,610 to 4,385 from 1850 to 1860, European Americans increasingly fixated upon a notion of Mexican difference. The state legislature, dominated by Northern Californians of U.S. provenance, in 1855 enacted the Greaser Act, which embedded "Spanish and Indian blood" as a marker of vagrancy. Flood and drought in the early 1860s devastated ranching and elite and middle-class Mexican Angeleno property holding. Emergent residential districts radiating from the Plaza also reflected ethnic and racial segmentation. Middle-class Mexican Angelenos and immigrants from Sonora constructed adobe dwellings in a district that came to be known as Sonoratown and that was perceived by Yankee arrivals as a key marker of Mexican difference. Yankee immigrants constructed dwellings west and south of the Plaza, while the blocks surrounding the Plaza emerged as a business district. A colony of French Angelenos—more than 10 percent of the city population in 1859—also lived adjacent to the Plaza and for decades constituted an important constituency for the Plaza Church. Meanwhile a Chinese residential neighborhood developed just southeast of the Plaza. In October 1871, European American and Mexican Angelenos united in a riot targeting Chinese following a shootout in the Chinese district in which a deputized European American saloon owner had been shot dead. Perhaps five hundred working-class, middle-class, and elite Angelenos collectively murdered by shooting, mutilating, and hanging at least thirty-one Chinese a short distance from the Plaza Church. It is likely that the rioters included Mexicans and Irish who worshipped at La Iglesia de Nuestra Señora de los Ángeles. The aftermath of the 1871 anti-Chinese massacre further increased racial distinctions in the growing city of Los Angeles. A grand jury indicted thirty-seven, with ten facing trial and eight convicted of manslaughter but successfully appealing their convictions. Non-Chinese Angelenos found a rationale for the massacre in purported Chinese lawlessness, and European Angelenos came to blame persons of Mexican descent for perpetrating it.[21]

The Americanization of Los Angeles, including the Americanization of the Catholic Church in California, had significant implications for La Iglesia de Nuestra Señora de los Ángeles. After 1850, following a pattern that developed elsewhere in the Southwest after U.S. annexation, virtually all of Los Angeles's Catholic clergy were of Spanish, French, or Italian nativity, with little effort made to cultivate a native Mexican American clergy. While the continental European clergy typically spoke Spanish and in the middle decades of the nineteenth century continued to enjoy close ties with the city's Californio elite, their ties to the Mexican American working class were less strong. In 1850 a Mexican bishop (Rev. Francisco Diego y Moreno) and priest (Fr. Gonzales Rubio) at the Plaza Church were replaced with a Spanish successor as bishop (Rev. Joseph Sadoc Alemany) and a French priest (Fr. Anocleto Lestrade, a Picpus Father) at La Iglesia de Nuestra Señora de los Ángeles. In 1854 a Neapolitan Vincentian priest, Fr. Bernardo Raho, took charge of the Plaza Church. Fr. Raho would oversee a drastic remodeling in 1861 that would de-emphasize the Plaza Church's Hispanic elements after heavy rains damaged the front of the church. The Victorian remodeling added a new façade, with brick replacing adobe, a fresco above the door by the French-born artist Henri Penelon, and ornamental pilasters ("Cleopatra's Needles"). In 1859 Raho also instituted a parish grammar school, Escuela Parroquial Nuestra Señora de los Ángeles, that enrolled Spanish-speaking and Yankee pupils under a Mexican headmaster, with Protestant youngsters permitted to sit out the course on Christian doctrine. Catalans succeeded Fr. Rado as rectors at Nuestra Señora de los Ángeles: Francisco Mora, who would become bishop of Monterey–Los Angeles in 1878, and Peter Verdaguer, who left to become the bishop of Brownsville, Texas, in 1891. In 1852 the Baltimore Plenary Council of Bishops had sought stronger jurisdiction over Catholic Spanish speakers in the Southwest by assuming control of the Pious Fund, the offshoot of the Mexican state's secularization of the missions. Bishop Alemany's reimposition of tithing and aranceles and insistence that priests should deny the sacraments without payments created acrimony with Mexican Catholics (Native neophytes were exempted from the fees). The priest at the Plaza Church, Padre Lestrade, assessed three hundred dollars for a funeral and fifty dollars for a wedding, eliciting strong complaint in *El Clamor Público*, and many Mexican Catholics turned to civil marriages to avoid the large fees sought by the church. An incident involving Fr. Estrade revealed tensions among recently arrived Americans, Mexican residents, and European Catholic clergy who leveed large fees for the sacraments. William W. Jenkins, a deputy constable, shot and killed Antonio Ruiz, who had resisted the confiscation of his property for failure to pay taxes. As Lestrade presided at Ruiz's funeral, friends of Ruiz reportedly met and decided to rob the rectory. Thirty-six armed vigilantes from El Monte rode to Los Angeles to assist in the arrest of the ringleader in the episode.[22]

The Californio elite retained their close ties to the city's Catholic hierarchy after Americanization, presiding for example as godfathers for the reconsecration following the remodeling of the Plaza Church in 1856 after the new bishop, the Spanish-born Taddeus Amat, a theologian who had served as rector of a Philadelphia seminary, moved the episcopal residence from Santa Barbara to Los Angeles. Yet a gap between the official, Church-sanctioned rituals and popular religiosity among

Mexican Angelenos became evident early in the American period, with clergy occasionally declining to participate in fiesta processions after complaints from the Californio and American-born elites regarding what they viewed as a plethora of processions. In September 1850, a Congregationalist-Presbyterian newspaper published in San Francisco, the *Pacific*, noted, "The anniversary of Our lady of the Angels has been celebrated today with some pomp, although the priests declined sanctioning the usual procession. The reason given was that the newspaper had criticised the processions as usually gotten up and they were not disposed to provoke further criticism."[23]

To Americanize the Church in Southern California, Bishop Amat sought to purge the Church of elements of Mexican folk religiosity that might arouse Protestant American hostility and that did not accord with his understanding of an increasingly standardized mode of "American" Catholic ritual. In synods of the Southern California clergy, Amat banned the irreverent Christmas procession Los Pastores that had been performed around the Plaza Church (and had been admired by Harris Newmark but had embarrassed Francisco Ramirez), the rowdy Holy Week faux execution of Judas Iscariot that had been performed by soldiers in the plaza, and a variety of funeral customs that included imbibing and dancing at wakes, and gunshots and firecrackers in funeral processions. Amat was particularly scathing toward the Mexican Franciscan friars who had long shepherded the region's religious institutions, arguing that they had demonstrated poor pastoral care. In Amat's view, the Franciscans had tolerated superstitious practices and administered the sacraments to sinners, and he suspended the Mexican friars' priestly faculties for several years beginning in 1858. Despite tensions with continental European clerics, sacraments conferring rites of passage remained central to Mexican American Catholicism in Los Angeles. This was indicated in 1854 when several dozen Mexicans furtively buried in the church graveyard a Mexican woman denied a church burial because she had purportedly died in sin, an episode that enraged Anglo-American Catholics and the Californio elite. The Americanization and Romanization of Los Angeles Catholicism alienated Mexican Americans, leading some to shift observance of customary religiosity to private homes and in some cases to convert to Protestantism. Indian worshippers were even more impacted by Americanization, with neglect by the Church and violence and disease taking a heavy toll. Native baptisms in Los Angeles and San Gabriel plummeted from 475 children in the 1850s to 81 in the 1870s. In 1874 Bishop Amat removed the cathedral from the Plaza Church to the newly constructed classical baroque St. Viviana's Cathedral in the southwestern portion of the city. With the construction of St. Viviana and of additional Catholic churches that served mainly English-speaking populations, the Plaza Church became by the late nineteenth century a parish that served predominantly but not exclusively Spanish speakers. The city's increasing residential segregation was now mirrored in its Catholic worship spaces. Even as the Plaza was converted in the 1870s into an urban garden park inspired by Frederick Law Olmsted and then saved in 1896 from conversion into a public market, it came in the late nineteenth century to be a venue for the expression of Mexican identity among Californios and recent Mexican immigrants within an Americanized city. The Plaza Church itself, newly remodeled in the late 1860s to redress crowding on Sundays with the addition of pews, chandeliers, murals, and a new ceiling and belfry, was a source of pride for Mexican Americans even as its long prominence in the spatial hierarchy of Los Angeles Catholicism was eclipsed by newer, Anglo-dominated sacral structures.[24]

Over the final three decades of the nineteenth century, Los Angeles grew exponentially and European American arrivals shifted the demographic balance, consigning persons of Mexican descent to a racialized minority status associated with Sonoratown. In 1875 Los Angeles was connected to the transcontinental railroad and its population spiraled upward, reaching fifty thousand in 1890, then a hundred thousand in 1900. In the 1870s European Americans achieved control of the Common Council as Mexican Californian political representation declined, in part through a deliberate redrawing of wards to reduce representation of persons of Mexican descent. While Spanish speakers of Californian and Mexican birth concentrated north of the Plaza and a Chinese community continued to grow southeast of the Plaza after the 1871 massacre despite official hostility, U.S. immigrants moved farther away, establishing commercial and residential districts in a southwesterly direction. The Plaza, including La Iglesia de Nuestra Señora la Reina de los Ángeles, remained a heterogenous space in which diverse Angelenos mixed through the 1880s even as the city's expanding neighborhoods became increasingly homogeneous and the city underwent a "Protestantiza-tion" in which Catholics lost their majority and cultural leadership in the city to ascendant Protestant newcomers and their denominations. However, by the last decade of the nineteenth century the racially mixed Plaza, with its proximity to adjoining Mexican and Chinese neighbor-hoods, came to be seen by European Americans as undesirable, and they withdrew to other spaces, particularly to the Central Park (later renamed Pershing Square) several blocks to the southwest. This ethnic-racial spatial configuration would achieve even greater mass with Los Angeles's continued growth to half a million by 1920 and to 1.3 million by 1930. Mexican, Chinese, Japanese, Filipino, and African American immigrants concentrated in boardinghouses in the central district sur-rounding the Plaza, which in its racial heterogeneity was increasingly perceived as unpleasant and dangerous by European Americans. More-over, the migration of a hundred thousand Mexicans from Mexico to Los Angeles between 1910 and 1930 would have significant implications for La Iglesia de Nuestra Señora la Reina de los Ángeles's ministry to Mexican Catholics and the elaboration of Mexican Catholic religiosity at La Placita in the early to mid-twentieth century.[25]

II

In a letter written in June 1960, Mrs. Ana Begue de Packman remem-bered a High Mass at the Plaza Church on a Sunday morning in the early 1890s while Fr. Sylvester Liebana was pastor. Begue de Packman recalled prominent Californio, French, and Yankee families arriving promptly and filling "velour-cushioned pews," wary of Padre Liebana's (known for his "Spanish austerity") scolding of late-arriving "stragglers from the pulpit." Begue de Packman reminisced that "at the first bars from the organ, a cadence of voices harmonized. The padre ascended the altar to celebrate the Mass."[26]

Begue de Packman, a descendant of Los Angeles's earliest pobladores and a longtime secretary of the Historical Society of Southern Califor-nia, elided the substantial Mexican element among the Plaza Church's late nineteenth-century worshippers in her account. But her letter re-flects the Plaza Church's key constituencies on the eve of incipient ethnic shifts around the Plaza and among its Catholic worshippers. In the 1890s

Los Angeles city builders turned to an "open shop" strategy to counter strongly unionized San Francisco, luring an extensive immigrant prole-tariat from Mexico, Asia, and Southern and Eastern Europe to low-wage jobs in the rapidly growing fragmented metropolis. Mexican newcom-ers, including workers, middle-class professionals, and radicals fleeing the Mexican Revolution, remade Sonoratown, just north of the Plaza, as a distinctly "Mexican" district. Sonoratown itself would be displaced over the next two decades by commercial and industrial development, but this merely reinforced the Plaza's centrality to the Mexican culture and community in Los Angeles amid significant Mexican in-migration, particularly after World War I, when new immigration laws sharply curtailed most foreign immigration but did not restrict Mexican ar-rivals. Mexican journalist Daniel Venegas's 1928 tragicomic novel *The Adventures of Don Chipote* captured the Plaza's key role for Mexican im-migrants' sensibility of *México de afuera* (Mexico outside), the exiled's longing for Mexico and effort to reconstruct a meaningful symbolic Mexican landscape in the United States. The novel's protagonist, Don Chipote, a migrant farmworker, is disoriented and disillusioned by the urban chaos of Los Angeles but is lifted by encountering the Plaza's fa-miliar Mexican environment. He is deeply moved by the sound of the bells of La Iglesia de Nuestra Señora la Reina de los Ángeles calling the faithful to pray the Rosary. Perhaps not surprisingly, devotion to the Virgin of Guadalupe emerged as central to México de afuera in Los An-geles, a potent symbol of Mexican Catholicism and Mexican nationalism that may have had particular meaning in exile as Mexicans contested the role of Church and state within Mexico in the first decades of the twentieth century.[27]

Meanwhile Italians predominated in a residential district along the Los Angeles River a bit beyond Chinatown, with immigrants from southern Italy in the early twentieth century joining an existing Italian community composed of nineteenth-century immigrants from north-ern Italy. The Plaza's Italian and Mexican communities worshiped to-gether at La Placita, intermarried, and contributed anarchist-syndicalist and socialist and communist activists to the Plaza's burgeoning com-munity of radicals. Italian associational life was centered in Italian Hall, constructed across Main Street from the Plaza Church in 1907.[28] The radicals' secularist and anticlerical tendencies of course sometimes clashed with the Catholic religiosity of the Plaza Church. For example, a supporter of the Mexican Liberal Party spoke in the Plaza in the 1910s during the era of the Mexican Revolution, declaring, "That old Roman Church opposite us is a nest of deceivers."[29]

The multicultural nature of the Plaza Church's worshippers received particular recognition when the Vatican's apostolic delegate to the United States, Diomede Falconio, visited in May 1903. Speaking to "fully 2000 people of the Latin races" (in the words of a *Los Angeles Times* reporter) on the patio of the rectory, the Irish American administrator of the diocese, the Very Rev. Patrick Hartnett, noted his own lack of Latin blood but asserted that "all the good in civilization today can trace its origin to Latin Rome" and lauded the French, Spanish, and Italian contributions to Catholic Christendom, failing to mention the strongly Mexican (and racially mixed) aspect of the Plaza Church's worship community. Celebrating Catholicism's Latin European roots, Fr. Juan Caballeria, a Catalan who would soon be appointed pastor, spoke in Spanish, the editor of Los Angeles's Italian newspaper spoke in Italian, and the French consul delivered an address in French.[30] Yet the substantial Mexican identity among the early twentieth-century Plaza Church's worshippers was evident in others ways. Since 1897 the parish had operated *El Hogar Feliz* (the Happy Home), a settlement that offered industrial courses, religion classes, and social activities for Mexican immigrant children.[31] In December 1903 special Masses observed the Feast of Our Lady of Guadalupe, while in May 1906 a church fund-raiser to pay off debt "enacted . . . old Mexican and Indian dances" in the Plaza, and in September 1907 the Plaza Church's patio hosted a program of recitations and music celebrating Mexican independence.[32] In August 1906 Fr. Caballeria, who had succeeded Emile Coté, a French Canadian, presided over a service at the Plaza Church commemorating the hundred twenty-fifth anniversary of the Los Angeles pueblo and the dedication of El Camino Real, a highway from San Diego to San Francisco recapitulating the "path of the padres." Mingling a fascination for the romance of the Spanish past with a patronizing characterization of the Mexican racial other, a *Los Angeles Times* correspondent noted the participation of "the sons and daughters of natives, but with a sprinkling of those of fairer skin . . . closely following the padres came the children in their bizarre dresses and then came a great throng of gray-haired old Mexicans."[33] During his pastorate, Fr. Caballeria would preside over a restoration of the Plaza Church that sought to restore Spanish-era paintings and statues and renovate a chapel dedicated to Our Lady of Guadalupe, serving both mission-era nostalgia but also Mexican Catholic religiosity.[34]

The Claretians, rooted in mid-nineteenth-century Barcelona and active in Mexico, assumed care of the Plaza Church and of the San Gabriel Mission by the end of the first decade of the twentieth century. The Plaza Church's former pastor, Brownsville, Texas, bishop Peter Verdaguer, had known the Claretians' founder Anthony Claret in Catalonia and in 1902 invited the order to work in his far-flung south Texas diocese, initiating the Claretians' ministry with Spanish speakers in the American Southwest, including eventually Los Angeles. While the Claretians offered crucial ministry to Mexican Americans in the Southwest, the order comprised primarily Spanish-born priests in the early to mid-twentieth century and sometimes evinced an Hispanophilism (preference for Spanish origins) that viewed Mexican-descended cultures and Mexican Americans in inferior, condescending terms.[35]

World War I and its aftermath brought significant challenges to the Plaza and its venerable Catholic Church. In the mid-1920s La Iglesia de Nuestra Señora la Reina de los Ángeles's long role as the central worship site in the Plaza was challenged by the construction of La Iglesia Metodista de la Placita, the Plaza Methodist Church, a large Spanish-Moorish structure that evoked Mexican church architecture. The well-funded Methodist church and its adjoining Plaza Community Center offered an array of Americanization and social service programs rooted in the social gospel. In 1916 a Claretian priest at the Plaza Church, Manuel Milagro, in an annual report to superiors in Madrid hoped that the impending ambitious Methodist project would fail, but noted that it would probably succeed given the Methodists' abundant resources. More broadly, the Plaza itself, demarcated as a free-speech zone by the city of Los Angeles, became the focus of a crackdown on radicalism and a xenophobic "Brown Scare" that targeted Mexicans and Mexican radicals from 1913 until 1918, efforts spearheaded by *Los Angeles Times* publishers General Otis and Harry Chandler after a series of bombings in Los Angeles in the early 1910s.[36]

Ministry to Mexican immigrants and the Mexican American community remained central at the Plaza Church in the World War I and interwar periods and amid the challenges posed by Protestant missions and the Brown Scare. A weeklong Fiesta in June 1913 raised funds to pay for the enlargement of the church facilities—expanding occupancy from five hundred to one thousand by removing rear walls and the sanctuary and adding new pews and altars—as well as the installation of a two-manual organ. The Claretians presided over festivities that blended Spanish mission nostalgia with Mexican culture, including dancers from Jalisco and Guanajuato.[37] In July 1917, a church fund-raising concert sought to defray debt accrued from rectory renovations and the "creation of quarters necessary for carrying on the institutional work among the large foreign population that resides within the parish," the *Los Angeles Times* reported.[38] In 1917, the archbishop of Durango, Mexico, Francisco Mendoza, presided over the annual Epiphany distribution of gifts to parish children, an annual tradition at La Placita that reflected regional Mexican custom. Archbishop Mendoza was a frequent visitor, evidence of the Claretians' strong Mexican ties, also presiding for instance over a Novena for the Immaculate Heart of Mary and the blessing of La Placita's new altar in August 1916.[39] Mission nostalgia and romanticized treatments of Spanish and Mexican culture similarly themed fundraisers for a 1921 renovation and the construction of an adjoining parish school, indicating that the Claretian fathers serving Mexican immigrant and Mexican American parishioners had found a successful formula for fund-raising among white Angelenos which anticipated a profound refashioning of the Plaza by the city's business elite a decade later.[40]

The Plaza and its environs would see profound changes in the early 1930s, with business interests, city planners, and preservationists dramatically remaking the Plaza and its surrounding Mexican and Chinese neighborhoods in part due to concerns about radicalism and disease in dilapidated Sonoratown and Chinatown. After a long debate throughout the 1920s, a redevelopment plan constructing Union Station near the Plaza and a Civic Center a few blocks west came to fruition in the 1930s. While the plan ultimately preserved the Plaza and the Plaza Church, thousands of Mexicans were displaced east of the Los Angeles River into areas such as Boyle Heights, and old Chinatown was leveled, with elements of the displaced Chinese community reconstituting New Chinatown in 1938 in what had been Sonoratown, north of the Plaza. As historian William David Estrada astutely observes, some of the very same business interests and city planners (most notably the Chandlers) involved in the redevelopment would play instrumental roles in "constructing simulated Mexican and Chinese landscapes in the void left where the neighborhoods once stood." Backed by Harry Chandler, publisher of the *Los Angeles Times*, a San Francisco–raised preservationist, Christine Sterling, led a successful effort to create Olvera Street, a romanticized Mexican marketplace theme park of merchants in costumes, restaurants, and shops adjoining the Plaza. Sparked by her efforts to save Los Angeles's oldest house, the Avila Adobe (1818), Sterling and Chandler were joined among others by Rodolfo Montes, an exiled Mexican real estate developer who saw Olvera Street as a way to reconstruct México de afuera, a symbolic Mexican landscape. Before his death in 1934, Montes and his family would frequently visit Olvera Street and became regulars at Sunday Mass at La Placita. Financed as a for-profit corporation headed by Harry Chandler, Olvera Street opened on Easter Sunday 1930.[41]

Across the street from the Plaza and La Placita, Olvera Street embodied intense contradictions. Created amid mass displacement and the deportation of thousands of Mexicans from Los Angeles in 1930–31 and continuing efforts to police the Plaza's historic radicalism, the tourist attraction encompassed a romanticized version of Los Angeles's past created by Anglos that both glorified the American conquest (by highlighting, for example, the Avila Adobe's role as headquarters for the American occupation in 1847) and involved important efforts to preserve Los Angeles's Spanish and Mexican past. The popular theme park offered non-Hispanics a safe and sanitized Mexico north of the border that may have in fact encouraged interaction with Mexicans working in Olvera Street and eased rampant anti-Mexican sentiment. As Estrada aptly notes, Olvera Street "celebrated a mythic preindustrial past that was both appealing and useful to Anglos while at the same time obscuring the contemporary reality of Mexicans in Los Angeles." Mexicans in turn, Phoebe S. Kropp argues, "asserted claims on the space and its representations, demonstrating that they still regarded the street as their own. For them, Olvera Street was not a world apart from the modern city."[42] Christine Sterling and Harry Chandler, with funding from railroad interests involved in the creation of Union Station, also constructed China City, a Chinese-themed marketplace just beyond Olvera Street and the Plaza Church along Main Street that would be destroyed by fire a year after its opening in 1938 and then leveled by fire again in 1949 and not rebuilt.[43]

An Anglo-concocted romanticized understanding of Los Angeles's Spanish past similar to Olvera Street was enacted in the September 1931 Fiesta de Los Angeles, marking the hundred fiftieth anniversary of the birth of Los Angeles, with the Plaza Church again playing a supporting role. The pageant attended by almost six hundred thousand emphasized the city's founding by light-skinned "Spaniards," with whites depicting the original pobladores, obscuring the mixed-race ancestry of the city's actual founders and excluding black and mestizo Angelenos who might have more accurately portrayed Los Angeles's initial settlers. The festivities included vespers in the Plaza Church attended by descendants of early Californio families, a procession to the Avila Adobe where Miss Los Angeles was crowned in front of hundreds, and a procession back to the "patio of the Plaza Church," where Mexican songs and dances were performed. The Plaza Church, serving mainly Mexican worshippers, many of them impacted by deportations, played a key role then in the staging of a pageant representing an Anglo-fantasized understanding of Los Angeles's Spanish and Mexican origins that emphasized, like Olvera Street, a romantic, safe image of Mexico, but avoided meaningful engagement with the realities facing Los Angeles's Mexican community.[44]

More generally, as Olvera Street and the Fiesta de Los Angeles offered Anglo-fantasized representations of a romantic, quaint Spanish past and benignly picturesque Mexican culture, La Placita provided a setting in the 1930s that both confirmed Anglo Angelenos' fantasies and served the needs of predominantly Mexican parishioners and may have at least temporarily blunted anti-Mexican prejudice. Hispanic Catholic heritage as Anglo Angeleno wish fulfillment in quest of a usable past pervades Marion Parks's description of the Plaza Church in a guidebook to historical Los Angeles that she published in conjunction with the 1932 Los Angeles Olympics. Parks's picturesque description belied the reality that little of the Spanish and Mexican era Plaza Church survived renovation in the nineteenth century. "A long tale of romance, pathos, and change is conserved within its thick adobe walls," Parks wrote. "Memories of chants and liturgies—for the living, the new-born, and the dead; for the most distinguished and picturesque personalities of a crowded century—echo underneath its roof."[45] A remodeling in the early 1930s further reinforced the Spanish mission theme, replacing roof shingles with tiles.[46] Similarly, in December 1935, the Native Daughters of the Golden West melded elite Anglo women's charity, preservationism, Spanish mission nostalgia, and Plaza Church history in a fund-raiser for restored entrance doors for the church. In a play authored by Susanna M. Ott, the head of the Los Angeles Public Library's history department, a cast of Anglo Angelenos portrayed Fr. Junípero Serra amid a traditional Christmas Pastores miracle play. Performers on the program also included descendants of early recipients of the sacraments at the Plaza Church.[47] In another example of the encounter of the Plaza Church's Mexican past and present with Anglo Angelenos' quest for an authentic experience in the fragmented metropolis, Timothy G. Turner, a *Los Angeles Times* reporter, detailed what he perceived as colorful observations from a bench in the "old Plaza, the hub of foreign Los Angeles" on New Year's Day 1937. Turner noted that large numbers of Mexican women "with black rebosos over their heads . . . filed into the Old Plaza Church for the 7 o'clock mass," after which the parish's "Sociedad de Damas" served menudo, coffee, and tacos on the church patio.[48] More generally, thousands of Mexicans and Mexican Americans participated in Corpus Christi processions in the 1930s that originated at the Plaza Church and that incorporated archdiocesan officials and organizations, a moment of public Catholic unity that transcended Los Angeles's ethnic, racial, and class segmentation and the often patronizing Anglo gaze.[49]

World War II and the postwar period saw further consequential shifts for the Plaza and its Catholic church. A rise in anti-Mexican prejudice, particularly the stigmatization of Mexican American youth, as Anglos from elsewhere in the country surged into the metropolis's wartime industries and military bases had particular implication. In August 1942, in what became known as the Sleepy Lagoon case, seventeen Mexican American young men were arrested in the death of a Mexican American youth. The intense publicity surrounding the trial of the men, which stressed innate Mexican criminality (purportedly due to Native/Indigenous ancestry) and involved only the slightest semblance of due process, gave rise to the image of the zoot-suited Mexican American hoodlum, despite the relative dearth of involvement of young Mexican Americans in gangs in wartime Los Angeles. From June 3 through 13, 1943, Anglo servicemen, including sailors from the Chavez Ravine Naval Base a short distance from the Plaza, attacked and stripped Mexican American youths throughout downtown, including on Main Street near the Plaza Church, in what became known as the Zoot Suit Riots. The riots ceased after military officials restricted servicemen from going downtown. Los Angeles officials found cause for the riots in supposedly degenerate Mexican American youth and the zoot suits they wore, which the city banned.[50]

Amid the wartime hostility directed at Mexican American youth, the Plaza Church remained a refuge for more positive images of Mexican Americans, including their participation in displays of "public Catholicism" that united believers of diverse backgrounds in spectacles of Catholic wartime patriotism. Indeed, as the oldest Catholic church in the city, the Plaza Church remained a focal point for prominent archdiocesan events that occasionally brought Catholic Angelenos from myriad neighborhoods to the predominantly Mexican American parish, easily the most prominent of the sixty-four Mexican parishes in the Los Angeles archdiocese in the 1940s.[51] For instance, on June 27, 1943, just two weeks after the Zoot Suit Riots, thousands participated in a procession of the Blessed Sacrament beginning at the Plaza Church. Catholic Army and Navy servicemen marched alongside as the Blessed Sacrament was carried on a float, with girls carrying the flags of twenty-one Latin American nations in costumes of those nations accompanied by a Boy Scout honor guard. Archdiocesan and military officials watched the procession from a reviewing stand at the Main Street entrance to the Plaza Church. The spectacle of Pan-American Catholic unity marking the Feast of the Sacred Heart offered a striking counterpoint to Anglo servicemen's recent riotous demonization of Pachucos and Pachucas— countercultural, zoot-suit-wearing Mexican American youth—on the very same streets.[52]

The Blessing of the Animals (Benedicion de los Animales), a springtime ritual at the Plaza Church, served a similar function to Olvera Street (and indeed was sometimes coordinated by Christine Sterling, Olvera's Street founder), bringing Mexican and Anglo Angelenos into the same space in an experience of picturesque Mexican culture that may have at least temporarily defused the intense anti-Mexican sentiments of 1940s Los Angeles. For instance, several thousand observed the ritual performed in Latin on the Plaza Church's patio in February 1940. The Plaza Church's pastor, Fr. Esteban Emaldia, CMF, blessed and sprinkled cows, horses, goats, dogs, cats, and birds, after which humans and animals partook of a collective meal on Olvera Street. A *Los Angeles Times* reporter grasped the ritual's capability for at least a moment of transcending the city's profound social segmentation. "Blessing and a common interest in animals has made strange friendships on the street. The motion-picture people, the family next door, and the Mexicans talk together of their pets."[53] By the late 1940s, most likely under Sterling's direction, the ritual more strongly stressed its quaint Mexican character and the Anglo gaze, with pet owners in Mexican and Indian costumes assembling on Olvera Street before processing over to the Plaza Church for the priest's benediction in Latin, with an audience of more than a thousand watching.[54] Beyond the theme park character of Sterling's orchestration of Mexican popular religiosity for Anglo consumption in coordination with La Placita's Claretian fathers, Los Angeles's English-language newspapers in the 1940s also occasionally reported Mexican Catholic religiosity at the Plaza Church that had little to do with the cultural needs of Anglo observers. In April 1943, for instance, hundreds of parishioners participated in a Good Friday pageant, with members of "various men's organizations" carrying life-sized statues of "Christ carrying the cross, the Blessed Mother, St. John and the crucifixion" followed by "adoration of the Holy Eucharist" in the church.[55]

After the war, Mexican youth involvement in gangs and police brutality against Mexicans increased even as Olvera Street and the adjoining Plaza remained a theme park for a quaint and safe Anglo experience of Mexican culture. The "Mother of Olvera Street," Christine Sterling, led an effort that succeeded in designating the Plaza a state historic park in 1953, in her words for the sake of uniting the Americas, preserving history, promoting tourism and the education of schoolchildren, offering a site for fiestas, and securing "a permanent labor supply of Mexicans." Yet the construction of the Hollywood Freeway leveled remaining surrounding neighborhoods and historical structures, including the 1838 Lugo House on the eastern edge of the plaza. State park designation—marked by a Te Deum service at the Plaza Church attended by Sterling—to an extent deadened the vibrant civic of the Plaza, incorporating all of the Plaza's buildings except its two churches, even as freeways hollowed out downtown. Sterling herself became the state park's manager, with the park's governance organized as the nonprofit El Pueblo de Los Angeles. Indulging the romance of the Spanish missions, and in a now familiar move questionably conflating the histories of the missions with that of Los Angeles, Sterling had a statue of Junípero Serra transplanted to the Plaza, despite the fact that Fr. Serra had little to do with the history of the Los Angeles pueblo. The statue was dedicated on the hundred seventy-fifth anniversary of Los Angeles in August 1956, with vespers in La Placita followed by a procession to the statue.[56]

As we have already seen, Sterling played a role in many public ceremonies rooted in Mexican popular religiosity involving the Plaza Church, an odd symbiosis of Sterling's voyeuristic tourism and the Claretian Fathers' Hispanic Catholicism that combined elite white Anglo patronage with a genuine effort to assist the Mexican American community and convey positive, if narrow and distorted, images of Mexican culture in an era of strong anti-Mexican prejudice. The complexities of the relationship among Sterling and Olvera Street and the Plaza Church and its largely Mexican-descended congregation were on display again on the Feast of Our Lady Guadalupe in December 1949. The feast day began with a High Mass in La Placita celebrated by Archbishop James Francis McIntyre that included a Spanish-language homily delivered by Bishop Joseph T. McGucken. Representatives of the Mexican consul and nineteen other Latin American consulates attended and the Mexico City Boys' Choir sang religious songs before the full church. The Guadalupe observance concluded with a procession of banner-carrying Olvera Street residents and shopkeepers into the courtyard of the Plaza Church, where La Placita's pastor, Rev. Joseph M. Llobet, blessed roses and gave them to the participants in the procession. The feast day's observance thus included a liturgy presided over by archdiocesan officials, gestures of Pan-American good will, and a ritual of Mexican popular religiosity that incorporated Olvera Street and La Placita clergy. While Sterling's efforts included strong elements of self-interest (in Olvera Street's success) and paternalism, she also demonstrated genuine concern for the Mexican American community and worked with La Placita clergy to facilitate public acts of Mexican popular religiosity that responded to the interests of Mexican American parishioners along with the at times patronizing curiosity of Anglo observers seeking a curated experience of "authentic" Mexican culture, including religious customs.[57]

The 1950s saw further challenges for Mexican Angelenos and collaboration between Sterling and the Plaza Church. In 1954 Operation Wetback entailed the deportation of a million Mexicans from the United States, with significant implications for Mexican Angelenos, including those who worshipped at La Placita, with many apprehended in the Plaza and deported from Union Station across the street. In 1959 Sterling joined Mexican Angelenos and La Placita clergy in protesting the razing of Chavez Ravine (including her own reconstructed adobe home) for the construction of Dodger Stadium, an exercise of eminent domain that displaced a Mexican American community rooted in the destruction of Sonoratown in the 1920s. In 1959 Sterling moved into the Avila Adobe on Olvera Street and presided over a new program of Plaza restoration in the El Pueblo de Los Angeles Historical Monument. On May 13, 1959, La Placita's bells pealed and Rev. Victor Martin and altar boys "walked across the Plaza" and blessed the newly restored Simpson-Jones Building with prayers in "Latin, English, and Spanish." Sterling, the Mother of Olvera Street, died in the Avila Adobe on June 21, 1963.[58]

III

The 1960s brought significant transformation of the Plaza and its Catholic congregation, developments tied to the Second Vatican Council (Vatican II), the Civil Rights Movement, and the emergence of a Mexican American social consciousness and activism that would grow into the Chicano/Chicana movement of the late 1960s and 1970s. Crucially, Democratic presidential nominee John F. Kennedy visited the Avila Adobe and the Plaza Church on the eve of his election as the first Catholic U.S. president in 1960. Mexican American Angelenos fondly remembered Kennedy's visit to the Plaza and its Catholic church as conferring a recognition of the growing political importance of the Mexican American community along with an acknowledgment of the Mexican American role in Los Angeles's history.[59] In the 1960s La Placita remained central to Mexican Angelenos' Catholic identity even as the parish's prominence as the city's first Catholic parish continued to draw Catholic Angelenos from around the metropolis despite the lack of appeal of downtown after urban renewal. For instance on August 3, 1960, "many of the city's 600,000 Mexican descent citizens" participated in a procession from Olvera Street to the Plaza Church in honor of the city's patronal Feast Day of Our Lady of Angels of Porciúncula and in quest of the Porciúncula indulgence offered at La Placita that bestowed blessings and remitted punishments for sins.[60] In 1964 the Plaza Church administered approximately six thousand baptisms, the most of any parish in the Archdiocese of Los Angeles, reflecting the parish's popularity among Mexican Angelenos for the reception of sacraments connected to the familial life cycle.[61] In the early 1960s the Plaza Adoration Society, founded under pastor Victor Marin in 1939, brought thirteen hundred Catholic laymen to the Plaza Church for hour-long stints of perpetual adoration of the Eucharist, linking suburban Catholics and working-class Catholics coming off "swing shifts near-by" in overnight devotions that transcended the profound divisions and disparities of the urban renewal era and sought to renew "family life and community" in accord with the Church's patriarchal family ideology.[62]

Amid the dramatic liturgical changes of Vatican II in the 1960s, including having priests face the congregation and the use of vernacular languages instead of Latin, the Plaza Church underwent a major restoration, the most significant changes to its plant since the 1910s. In 1956, the city's Department of Building and Safety had expressed doubts about the building's safety, with investigation revealing problems with the masonry supporting the roof and the roof supporting its tiles. In the ensuing debate, some advocated demolition of the old church and the construction of an entirely new edifice. In 1962 Los Angeles's Cultural Heritage Board declared that what remained of the original mission church's structure should be preserved and in April 1964 approved a plan of restoration of the original church and reconstruction of the addition. Accordingly, in the mid- to late 1960s the original structure was reinforced against potential earthquakes and the interior renovated with the west wall restored. Builders demolished the 1912–13 addition and a new more capacious church was constructed that shared a sacristy with the original church, now repurposed as a chapel. In 1966, Robert Bobrow, a Los Angeles architect, characterized the project as a "pseudo-restoration" that combined a respect for "historical authenticity" with the parish's practical space needs and the reality that a full restoration was impossible because only a small amount of the early to mid-nineteenth-century Plaza Church actually had survived to be restored.[63] Yet John Dewar, an associate curator of Western-American art at the Los Angeles County Natural History Museum, offered a harsher verdict. In 1970 Dewar argued that the $600,000 renovation was "little more than a job of interior decoration" with little or no effort made to accomplish a "historical reconstruction of the original church or even any of its later phases." Dewar explained that he had visited during the early stages of preparation for the restoration "and found workmen engaged in wrecking the interior rather than preparing for a study of it." Dewar believed that a thoughtful effort at a historical reconstruction would have been feasible but was simply never attempted.[64]

Further shifts in the latter decades of the twentieth century reinforced the role of Los Angeles's oldest Catholic church as the central sacral space for Mexicans and Latinos in the city. Extensive immigration from Mexico and Central America in the 1970s, 1980s, and 1990s enlarged and diversified Los Angeles's Latino community, which would attain majority status in Los Angeles City and County by 1998. In 1977 Mario Valdez, the managing director of the Plaza's corporation El Pueblo, estimated that 80 to 90 percent of those who attended Masses and other ceremonies at the Plaza Church were Mexican or Mexican American, with their families linked sacramentally to La Placita. "Their parents or relatives got married at this church. Maybe they were baptized here."[65] Father Al Vasquez, pastor from 1973 to 1981, estimated that 99 percent of the worshippers during his pastorate were of Mexican descent. Under Vasquez, parish services expanded to include a Centro Pastoral in the church's courtyard that offered meals and food for the homeless and poor. In the early 1980s La Placita drew Mexican-descended worshippers from many Los Angeles Catholic parishes, with ten to twelve thousand persons typically attending eleven Sunday Masses, including several standing-room-only Mariachi Masses.[66]

By the early 1980s La Placita's long popularity as the site for baptisms among Mexican and other Latinx Angelenos had increased exponentially, with the Plaza Church baptizing a record 13,800 infants in 1981, the largest number of any parish in Los Angeles and possibly in the country. In 1983, the parish's 11,800 annual baptisms composed a fifth of all baptisms in the archdiocese. La Placita priests administered more than 200 baptisms a weekend in four group sessions. Given the space demands, only parents and godparents were guaranteed tickets for the ceremony, and infants received a computer-generated baptismal certificate afterward. In 1984 Juan Muniz, the proud father of a recently baptized six-month-old son, explained the appeal: "Here everyone is Latino, so you just feel more *a gusto* (comfortable). Everybody understands what a *bautizo* means, the festival of it all as well as the religious ceremony." While a few parents complained that the mass baptisms of fifty to seventy infants at a time felt overly standardized and commercialized, other parents argued, "It's more traditional here, more typical of the *bautizos* in Mexico. The priests are more involved here, and it just feels more like family." Responding to criticism from pastors at other parishes in the city who contended that the Plaza Church was more popular for baptisms because it did not require baptism classes for parents, La Placita in the early 1980s responded to archdiocesan pressure by cutting back on baptisms for out-of-town Catholics and nonparishioners who did not speak Spanish and worked to inform pastors of other parishes when infants living in their parishes were baptized at La Placita. La Placita clergy denied that the baptisms were lucrative for the parish, as the parish required only a ten-dollar donation per baptism. Beyond baptisms, La Placita on weekends also offered many quinceañeras and weddings, hours of CCD (religious education) classes, and twenty-one hours of confession. Despite some pushback from elsewhere in the archdiocese, La Placita by the early 1980s had clearly augmented and extended its longtime role as a key focal point for Mexican- and Central American–rooted sacramentalism in Los Angeles.[67]

Fr. Luis Olivares, an activist pastor, came to La Placita in 1981. Olivares had been born in 1934 in San Antonio to political refugees from the Mexican Revolution. From south Texas, Olivares's parents had assisted Catholic clergy fleeing the anticlerical Mexican government's persecution in the Cristero War (1926–29), a family history that helped to shape the future priest's eventual emphasis on hemispheric social justice across the Americas and the need to assist refugees. Olivares entered the Claretian seminary in Compton, California, at age thirteen in 1948 and was ordained a priest in 1961. Rising rapidly in the order, Olivares became the Claretians' treasurer by the mid-1960s. In 1975 Olivares met César

Chávez, the United Farm Workers organizer and Chicano activist, and was converted to what his biographer, Mario T. García, terms "faith politics," a faith-based commitment to seeking social justice.[68]

Olivares's political awakening took root in a milieu of Mexican American Catholic activism in Los Angeles influenced by the Chicano movement and Latin American liberation theology, particularly its advocacy of a preferential option for the poor and its stress on combating the social sin of injustice rather than merely on a Catholic Christianity of individual salvation. In 1969 Mexican American Catholic activists organized as Católicos por La Raza had sought greater efforts by the Church to meet the social needs of parishioners in East LA and a greater role for Mexican American clergy and the laity. Demonstrating outside and eventually disrupting Cardinal James Frances McIntyre's Christmas Midnight Mass at St. Basil's Catholic Church on Wilshire Boulevard in 1969, twenty-one activists were arrested and jailed. The archconservative McIntyre denounced the Católicos from the pulpit, but retired within a month after pressure from the Vatican. In the ensuing effort by the archdiocese to respond to Mexican American concerns, Father Juan Arzube (of Ecuadorian descent) was appointed auxiliary bishop in 1972 and helped to facilitate greater respect for Mexican American Catholic religiosity and grassroots organizing of Mexican American parishes in Los Angeles. Stepping into this ferment, Olivares became pastor of Our Lady of Solitude (La Soledad) Church in East LA. There Olivares became involved with the United Neighborhoods Organization, which used churches to seek better infrastructure and schools in the barrio. With the financial acumen acquired in his role as the Claretians' treasurer, Olivares led a successful, high-profile campaign against discriminatory auto insurance rates in East LA, ultimately compelling the insurance industry to offer fairer rates to barrio residents.[69]

During the 1970s Olivares also became active in and eventually president of PADRES (Padres Asociados para Derechos Religiosos, Educativos, y Sociales), an organization of Chicano priests founded in 1969 in San Antonio seeking greater representation of and support for Mexican American clergy and Mexican American Catholics within the institutional Church. Although PADRES would eventually be countered by more conservative Latino bishops and clergy aligning with Pope John Paul II's dislike of the liberation theology emanating from Latin

America, work with PADRES assisted Olivares's growing interest in the liberationist model, his own identification with the Mexican American and larger Latino community and their distinct Catholic traditions, and his awareness of the emerging backlash against undocumented Mexican laborers.[70]

Olivares was unafraid of controversy when defending the Latino community and what he viewed as its needs. Even before officially taking on the pastorate at La Placita, Olivares waded into a dispute with preservationists who sought to delay work on a new parish center after an archaeological investigation discovered remnants of the Plaza Church's first rectory. Fr. Vazquez, the outgoing pastor, told the Cultural Heritage Board that the eleven-thousand-member parish desperately needed a new center and that delays would be costly. Olivares followed up by telling the board, "Latino people are attached to the (Plaza) church and feel at home there." Conceding the historical value of the rediscovered padres' house, Olivares asserted that the needs of the Latino community took precedence over preservation concerns. "We're (now) talking about a living church—people, baptisms. . . . They don't want to look at a lot of old rocks." The priests presented the Cultural Heritage Board with the signatures of two thousand parishioners opposing delays in construction of the parish center. The board agreed to let the church begin construction of the center while also allowing further archaeological digs.[71]

After assuming the pastorate at La Placita, Olivares quickly asserted a new pastoral style. In the early 1980s Olivares apparently became the first pastor in the archdiocese to employ girls as altar servers. Citing the difficulty of staffing the parish's large number of weekend Masses and the practice of incorporating the family members of his Mexican American parishioners in liturgies, Olivares declined to halt the practice when pressed to do so by Cardinal Timothy Manning.[72] A charismatic speaker with a sometime humorous and earthy bent, Olivares delivered compelling ground-level homilies (away from the pulpit) in Spanish that emphasized social justice and the linkage between the gospel and society.[73]

Fr. Olivares began ministering to the inflow of Salvadoran refugees in Los Angeles that followed the assassination of Archbishop Oscar Romero and the murder and rape of four American churchwomen in El Salvador in 1980. Working with assistants such as Fr. Mike Kennedy, a Jesuit, Olivares sheltered Salvadoran refugees on church property and in

1984 opened the Centro Pastoral Rutilio Grande (named after a slain Salvadorian Jesuit who was a close associate of Archbishop Oscar Romero), which provided social and legal services to Central American refugees. Seeking "liberation from the base," Olivares and Kennedy incorporated Salvadoran refugees and their personal narratives of oppression into liturgies and facilitated Mexican American parishioners as members of base communities assisting Central American refugees. Salvadoran iconography such as a Salvadoran cross and a side altar dedicated to Archbishop Romero were incorporated in La Placita's sacral spaces. On the Feast of Our Lady of Guadalupe, December 12, 1986, the Salvadoran archbishop Arturo Rivas y Damas celebrated Mass with Fr. Olivares and Fr. Kennedy at La Placita, cementing Mexican and Salvadoran unity on the feast day most central to Mexican devotions.[74]

In the mid- to the late 1980s, Olivares celebrated a liberation-theology-inflected, pan-Latin Catholic religiosity at La Placita, with shrines dedicated to devotions important to Guatemalan, Salvadoran, and Peruvian Catholicism, even as a Mexican Catholic sensibility remained central to devotions and worship in the parish. While some parishioners complained during these years that the parish's Mexican identity was being diluted, Olivares's efforts to cultivate a pan-Latino identity at La Placita, what he called "la cuna del hispanismo," that is, the font of Hispanic/Latino identity in Los Angeles, were largely successful. By the mid- to late 1980s, Salvadorans and other Central Americans may have composed perhaps 10 percent of La Placita's worshippers. Most vitally, worship at La Placita melded a Latino Catholic religiosity emphasizing what Timothy Matovina terms "direct . . . encounters with God, Mary, and the saints in everyday life," a communitarian approach rooted in Hispanic Catholic traditions countering American culture's emphasis on the autonomous individual, and a strong social justice focus on combatting hemispheric oppression. Moreover, Latino Catholic worshippers welcomed La Placita's effective status as a Latino national parish where Hispanic traditions were deeply valued and where the sometimes difficult encounter with a middle-class, Euro-American U.S. Catholicism unfamiliar with and sometimes hostile to Latino Catholic religiosity was less relevant than in many American parish settings.[75]

Angered by the Reagan administration's support for violent authoritarian governments in El Salvador and Guatemala, and its refusal to recognize Salvadorans and Guatemalans as valid political refugees, Fr. Olivares declared La Placita a public sanctuary for Central American refugees on the Feast of Guadalupe, December 12, 1985, an occasion that emphasized pan-Latino solidarity. Although it had already been informally sheltering Central American refugees, La Placita became the first Catholic parish in Los Angeles to publicly declare sanctuary, participating in a movement that had begun with Arizona Quakers in 1982 and had extended nationally to some mainline Protestant denominations, Jewish congregations, and individual Catholic parishes and bishops (although not the U.S. Catholic bishops as an organization, who sought to avoid public defiance of the Reagan administration). Embraced by Hollywood activists such as Martin Sheen, the high-profile, media-savvy Olivares would also receive death threats from Salvadoran death squads in 1987.[76]

After the passage of the 1986 Immigration Reform and Control Act (IRCA), which included an amnesty provision for undocumented persons who had arrived before 1982, Olivares extended sanctuary to Mexican undocumented laborers and their families who had arrived after the amnesty deadline. At Mass on the Feast of Guadalupe in December 1987, Olivares urged defiance of IRCA, advocating the hiring of the undocumented excluded from the law and publicly noting that he had hired undocumented Mexicans to work at La Placita. Moving beyond much of the Sanctuary Movement, which focused its efforts on Salvadoran and Guatemalan refugees, Olivares emphasized a capacious notion of sanctuary at La Placita that linked Central American refugees and undocumented Mexicans as "children of God" victimized by oppressive governments, the Reagan administration's immoral policies, and global inequality. Criticized by immigration authorities as a "renegade priest" and by Olvera Street merchants who feared that La Placita's openness to refugees, the undocumented, and the homeless was encouraging crime and driving away tourists, Olivares ignored Archbishop Roger Mahony's insistence that he no longer make public statements on refugee and immigrant issues. Spanish- and English-language press coverage had played up a rivalry between Olivares and Mahony, a liberal archbishop who had urged lawful assistance to refugees and the undocumented and may have resented Olivares's stature among Latino Angelenos. Olivares's biographer Mario T. García argues that Olivares's pre–Vatican II

seminary formation inclined him toward respect for Mahony's authority, but Olivares's sense of the moral imperative to speak out and act
against injustice led him to push beyond Mahony's cautious approach.
Quite possibly due to pressure from the archdiocese, the Claretians announced Olivares's transfer to Fort Worth in 1989. However, the liberationist priest was soon hospitalized in Los Angeles and then moved to
the Claretian Provincial House after contracting AIDS, possibly from
a contaminated needle in a medical injection to treat his diabetes in
El Salvador. Fr. Olivares died on March 18, 1993, and was buried at San
Gabriel Mission after an overflow funeral Mass attended, among others,
by refugees and the undocumented.[77]

A rough transition followed Olivares's departure from La Placita. His
successor as pastor, Father Al Vasquez (also his predecessor), ended the
parish's sanctuary status, its role as the host for political demonstrations,
and its welcome to street vendors and removed a portrait of Archbishop
Oscar Romero from the church's walls. While praising Olivares's prophetic voice and retaining some ministries for the homeless, Vasquez
argued that a small but violent criminal element among the refugees
had taken advantage of sanctuary and that the parish's limited resources
had proven inadequate for the needs of Salvadoran refugees, leading to
repeated sanitary and housing violations. Vasquez hoped to restore La
Placita's role as a focal point for Mexican Catholic culture, including the
incorporation of Indian dancers and folk arts into Masses and collaboration with Olvera Street merchants in a Mexican Christmas festival. Some
parishioners praised the changes, arguing that the Salvadoran refugees
had become too much of a focus for the parish. However, Camilo Castillo, a Salvadoran refugee who had worked at the parish under Olivares, deplored the reversion back to La Placita's formerly apolitical profile
centered on Mexican Catholic religiosity. "Frankly it seems like they're
trying to make a Disneyland out of La Placita. The voice that once spoke
out in favor of the undocumented is no more." A former church worker
commented on how homilies had quickly moved away from a social
justice focus after Olivares's departure: "They used to talk about the
problems of the refugees. Now the priests talk about some God who
seems to have little to do with us." Activist parishioners belonging to
Comunindad de Base (the Base Community) disrupted some Masses
in protest of the changes.[78] During the same years, an Anglo backlash

against new Latin American immigration contributed in 1994 to the passage of Proposition 183, denying public benefits to undocumented immigrants, a measure later found unconstitutional in federal court. More broadly, the resurgence of U.S. conservatism beginning with the Reagan administration in the 1980s, the emphasis of John Paul II's papacy on respect for the authority of Church leaders, and other structural changes in the late twentieth-century American Catholic Church undercut the Chicano movement and liberation-theology-inspired activist Hispanic ministry approach that Luis Olivares and other clerics had embodied, although the activist approach would see a revival after the turn of the twenty-first century at La Placita.[79]

The Plaza and La Placita have seen further transformations in the twenty-first century. Mexican and Central American immigrants have fueled a revival of the Plaza, with the Our Lady of Guadalupe and Juan Diego (Guadalupe's Europeanized Indian seer, canonized in 2002) devotions a particular focus. Immigrant vendors sell myriad Guadalupe and Juan Diego items, and visitors pay their respects at La Placita's large outdoor Virgen de Guadalupe shrine. In 2008 historian William David Estrada noted that the emergence of a new corporate Bunker Hill business district and renovated Pershing Square, seeking to wall off public space from Los Angeles's immigrant proletariat and the homeless, had left the Plaza one of the few remaining public spaces available for the city's disenfranchised. Estrada wrote about his 1994 interview with a twenty-two-year-old recently arrived Mexican immigrant, Luis, who found Los Angeles disorienting but found the Plaza and La Placita comforting in that they reminded him of his origins in rural Mexico, indicating that the Plaza and its church retained their long ability to signify México de afuera.[80]

A renewed social justice focus at La Placita ensued after the Claretian Order, which like many American religious orders in the early twenty-first century was declining in numbers, decided in 2001 to make immigrants, the poor, and the cultivation of lay leadership its key priorities. In 2003 La Placita's pastor Fr. Dennis Gallo noted that the parish served as a gateway to Los Angeles for many Latino immigrants, who retained ties even as they moved out of the neighborhood, coming in on Sundays by train. "They come from all over; their culture is respected and valued. This is their parish, their home." In the 2000s Fr. Richard Estrada contributed to La Placita's involvement in the New Sanctuary Movement, which aided undocumented persons facing deportation with families in the United States. Estrada helped to organize the parish's participation in the massive Immigration March of 2006. La Placita's Catholic activist tradition critiquing "social sin" found further revival in 2011, when Estrada opened the church to the Occupy LA movement, which critiqued the abuses of early twenty-first-century American capitalism, including concentrations of wealth and corporate influence. Despairing at the Catholic Church's unwelcoming approach to gay and lesbian parishioners and to women in leadership roles, Estrada left the Claretian Order and became an Episcopalian priest in 2013.[81] In 2010 the city of Los Angeles renamed a short street adjoining La Placita Paseo Luis Olivares, nearly two decades after the liberationist priest's death and following the dismantling and then reengagement of his legacy at the parish. After the renaming, the former pastor's brother, Henry Olivares, noted, "Dedicating a street in Los Angeles is the basic recognition from the city where my brother labored and struggled for justice for its poorest residents."[82] Celebrating the centenary of the Claretians' ministry at the Plaza Church in 2010, La Placita's pastor, Fr. Roland Lozano, reasserted the parish's commitment to social justice. "The city has changed. The church has changed," Lozano said. "But one thing has not changed: The dedicated mission of Claretian missionaries to immigrants, the poor, the defenseless, those who have no voice."[83] However, in July 2015, the Claretians departed La Placita after 105 years, with diocesan priests assuming care of Los Angeles's oldest Catholic parish.[84]

In the early twenty-first century, La Placita, among the oldest structures in Los Angeles, stands at the contentious meeting point of the city's past and present, even as its clerics and parishioners have continued to negotiate a Catholicism responsive to Hispanic traditions, the ideological polarities of American Catholicism, and the economic and social needs of immigrant and working-class Latinx Angelenos. In recent years condo developments have brought the gentrification of downtown to the very edge of La Placita and Chinatown, suggesting an impending renewed clash of notions and practices of urban space in the oldest part of Los Angeles and its church.

In sum, La Placita's lengthy history reveals the dynamic persistence of Mexican American Catholicism in Los Angeles and the American West and the ability of Latinx Catholics to retain and refashion their religious traditions amid great political and cultural flux, the emphasis of American culture on individualistic capitalism, and at times the denigration of Mexican culture and immigrants. Los Angeles's oldest Catholic church has had many functions: a key site for Spanish colonialism, Mexican era Catholicism, and Mexican Catholic survival in an Americanizing and Protestantizing city; a Mexican Catholic refuge for waves of Mexican immigrants; a romanticized fantasy of a Spanish Catholic past for Anglo Angelenos; and a central locale for pan-Latino Catholicism and activism for immigrants' rights and hemispheric social justice. Amid complex relations over time with an American Catholic Church hierarchy sometimes hostile or indifferent to Mexican American Catholicism, La Iglesia de Nuestra Señora la Reina de los Ángeles has throughout its history been shaped by transnational relationships facilitating a creative synthesis not only with Rome but also with the cultures of other Catholic homelands such as Spain, Mexico, and more recently El Salvador.

5

Holy Cross on West Forty-Second and the Transformation of New York City's Irish American Catholicism

1852 - 2015

Irish-born Archbishop John Hughes created Manhattan's Holy Cross Parish in 1852 to serve the thousands of Irish Catholics moving north of Lower Manhattan into what became known as Longacre Square (later Times Square) and the developing neighborhood of Hell's Kitchen. Holy Cross maintained a strong Irish American identity into the mid-twentieth century, and its path charted the transformation of the disciplined folk piety created by the "devotional revolution" in Ireland in the nineteenth century into an American Catholicism dominated by Irish American clergy who sought to defend communalistic Catholic distinctiveness amid the rapid urban growth and burgeoning individualistic capitalism of a historically Protestant nation.[1] In the early twentieth century, clergy and laity at Holy Cross converted Irish Catholic longing for an independent Irish nation and ambivalence about American society into a powerful synthesis of Irish American culture and American patriotism. In subsequent decades, Irish American Catholics at Holy Cross also participated in an emergent reactionary critique of the changing sexual mores and increasing ethnic and racial diversity of urban America. The white ethnic Catholic stance on American social change, carried in this case from Manhattan to New York City's outer boroughs and then out to its suburbs, would become a key rhetorical and ideological element of resurgent American conservatism in the late twentieth and early twenty-first centuries.

While Irish Catholicism predominated in the Church hierarchy and became the dominant ethos of Catholicism in the Northeast, other immigrant Catholic groups participated in the region's developing Catholic cultures in the nineteenth and early twentieth centuries, including Germans, French Canadians who immigrated to industrial labor settings in New England, black Catholics from the Caribbean and the American South, and Catholics from Southern and Eastern Europe, most notably

131

Italians. Eventually Puerto Rican, Dominican, and other Latinx Catholics would join the complex mosaic of Catholic cultures in Pennsylvania, New York, and New England, where in the early twenty-first century Catholics composed from one-third to more than half of the population.[2] While Holy Cross's historical experience hardly encompasses the diversity of northeastern Catholicism, it does chart the evolution of Irish American Catholicism and its encounter with New York's multiethnic Catholicism and polity and with important aspects of the working out of the relationship of Catholicism and American identity. As we have seen throughout this book, the Northeastern Catholic experience cannot be taken as representative of American Catholicism, but it was a central and influential thread in the making of American Catholicism.

I

Holy Cross was founded as New York Catholicism emerged from minority, ostracized status, a legacy of the English anti-Catholicism of the colonial era, to embattled majority status with the arrival of large numbers of Irish and German Catholics in the antebellum era. In the late seventeenth century, Catholics composed less than 5 percent of the diverse New York colony. New York had an Irish Catholic governor, Thomas Dongan of Kildare, from 1683 to 1688, whose tenure included the adoption of a Charter of Libertys and Privileges establishing religious freedom. James II removed Dongan in 1688 after Dongan sought to supplant French clerics in New York with British Jesuits, a plan inconsonant with James's efforts to maintain amenable relations with King Louis XIV of France. After the Glorious Revolution later in 1688 and James's own removal, an energetic antipapist colonial government came to power in New York, ending religious toleration and seeking to arrest all Catholics. Catholics fled to other colonies, particularly Pennsylvania, with its Quaker-rooted tradition of tolerance. In 1741, New York City authorities blamed multiple fires and an alleged plot for a slave rebellion on a "Popish" plot fomented by Spanish priests. Authorities executed thirty African Americans and four whites, including an Anglican clergyman, John Ury, accused of being a Catholic priest.[3]

Maryland was the exception to the Protestant character of the English colonies, with its founding proprietor in 1634 Sir Cecil Calvert, Lord

Baltimore, the son of a well-known English Catholic convert. Yet Catholics did not approach a majority in early Maryland, and while several Jesuits participated in the group that settled St. Mary's, Maryland, where they founded the first Catholic site of worship in the English colonies, the early Maryland government sought to keep Catholic worship private. Catholic Calverts promoting limited religious liberty and Puritans seeking anti-Catholic measures contended for power in Maryland in the mid-seventeenth century. The Calverts were deposed in the Glorious Revolution, and the Church of England became the colony's state church in 1702. While official anti-Catholicism persisted, a Catholic elite retained Catholic identity and private Catholic worship continued. Charles Carroll, a prominent Maryland Catholic slaveholder, attended the First Continental Congress and signed the Declaration of Independence, the only Catholic signee. His cousin John Carroll, a Jesuit, would serve as the first bishop in the United States, elected in republican fashion by the U.S. clergy in 1789 as the bishop of Baltimore, a see that included the entirety of the United States. Carroll's election as bishop was approved by Pope Pius VI, and he was installed in 1790, serving until his death in 1815 and laying a pivotal foundation for Catholicism in the early United States in a republican mode. Catholic religious orders, the Jesuits and the Sulpicians, held enslaved African Americans as human property in eighteenth- and early to mid-nineteenth-century Maryland. Meanwhile the Maryland tradition originating in early modern English Catholicism would be carried westward to the Lower and Upper South and the Lower Midwest, most notably the Ohio Valley and Kentucky, with the diocese of Bardstown, Kentucky, established in 1808.[4]

In light of the legal proscription of Catholicism in New York in the eighteenth century, New York City's Catholic community developed little until the American Revolution's emphasis on religious freedom and the separation of church and state, while Catholics in New York remained legally encumbered until the early nineteenth century. In the eighteenth century, small numbers of New York City Catholics maintained a Catholic identity in a "priestless church" (to use James M. O'Toole's phrase), some attending Trinity Church, an Anglican congregation, on Sundays, but traveling for instance to Philadelphia once a year for Easter Mass at a Catholic church. New York's Catholics took both sides in the Revolution, while the British controlled the city until end of the Revolutionary

War. John Jay, a descendant of French Protestant Huguenots and later the first chief justice of the United States, failed in efforts to restrict the religious freedom of New York Catholics in the State Constitution of 1777, yet he managed to restrict the rights of foreign-born Catholics to naturalize as citizens, a measure superseded by the U.S. Constitution in 1789. New York's anti-Catholic proscription took on further life in 1788, when the New York State legislature imposed a requirement that officials "renounce and abjure all allegiance and subjection to all and every foreign King, prince and State, in all matters ecclesiastical as well as civil," a measure that effectively precluded Catholic officeholding until its removal by the state legislature in the early nineteenth century.[5]

New York City's Catholic institutional life originated in the late eighteenth century. Church officials dedicated the city's first Catholic congregation, St. Peter's Church, in 1786. John Carroll, at the time the Vatican's superior of the missions in the United States, waded into the parish's affairs when the church's two Irish Capuchin priests quarreled and lay trustees sought to appoint the pastor (which Carroll disallowed). Carroll would intervene again at St. Peter's in 1807, removing the long-time pastor, William O'Brien, an Irish Dominican, for "misconduct," but in the meantime the parish developed along diverse lines, with many Irish parishioners (75 percent), but also French-speaking Catholics from France and Saint-Domingue (14 percent), Germans (5 percent), African Americans (3 percent), and small numbers of Catholics of Italian, Spanish, and Portuguese descent as well as a handful of American-born white Catholics. Pierre Toussaint, born a slave in Saint-Domingue and manumitted in New York in 1807, was a longtime pewholder at St. Peter's. A hairdresser to New York's white elite, Toussaint engaged in many charitable works, including nursing cholera victims, aiding orphans, and helping to fund the construction of the original St. Patrick's Cathedral. Pope John Paul II declared Toussaint Venerable (the second stage of potential canonization as a saint) in 1997. As Toussaint's canonization cause was discussed in the 1990s, some, including portions of the Haitian American Catholic community, found a saintly model in Toussaint's piety and charity, while others argued that his failure to participate in the Haitian Revolution indicated that he was a "docile slave" who did not overtly challenge slavery in Saint-Domingue or in the United States after his manumission and was thus a questionable choice for sainthood.[6]

New York City's Catholic community saw further development in the first decades of the nineteenth century. In the absence of the first bishop of New York, Richard L. Concanen, an Irish Dominican who died en route from Italy, an Alsatian Jesuit, Anthony Kohlmann, served as vicar general, 1808 to 1815. Kohlmann oversaw the construction of the new diocese's second Catholic church, the original St. Patrick's Cathedral, near the northern boundary of the city at Mott and Prince streets. Kohlmann also prevailed in a key legal case that upheld the inviolability of the secrecy of the confessional. One of Kohlmann's lawyers, William Sampson, an exiled Protestant member of the United Irishmen, drew on arguments from the Irish struggle against British rule, noting that the secrecy of the Catholic confessional had even been respected amid the legal proscriptions of Catholics in eighteenth-century Ireland.[7] In 1815 Vatican authorities appointed New York's second bishop, John Connolly, a Dominican from County Meath, and in 1826 its third bishop, John Dubois, a Paris-born exile from the French Revolution resident in the United States since 1791. In 1827, with four Catholic churches in New York City, Dubois guessed that there were thirty-five thousand Catholics in the city (17.2 percent of the population), while in 1834 Dubois estimated that thirty thousand Irish Catholics lived in the city. Impoverished Irish immigrants tended to live in the overcrowded Fourth, Fifth, and Sixth Wards, working as manual laborers and domestic servants. Germans concentrated in the Lower East Side's Kleindeutschland, with a third of them German Catholics from the Rhineland and Bavaria. While Germans at St. Peter's Church had sought their own German-language parish as early as 1808, the first German national parish would be established with St. Nicholas Parish in 1835, with Most Holy Redeemer, another key German parish, established a short distance away on East Third Street in 1844. French Catholics, long a presence in the city, had contended with Irish Catholics when they resisted the appointment of Dubois instead of another Irish bishop. The French-speaking community, composed of Catholics from France and Saint-Domingue but decreasing in numbers by the mid-nineteenth century, established a French national parish, St. Vincent de Paul, on Canal (later West Twenty-Third) Street in 1841.[8]

Converts, particularly Episcopalians, also added to the ranks of New York City's Catholics. Elizabeth Ann Seton, the daughter of a prominent physician and widow of a businessman, was received into the Catholic Church at St. Peter's Church in 1805. Mother Seton made vows in Emmitsburg, Maryland, in 1808 and founded the Sisters of Charity of St. Joseph the next year. Pope Paul VI canonized Seton in 1975, making her the first native-born American to be made a saint. As a founder of an American congregation of religious women, Mother Seton agreed with John Carroll that the United States' rapidly growing republican conditions called for active religious sisters rather than cloistered nuns. Writing to another religious sister, Cecilia O'Conway, Seton wrote, "This is not a country my dear one, for Solitude and Silence, but of warfare and crucifixion." Mother Seton countered Protestant notions that women's role should be confined to the home, arguing instead that Catholic religious sisters might bring their maternal gifts as "brides of Christ" committed to virginity to their work outside the home in schools, in hospitals, and with orphans and the poor.[9]

Ulster-born John Hughes became the fourth bishop of New York in 1842. Born to a "respectable" tenant farmer in County Tyrone in 1797, Hughes was shaped by the impoverished and disenfranchised status of Catholics who contended with the penal laws in Protestant-majority Tyrone. Arriving in the United States in 1817, Hughes worked for a few years as a gardener and stone cutter and then in 1819 entered St. Mary's Seminary in Emmitsburg, Maryland, where he began his studies in a remedial course. Ordained in 1826, Hughes served twelve years as a diocesan priest in Philadelphia, where he contended with anti-Catholic Protestant nativists, including rioters and polemicists, and lay trustees who asserted what they viewed as their democratic republican role in Church governance. As bishop and later archbishop in New York, the politically skillful "Dagger John" strongly centralized diocesan authority and asserted a pugnacious Catholic identity heavily influenced by his Irish Catholic background. Like Daniel O'Connell, the leading advocate for Catholic Emancipation from the penal laws in Ireland, Hughes sought to claim civil and religious rights for New York Catholics. Lay trustee efforts to select pastors had stemmed from American Catholics' synthesis of notions of a robust lay role brought from Europe, the initial shortage of priests in the United States, inculcation of America's democratic republican ethos, and imitation of Protestant neighbors. However, drawing from the example of Catholics embattled by hundreds of years of British oppression in Ireland, Hughes argued that lay trustees were asserting the supremacy of civil law over Church law, acting like Protestants, and undermining the authority of the Catholic Church. In the early 1840s, Hughes virtually eliminated the independent authority of lay trustees in New York, with power over parish property and finances concentrated instead in the hands of the pastor and the bishop. In line with his emphasis on respect for diocesan as well as papal authority, Hughes sought to end what he viewed as irregular and disordered clerical practices and strove to promote a standardized liturgy and sacramentals. Accordingly, he halted priests' officiation at home baptisms, marriages to non-Catholics, and funerals in city rather than Catholic cemeteries.[10]

Hughes next turned to the public education of Catholic children in New York City. Objecting to the use of the Protestant King James Bible and anti-Catholic textbooks in New York City's nominally nondenominational common schools, Hughes drew again from Irish Catholic experience, the struggle against compelled Catholic support for the Protestant Church of Ireland. In the Great School Controversy of the 1840s, Hughes managed to end the Public School Society's monopoly over public education in New York City but failed to achieve public funding of Catholic schools. Helping to set a pattern for American Catholicism, Hughes shifted instead to an effort to construct a separate Catholic parochial system supported by Catholic parishes, an approach that would be promulgated by the Third Plenary Council of Catholic bishops in Baltimore in 1884. Hughes, by this time a naturalized American citizen invoking his experience as an Irish Catholic immigrant, contended with nativist Protestants asserting that his defenses of Catholic rights were eroding American institutions rooted in a Protestant heritage. Hughes asserted a capacious Americanism encompassing equal rights for immigrants and religious freedom for all, but also his view of the superiority of a Catholicism that might convert back wayward Protestants. The New York archbishop famously expressed his willingness to use defensive violence if necessary to protect Catholic property in the city from nativist mobs. Not opposed to capitalism per se, Hughes worried about how it degraded white workingmen, including his Irish immigrant countrymen, and he emphasized instead a communitarianism rooted in ethnic and religious bonds that might counter the harsh effects of a ruthless, rootless individualistic capitalism.[11]

II

In 1852 Archbishop Hughes appointed Fr. Joseph Anthony Lutz, who would become the parish's first pastor, to lead the effort to organize Holy Cross Church, one of seventeen parishes that Hughes would create in Midtown and Upper Manhattan between 1840 and 1860 as New York City and its burgeoning Catholic population, largely recent Irish and German immigrants, burst out of overcrowded Lower Manhattan districts. From 1840 to 1860, largely due to the arrival of Irish refugees fleeing the Great Famine of 1845–49, but also due to ongoing German immigration, the numbers of New York City's Catholics expanded from between eighty and ninety thousand to between three and four hundred thousand. Holy Cross represented a northward extension of antebellum New York's predominantly Irish Catholicism, which had taken root in twenty-two territorial parishes largely synonymous with Irish identity. After early conflicts within downtown parishes between Irish and German Catholics, German Catholics were accommodated by 1865 in seven national parishes.[12] Holy Cross Church would be dedicated to a devotion that stemmed to the purported discovery of the True Cross in Jerusalem by Emperor Constantine's mother, St. Helena, in 326 CE. Constantine would soon construct the Church of the Holy Sepulchre on the site, encompassing the location of Christ's crucifixion, burial, and resurrection. The Feast of the Holy Cross, on September 14, may have originated with the dedication ceremonies for the church in 335 CE. The subsequent popularization of the cult of the True Cross would assist the rising stature of Jerusalem as an episcopal see in the fourth and fifth centuries and later help to inspire Crusades by medieval Europeans seeking to reclaim the Holy Land from Islamic control.[13] On November 25, 1852, Bishop Richard Vincent Whelan of Wheeling, West Virginia, laid the cornerstone for the church to be built on West Forty-Second Street between Eighth and Ninth avenues and Hughes preached the homily. Offering services out of a temporary chapel on West Forty-Second Street, Lutz oversaw fund-raising, including a Benevolent Lares' Fair that was advertised in the city's Irish Catholic press. At the same time the apparently hasty construction of the church commenced, in line with Hughes's desire to respond to the city's rapidly growing Catholic population by putting up "plain and solid" churches designed more out of "pressing want than any aesthetic idea," as Gilded Age New York church historian John Gilmary Shea expressed it.[14]

It is unclear why Hughes appointed Fr. Lutz, a German, to pastor Holy Cross, which would quickly develop an Irish congregation and identity; in any case, an Irish assistant priest, Rev. Patrick Mahony, would serve along with Lutz when the church opened in 1854.[15] Perhaps Hughes chose Lutz because he spoke good English, which he had acquired over several decades in working as a priest in the United States not exclusively with German Catholic communities but rather in a variety of capacities, initially in the diocese of St. Louis. Although there is no evidence that the bishops he served under found Fr. Lutz's work problematic, he nonetheless typified the foreign-born, often itinerant clergy who staffed the American Church in the early to mid-nineteenth century, priests whose flexibility aided bishops' efforts at planting Church institutions in far-flung, widely varying settings but whose mobility sometimes stymied the hierarchy's efforts at imposing authority, control, and stability.[16]

Lutz was born in 1801 in the village of Odenheim in the Baden Margraviate, a southwest German principality with a Catholic majority that flanked the east bank of the Upper Rhine. He was ordained in Paris and arrived in Missouri in 1826 with several other continental European priests recruited for St. Louis. In the St. Louis diocese, then under the leadership of Neapolitan-born bishop Joseph Rosati and newly separated by Rome from the New Orleans diocese, Lutz built and pastored parishes, worked Indian missions in Illinois, Kansas, and portions of the Northwest Territory, and served as pro-rector of the cathedral. Lutz initiated St. Louis's first German-language sermons and catechism lessons in 1834 as increasing numbers of German Catholics migrated to St. Louis and its environs. In St. Louis, Lutz acquired experience navigating the complex linguistic politics of transnational American Catholicism. In petitions to the bishop, English-speaking Catholics ("Americans," Irish, and Americanized French Creoles) had lamented that the predominance of French rather than English in services at the St. Louis Cathedral depressed church attendance and demoralized non-French-speaking Catholics. In 1832, Bishop Rosati assigned Lutz, who had honed his vernacular English in missionary trips where he worked with Indian agents and other English-speaking denizens of Indian country, to offer regular English homilies and catechism at the cathedral. Lutz was appointed vicar general for the Germans in St. Louis in 1846 but left that diocese the following year. After Lutz's arrival in New York in 1848, Bishop Hughes designated him pastor of St. John the Baptist, a German parish on West Thirtieth Street, where he served until 1852 and his appointment to organize Holy Cross further uptown. Lutz was available for Holy Cross because Hughes had placed the German parishioners at St. John's, resistant to the Irish bishop's efforts to extinguish lay trustee control, under interdict.[17]

As the building neared completion, the Church of the Holy Cross was formally dedicated on December 17, 1854. Rev. William Starrs, vicar general of the diocese, celebrated the Solemn High Mass with the assistance of Fr. Lutz. Rev. Patrick Moriarty, a Dublin-born Augustinian friar who led Villanova University and who would clash in the 1860s with the bishop of Philadelphia, James F. Wood, over Moriarty's vocal support for the controversial Irish nationalist Fenian movement, preached at the formal dedication Mass.[18] In the late 1870s John Gilmary Shea recalled the church's original brick building, which was heavily damaged by lightning in 1867, as constructed in Roman style, one hundred feet in depth and seventy-five feet in width, with a seating capacity of fourteen to fifteen hundred. Shea remembered that the original church lacked "elaborate ornamentation, but was grand and imposing; the tall spire, towering one hundred and sixty feet, making it a conspicuous object" looming over the still quite modest and low-flung Midtown environs that were filling in with Irish immigrants.[19] Holy Cross's Irish identity took fuller shape in the next several months as Hughes transferred Fr. Lutz and replaced him with clergy of Irish extraction, bringing in Rev. Thomas Martin, OSD from St. Brigid's, a downtown Irish parish, to administer the nascent parish and then appointing Patrick McCarthy as rector in November 1855.[20] John Gilmary Shea quotes Archbishop Hughes's description of Fr. Martin's parish-building efforts at Holy Cross, a characterization that highlights the importance of effective pastoral leadership but also hints at Hughes's understanding of the crucial importance of ethnic consciousness and solidarity in parish community formation. "[Fr. Martin] went to the then hardly formed congregation on Forty-second Street, where, without haranguing, he began silently and noiselessly to work to show them their way through their difficulties until the people began to understand themselves and to be a congregation—a numerous congregation."[21] Participating in Archbishop Hughes's effort to create a Catholic school system separate from and parallel to the public school system, by 1857 Holy Cross supported two schools, one for boys with one hundred sixty students and another in the basement for girls with two hundred students.[22]

Holy Cross took form as an Irish-identified parish as Irish Catholicism underwent a "devotional revolution" from a Gaelic Catholic religiosity rooted in pilgrimages to sacred sites and devotions at holy wells to a highly centralized Catholicism tied to Pope Pius IX's (1846–78) efforts to Romanize the Church through standardized fidelity to a Tridentine Catholicism (rooted in the Council of Trent). The Irish "devotional revolution" participated in Pius IX's efforts to cultivate a revival of devotional piety and to strengthen Church hierarchical authority, including the papacy. Paul Cullen, the archbishop of Dublin (1852–78), led these post-famine changes in Ireland, where the Synod of Thurles in 1850 supplanted the holy well with the parish as the focus of worship, mandated church baptisms and funerals (rather than wakes without funeral Masses), and encouraged regular Mass attendance and annual reception of the sacraments. Earlier in the nineteenth century, Daniel O'Connell's efforts for Catholic Emancipation had cemented a profound linkage between Irish nationalism and Catholic identity.[23]

Holy Cross was one of eight Irish parishes formed in New York City in the 1850s, corresponding with the burst of Irish immigration to the United States that occurred in the wake of the famine. By the end of the Civil War in 1865, twenty-three of New York City's thirty-two parishes (72 percent) were Irish identified. In his studies of Irish Catholics in New York City, Jay P. Dolan has argued that while a substantial portion of the Irish immigrant population in the city was unchurched, perhaps half of the population attended Mass regularly, filling parishes to overflowing at early Sunday Masses. At the Solemn Mass later in the morning, unskilled Irish immigrants filled the galleries while Irish skilled laborers and professionals sat in pews for which they had paid rents. Pew rents and fees for seating or even admission to Mass became standard in New York, a crucial means by which parishes raised funds. By the 1880s, those who sat in the galleries for the early Masses at Holy Cross were expected to pay five cents, while those who sat on the main floor of the church were to pay ten cents. Seats at the High Mass cost a dime more, ensuring a degree of social stratification by hour on Sunday morning. The early Masses tended to last a half hour, with priests celebrating Mass in Latin facing the altar with their back to the congregation and assisted by altar boys. Special weekday evening services occurred during the Lenten season, with such services held at Holy Cross on Tuesday evenings during Lent in 1857. The pomp of liturgy at Irish parishes, particularly during key moments in the liturgical calendar, contrasted markedly with the squalor of Irish neighborhoods such as Five Points and Hell's Kitchen. Sermons offered the opportunity for instruction in orthodox, Romanized doctrine. For instance, the *New York Herald* noted that Fr. McCarthy delivered an "eloquent discourse on the Immaculate Conception" on that feast day at Holy Cross in December 1866, twelve years after Pius IX had pronounced the dogma of the Immaculate Conception in 1854. The parish's choir and the "children of the sodalities" had preceded the Mass with a solemn procession and hymns. As the transatlantic Irish "devotional revolution" took root in New York under the aegis of bishop and then archbishop (in 1850) John Hughes at parishes that included Holy Cross, confession and the reception of communion became more frequent, funeral Masses supplemented but did not supplant wakes, and confraternities cultivated devotions to the Immaculate Heart of Mary and the Confraternity of the Sacred Heart. Holy Cross's sacramental register from the 1850s documents scores of Irish-surnamed infants baptized by Frs. Lutz and McCarthy, sometimes only a day or two after birth, according with the era's high infant mortality and the then-prevalent Catholic notion that the souls of infants who died before baptism entered a "limbo" short of heaven. In the transition from the mid- to the late nineteenth century, predominant images of Irish and Irish American priesthood transitioned from heroic images of ascetic priests serving the sick and poor to "priest-builders," "brick-and-mortar priests" constructing large churches and parish plants.[24]

It is highly possible that Holy Cross parishioners participated in the July 1863 Draft Riots, in which Manhattan's Irish Catholics took out their rage at Protestant, Republican, and African American targets who for them represented abolitionism, the unjustness of the war's toll on the Irish, and the purported subjection of Irish Democratic laborers to the nativist Republicans' agenda of racial equality. Nine blocks south of Holy Cross Parish, at West Thirty-First Street and Ninth Avenue, the County

Kildare–born pastor of St. Michael Parish, Arthur J. Donnelly, dissuaded a mob that probably included some of his parishioners from burning down a Presbyterian church across the street. The grateful Presbyterian minister gifted St. Michael's oak chairs that would be used in the sanctuary for decades afterward. A number of city priests had similarly talked down mobs, including a priest from the Church of the Transfiguration on Mott Street who helped avert the lynching of an African American family, and Isaac Hecker and the Paulists, who spent all night seeking to counsel Irish Catholics they knew away from violence.[25] Meanwhile Irish Catholic laborers lynched African Americans in a number of Midtown and Downtown locales, including on West Twenty-Seventh Street. Irish Catholic rioters took refuge in barricades they constructed on Ninth Avenue, from Thirty-Second to Forty-Third streets, a mere half block from the church on Forty-Second Street. Across Midtown, heeding the request of New York governor Horatio Seymour, a Peace Democrat, an ailing Archbishop Hughes on July 17 belatedly spoke to a crowd from his residence at Thirty-Sixth and Madison Street, requesting, amid the crowd's occasional interruption with racial epithets, that "the disturbances be stopped, for the sake of religion and the honor of Ireland." A day later, Hughes, long tolerant of but ambivalent about slavery, indifferent to African Americans and racial equality, and hostile to abolition but (unlike the Catholic press in New York) supportive of the Union and conscription, wrote to his longtime friend, U.S. Secretary of State William H. Seward, asserting that the root cause of the riots was Irish Catholic working-class fear of black labor competition.[26]

There is no record of how Fr. Patrick McCarthy sermonized at Holy Cross on Sunday, July 20, but across the city Catholic clerics condemned the riots.[27] Down Ninth Avenue at St. Michael Parish Fr. Donnelly, with considerable indirection, told his parishioners that had he seen little evidence that they had actively participated but he "cautioned . . . against all riotous proceedings . . . [and] condemned all assaults on a harmless, inoffensive people [negroes]." Donnelly continued, parrying Irish Catholic arguments that had been made for the riots, arguing to the contrary that indiscriminate antiblack violence could not be justified and that mob violence was a fruitless, destructive exercise inconsistent with morality and Irish claims to American respectability. "It was said that bad men used the negro as a tool but, if so, was that any reason why a whole race should be exterminated? If this devil was unchained with a view of getting rid of a 'bad law,' the plan would fail for the rule of a mob was dreaded by all well disposed persons next to the rule of hell itself." Donnelly admonished his flock to disassociate themselves from any neighbors in their tenement houses who had stolen property during the riots and to urge them to return it.[28] It is likely that Holy Cross parishioners were also among the crowds of Irish Catholics, many of them from Hell's Kitchen, who thronged Eighth Avenue from Twenty-First to Thirty-Third streets as Irish Protestant Orangemen paraded on July 12, 1871. William M. "Boss" Tweed, Tammany Hall, and city and state authorities had reversed a previous ban on the Orange Parade under pressure from Protestant New Yorkers who feared the growing influence of Irish Catholicism and Irish nationalism, including Fenianism. More than sixty died after militia opened fire on the crowd at Twenty-Fourth Street, in what became another signal event in Irish Catholic consciousness in nineteenth-century New York City.[29]

The Midtown Irish parish faced a significant challenge several years after the Draft Riots when lightning in an afternoon thunderstorm severely damaged the church's steeple on June 18, 1867. Highlighting its fears of further Irish Catholic urban disorder, the *New York Times* reported that "a roundsman and a section of men from the Twenty-second precinct were soon on the ground and preserved order, keeping the crowd back from the vicinity of the church."[30] With the remaining structure found to be poorly constructed and physically unsound, Fr. McCarthy decided to replace the existing structure with a new church. Employing a fund-raising method that would be used by other Irish parishes in the city, parishioners contributed to a New Holy Cross Church Debt Paying Association, with respective parishioners' weekly payments announced at Sunday Masses. Several years after the new church was dedicated on the Feast of St. Joseph on May 7, 1870, a parish committee seeking further means to defray the building cost held a benefit at Lyric Hall several blocks away on Sixth Avenue offering a "Panoramic view of Ireland: its scenery, cities, churches, & c." The benefit was skillfully framed to appeal to the worldview of Irish immigrants and their children, for whom a sense of exile from and longing for Ireland would remain a key mental and cultural framework until the early twentieth century.[31] Gilded Age lay New York City church historian John Gilmary

Shea described the new Holy Cross Church as "a spacious, cruciform building, in the transition style of Byzantine. . . . In construction it is one of the most solid and substantial churches in the city."[32]

An Irish Catholic sensibility synthesizing the continued resonance of Irish nationalism with navigation of the inequities of New York City's Gilded Age capitalistic order characterized the lengthy (thirty-seven years) pastorate of Charles McCready, who became rector at Holy Cross in September 1877. Born in Letterkenny, Ulster, in 1837, McCready began studies for the priesthood in Ireland at Maynooth but in 1864 came to the United States, where he completed his seminary studies at Mount Saint Mary's, Emmitsburg, Maryland. New York archbishop John McCloskey ordained McCready in Old St. Patrick's Cathedral in 1866.[33]

Shaped like many of his parishioners by the searing experience of the famine that occurred during his boyhood years and by the ongoing struggle against British rule, McCready along with many Irish-born clergy and laity was an ardent supporter of Irish nationalist causes, a means of expressing an exile's longing for Eire and of constructing an Irish national consciousness within a community of Irish and Irish Americans in the United States. For example, Fr. McCready attended an Irish nationalist fund-raiser at the Metropolitan Opera House in November 1890. Five Irish members of Parliament made speeches beseeching contributions of Americans "because our liberty has been denied to us, and because we have to fight against brute force on a gigantic scale." McCready contributed fifty dollars to the thirty-three thousand that was raised for the Irish home rule cause that evening. Other subscribers included myriad state and local officeholders, ward Irish National League branches, and many Catholic clergy of Irish descent.[34] Into the early twentieth century, the Holy Cross pastor participated in organizations such as the Society of the Friendly Sons of St. Patrick and the United Irish League of America that promoted visions of Irish nationalism in networks of Irish American Democratic politicians and Catholic clergy in New York City. At a meeting honoring New York Supreme Court justice James A. O'Gorman in February 1903, McCready delivered a speech citing the Irish ancestral hatred held for their British oppressors.[35] As one of the more prominent Irish Catholic clerics in New York City, McCready also retained clerical ties to Ulster. In July 1904, the Holy Cross rector attended the reopening of the cathedral in Armagh, Ulster, where a riot between Orangemen and Catholics ensued. The Armagh tie was renewed nearly four years later in April 1908, when McCready assisted at the altar at St. Patrick's Cathedral when Cardinal Michael Logue, the archbishop of Armagh and primate of all Ireland, celebrated Mass there.[36]

Even as Irish and Irish American Catholics in New York City retained ties to an Ireland seeking release from British colonialism, they expressed competing visions of engagement with an increasingly unequal American capitalistic society, with American politics and culture, and with episcopal authority. This was nowhere more evident than in the McGlynn affair, a contest over the ideological direction of the New York Archdiocese and of American Catholicism that involved Archbishop Michael Corrigan and Rev. Dr. Edward McGlynn, the fiery, radical rector of St. Stephen's Church on East Twenty-Eighth Street, one of the largest and most prominent parishes in the city. At St. Stephen's, McGlynn directed an extensive plant offering social services that anticipated the social gospel of liberal Protestant denominations in the late nineteenth century. McGlynn was a close friend of Holy Cross's pastor, Charles McCready. McGlynn had visited Ireland in the early 1860s and recruited McCready to the United States, and McCready had served as an assistant priest under him at St. Stephen's Church for six years beginning in 1871, an assignment that began with sick calls at Bellevue Hospital attending the many Irish Catholics injured in the July 1871 Orange Riot. McGlynn was born in New York City in 1837, and his parents had immigrated from Donegal (McCready's native county in Ulster) in 1824. McGlynn would preach at Holy Cross in December 1877 when a few months into his pastorate McCready initiated devotions to the Sacred Heart at the West Side parish.[37]

The dispute between Archbishop Corrigan and McGlynn crystallized emerging divisions between conservative and liberal Catholics in New York and nationally. McGlynn was one of a group of liberal New York priests known as the Accademia that among others included Paulists such as Isaac Hecker. Suspect in the eyes of the archdiocesan chancery for their liberal views, the Accademia had begun meeting in 1866 to discuss causes and ideas such as Fenianism, Radical Reconstruction, optional clerical celibacy, the possibility of a vernacular liturgy, and an understanding of the Church instead of the pope as infallible. McGlynn had antagonized Corrigan by publicly opposing public aid to religious institutions and criticizing parochial schools, and he had resisted building a school at St. Stephen despite the Third Plenary Council of Baltimore's mandate that every parish should open a school. Beginning in the early 1880s, McGlynn had wedded Irish nationalism with the socialist ideas of Henry George, who advocated a single tax on land to redress the rapidly growing inequality of Gilded Age America. To McGlynn, Henry George's ideas offered an analysis and solution for the profound poverty of many of his Irish parishioners at St. Stephen's. Tammany Hall, which had close links to Corrigan, feared Henry George's challenge in the 1886 mayoral election to the traditional Democratic dominance of the Irish Catholic vote, and McGlynn ignored Corrigan's command that he not publicly endorse George. Corrigan was an emergent leader among U.S. Catholic bishops of a conservative bloc that sought to perpetuate a unique and separate Catholic culture in the United States. The conservative bishops supported the primacy of papal and episcopal authority, sought to conserve existing social hierarchies, and resisted accommodation with liberalizing trends in American society. The conservatives contended with a liberal Americanist bloc (which included Baltimore's James Gibbons and Saint Paul's John Ireland) that embraced American republican ideology and sought greater accommodation with American culture and institutions and social reforms that might redress growing social disparities.[38]

Corrigan suspended McGlynn in November 1886 after the St. Stephen's pastor advocated the reading of Henry George's *Poverty and Progress* in a newspaper interview. Corrigan pressed the Holy See for action against the dissident priest, and in December the prefect of the Propagation of the Faith (also known as Propaganda) ordered McGlynn to report to Rome. McGlynn refused to go, citing poor finances, bad health, and commitments to his family. The St. Stephen's rector wrote to Archbishop Corrigan that he would persist in teaching "as long as I live, that . . . private ownership of land is against natural justice, no matter by what civil or ecclesiastical laws it may be sanctioned." He also declared that no one, whether "Bishop, Propaganda, or Pope," could rightfully punish him for views on "political economy" that had not been condemned by the Church. After McGlynn refused to report to Rome, insisting that conscience preceded obedience, he was excommunicated in

July 1887. Corrigan offered to make McCready the rector at St. Stephen after he removed McGlynn in 1887, a gesture that might have conciliated the many Irish Catholics in New York City upset at the archbishop's high-handed treatment of the popular McGlynn, but McCready declined to leave Holy Cross to supplant his longtime confidant.[39]

The contest between conservative and liberal wings of the late nineteenth-century American Catholic Church did not end with the excommunication of McGlynn. Corrigan demanded loyalty oaths from New York priests, strongly discouraged the attendance of Catholics at meetings of the Anti-Poverty Society (which had been formed by McGlynn and Henry George after McGlynn's suspension), and transferred clerics who had expressed support for McGlynn. German priests in the archdiocese and German American bishops such as the Milwaukee archbishop Frederick X. Katzer—who were wary of liberal Irish American Catholics' advocacy of an adaptation of the Church to American conditions—readily supported Corrigan. Yet liberal bishops such as John Ireland continued to press the case in Rome that Corrigan had acted precipitously and that McGlynn had not been treated fairly. In December 1892 the new apostolic delegate to the United States, Francesco Satolli, shocked Corrigan by restoring McGlynn to good standing. However, Corrigan was able to delay and maneuver Vatican politics to the extent that Satolli eventually asked him to appoint McGlynn pastor of St. Mary's in Upstate Newburgh. This reincorporation of McGlynn into the archdiocese in an obscure pastorate far from New York City diminished the radical priest's influence and did little to threaten Corrigan's. As the announcement of McGlynn's appointment to Newburgh impended in December 1894, the radical priest celebrated and preached at Christmas Masses at Holy Cross on West Forty-Second. McGlynn's return to the altar and pulpit in New York City after seven years—albeit temporarily—flowed from his long friendship with Holy Cross's pastor, Charles McCready. McGlynn died of kidney disease in Newburgh in January 1900.[40]

Beyond its reverberations in New York, the McGlynn affair had profound repercussions for American Catholicism. Historian Robert Emmett Curran persuasively argues that the affair's denouement ultimately bolstered conservative forces and weakened liberal ones, setting the American Church on the path to ultramontanism (an emphasis on infallible papal authority) through much of the twentieth century. Among the shifts in the wake of the McGlynn affair that strengthened conservatives and undercut liberals, Pope Leo XIII validated private property in *Rerum Novarum* (1891) and condemned Americanism (1899), while the institution of the Vatican's apostolic delegation to the United States (ironically inaugurated with Francesco Satolli's restoration of Edward McGlynn) granted the apostolic delegate veto power of episcopal appointments and undercut the previous relative independence of American bishops. While Leo had recognized the problem of working-class poverty and had emphasized the dignity of workers and their right to organize and seek a living wage in *Rerum Novarum*, the encyclical had dismissed McGlynn and Henry George's proposed solutions for the inequities of industrial capitalism. Besides endorsing private property, Leo had criticized the way in which socialism in his view emboldened the state at the expense of families and communities.[41]

Even as Fr. McCready treaded carefully amid the treacherous, prolonged ideological dispute between his friend McGlynn and Archbishop Corrigan, he zealously sought to uphold Holy Cross's interests as an Irish-identified territorial parish in Hell's Kitchen. With overlapping grids of parishes in the neighborhood organized along both territorial and national parish (ethnic) lines, ethnic and racial identity in Hell's Kitchen was synonymous with particular parish lines, largely avoiding questions of pluralism and ethnic and racial mixing amid the explosive urban growth of New York City into the early twentieth century. In the early 1880s, Holy Cross's northern boundaries reached Forty-Sixth Street, beyond which Sacred Heart on West Fifty-First (established in 1876) served Irish Catholics in the northern reaches of Hell's Kitchen. Below Holy Cross's southern periphery at West Thirty-Eighth, St. Michael's on West Thirty-First served Irish Catholics in the southern stretches of the neighborhood. German Catholics in Midtown West worshipped at St. Francis of Assisi and St. John the Baptist in the West Thirties and after 1858 at Assumption Parish on Forty-Ninth Street. On the northern fringe of Hell's Kitchen, the Paulists operated St. Paul the Apostle (founded in 1858) at West Fifty-Ninth and Ninth Avenue.[42]

McCready complained bitterly to the chancery and to his parishioners when a new territorial parish on West Fortieth Street, St. Raphael's, was created for Irish Catholics living west of Tenth Avenue. A 1902 parish history explained what McCready viewed as the injustice of the division, which he had protested in vain in letters to the chancery. "For three-fifths were taken from Holy Cross, and two fifths from St. Michael's, a larger parish . . . the church was located nine blocks from St. Michael's, and two from Holy Cross, and placed within one hundred feet of Holy Cross boundary." For decades after the division, priests from the adjoining parishes competed to offer the sacraments to Hell's Kitchen Irish affected by the boundary change, sometimes exchanging harsh words with each other and parishioners. For instance, in 1900 McCready wrote Fr. Malick A. Cunnion, St. Raphael's rector, protesting that St. Raphael's new church and rectory on West Fortieth would bring it even closer to Tenth Avenue and the Holy Cross boundary. McCready complained of many instances in which St. Raphael priests had tried to poach and pressure Holy Cross parishioners and described the most recent instance.

> Mrs. O'Brien, a parishioner and a pew-holder of Holy Cross for over thirty years, during a protracted, intermitting illness, was several times annointed [sic] by the priests of this church. By some chance the priests of St. Raphael's found their way there and administered the sacraments to the woman, knowing that she had been attended from Holy Cross. Mrs. O'Brien died last Sunday, and arrangements were made to have her buried from her own Church; on this becoming known to Fr. Bergin of St. Raphael's, he called at the residence of the deceased, administered a severe reprimand to her relatives for this action, and threatened to "compel" them to bring the remains to 40th Street. Such an action as this will hardly commend itself to you as neighborly, or Christian, or Priestly.[43]

As the pitched battle for Irish worshippers in Hell's Kitchen demonstrated, by the late nineteenth century ethnic and racial identity had become synonymous with parish identity in New York City, erasing the more fluid Catholic congregations of the early nineteenth-century city. In 1883, six Irish parishes including Holy Cross and St. Stephen had raised ten thousand dollars in a three-week Ladies' Fair to support St. Benedict the Moor Church, which had recently been founded on Bleecker Street in what may have constituted the first mission parish for black Catholics north of the Mason-Dixon line. The notion of a separate parish for black Catholics may have seemed consistent with the distinct ethnic organization of Gilded Age New York City's Catholic parishes. Yet, as seen in the case of New Orleans, the shift from black Catholic participation in racially mixed congregations (for example, at St. Peter's in Lower Manhattan in the early nineteenth century) to racially segregated worship spaces marked a significant move away from Catholic universalism to a Jim Crow Catholic religiosity that spanned the regions of the United States. In 1898, St. Benedict the Moor, following the northward movement of African Americans in Manhattan, moved from Lower Manhattan to West Fifty-Third Street. Over the next few decades, further Catholic diversification would occur in Hell's Kitchen as immigrants from additional ethnic Catholic constituencies found employment along or near the Hudson River docks. The new Catholic congregations included an Italian parish, St. Clares, on West Thirty-Sixth in 1903; a Polish parish, St. Clemens Mary, established on West Fortieth in the early 1910s; and a Belgian parish, St. Adalbert's, on West Forty-Seventh in 1917. The construction of the Lincoln Tunnel further reconfigured Hell's Kitchen Catholicism in the 1930s. The new tunnel adjoined St. Raphael's, taking out a significant portion of its territory, and St. Clare's was demolished. Accordingly, some fifteen years after Charles McCready's pastorate ended with his death in 1915, Holy Cross's longtime bitter rival for Hell's Kitchen Irish merged with St. Clare's to take on a new identity as an Italian parish.[44]

III

In 1921, Fr. Francis Duffy, one of the most well-known Catholic priests in the United States, became Holy Cross's pastor, serving until his death in 1932. Duffy's pastorate marked the fading of Irish nationalism and Irish Catholic distinctiveness and embodied a merging of Irish American identity with American patriotism. Duffy was born in Cobourg, Ontario, in 1871 to a father from County Monaghan, Ulster, and after studies in Toronto and New York was ordained in Cobourg in 1896. After time as a chaplain in the aftermath of the Spanish-American War and further studies at the Catholic University of America, Duffy became a professor at the New York Archdiocese's new Dunwoodie Seminary in Yonkers. At Dunwoodie Duffy helped edit a liberal theological journal, the *New York Review*, which ceased publication after Pope Pius X condemned modernism in 1907. Duffy expressed his view of Catholic theology when he wrote in 1901, "The old faith does not change and does not need to change, but we must find new approaches to it and new ways of presenting it." In Duffy's view, Church doctrine was not timeless and unchanging, as conservative neo-scholastic theologians held in the late nineteenth century, but rather developed over time in response to evolving conditions. The *New York Review* published the work of a number of theologians who would be rooted out after the papal condemnation as modernists; Archbishop John Murphy Farley in correspondence with the Vatican in 1913 characterized Duffy as someone who "has shown for years a strong learning toward the liberal tendency of the time called modernism." While serving as a pastor in the Bronx in the 1910s, Duffy became chaplain of the 69th Regiment of the New York National Guard, an Irish American infantry regiment that originated in the efforts of mid-nineteenth-century Irish nationalist exiles and that had seen extensive, decimating service in the Civil War. Duffy accompanied the Fighting 69th to the Mexican border in 1916–17 and to France (where the regiment was designated the 165th Infantry) after the American entry into the Great War in 1917. Duffy's heroism as chaplain in France made him perhaps the best-known American cleric during the war, exploits that would eventually be dramatized by Hollywood in the 1940 film *The Fighting 69th*, with Pat O'Brien as Father Duffy. Duffy's friendship with the well-known poet Joyce Kilmer, a Catholic convert who died fighting with the 165th Regiment in France in 1918, further increased the regiment and the chaplain's renown. Duffy and the 69th/165th Regiment's celebrated valor on the Western Front converted Irish American ambivalence about the war alliance with Great Britain into an embrace of American patriotism and civic culture.[45]

Duffy's stature generated pride among American Catholics at the Catholic contribution to the successful war effort and a sense that the historic marginalization of Catholics within the American polity could be fading. Several thousand, including leading politicians and entertainers, gathered at the Hippodrome on Sixth Avenue in December 1921 to celebrate the twenty-fifth anniversary of Duffy's ordination. Archbishop Patrick Joseph Hayes declared that the event displayed American unity, "a combined allegiance to the American flag that makes America great and will make America greater." The New York archbishop asserted that

Duffy represented the moral force of the United States in the aftermath of the Great War. "Father Duffy stands for the spiritual power of America which is needed at this particular period of the disarmament conference so that there may be no mistakes or false steps." Rabbi Joseph Silverman noted the unity of chaplains of various faiths in the war and how Duffy exemplified this cross-faith collaboration. In his remarks, financier and philanthropist Otto Kahn stressed that Duffy's contribution to American civilization drew from but transcended his Irish Catholic background. "In this age where materialism is rampant, Father Duffy is true and fine, high and right. He belongs to the Catholic Church and springs from the Irish race; but we claim him, all of us." The *New Yorker* writer Alexander Woolcott noted that Duffy's popularity among New Yorkers knew no class bounds and that everyone seemed to know him "when he walked down the street—any street. . . . Father Duffy was of such dimensions that he made New York into a small town." For Americans of Irish descent and for Catholics and non-Catholics alike, Duffy represented an idealistic, spiritual notion of American patriotism that drew on conceptions of military duty and valor and the selfless service of military chaplains and also on positive images of American Catholic priests as tireless social workers.[46] As Holy Cross pastor, Duffy ministered not only to the Irish American longshoremen of Hell's Kitchen but also to the menial fourth estate workers around Times Square. Duffy received special dispensation from the Vatican to offer a Printer's Mass at two thirty on Sunday mornings for nocturnal laborers of the *New York Times, Daily News, Daily Mirror*, and *Herald Tribune*.[47]

During his tenure as pastor at Holy Cross on West Forty-Second, Duffy continued his efforts to reconcile Catholicism with American culture and politics. In 1928 Duffy assisted Democratic presidential candidate Al Smith in rejecting arguments that a Catholic should not be president. Arguments against Smith's candidacy drew on a deep well of anti-Catholic thought in the United States rooted in both Protestant and secular critiques of Catholicism and newly weaponized by the second Ku Klan Klux, which in the 1920s rallied white Protestants around the country against blacks, Jews, and Catholics. While Protestant and secular anti-Catholic thinkers varied in their specific objections to Catholics and Catholicism, which they deemed biblically errant or dangerously reactionary, they shared the view that Catholic officeholders and voters

were beholden to a Roman pontiff who rejected the American distinction between church and state and were thus unfit for the independent
judgment intrinsic to American republicanism.[48] Smith, the governor of
New York, was a lifelong Catholic of Irish, German, and Italian descent
from the Lower East Side. While Smith's wet position on Prohibition
rankled some Protestants, his Catholic identity was equally if not more
problematic.[49]

In April 1927 Charles Marshall, a retired New York City lawyer and
Episcopalian layman, addressed Smith in an open letter in the *Atlantic
Monthly*. Drawing on several encyclicals of Leo XIII expressing what
Marshall characterized as the theory of "the Two Powers . . . [which]
inevitably makes the Roman Catholic Church at times sovereign and
paramount over the state," Marshall asked whether Smith accepted
Church teaching as "authoritative" when it contradicted civil law. After
discussing what he characterized as problematic aspects of the Catholic Church's historic relations with Anglicans, in the ongoing church-
state conflict in Mexico, and in regard to parochial schools in the United
States, Marshall concluded by suggesting that Smith's Catholicism would
pose a grave danger to American institutions if he were to be elected
president. "We have no desire to impute to the Roman Catholic Church
aught but high and sincere motives in the assertion of her claims as one
of the Two Powers. Her members believe in those claims, and, so believ-
ing, it is their conscientious duty to stand for them. We are satisfied if
they will but concede that those claims, unless modified and historically
redressed, precipitate an inevitable conflict between the Roman Catholic
Church and the American State irreconcilable with domestic peace."[50]

Realizing that a response to Marshall's high-profile challenge to
Smith's ability to serve as president in light of his Catholic faith was necessary, Smith and his advisors turned to Fr. Duffy for help in crafting a
rejoinder. Duffy's celebrity and unimpeachable patriotism were helpful,
as was his earlier career as a theology professor and his many years of
thinking about the role of Catholics in American public life. Duffy provided the ideas, while Smith and his advisor Joseph Proskauer crafted
the words for Smith's reply to Marshall in the May 1927 *Atlantic*. In his
rebuttal to Marshall, Smith began by noting he was only a layman and
not a theologian and had thus requested assistance from Duffy in fashioning his response. Smith stated that he had taken an oath as a public

official in New York State nineteen times and had never experienced a conflict between "my official duties and my religious belief." Smith wrote that as governor he enjoyed support from "all denominations," had worked for all state residents, had strongly supported the public school system, and had never been pressured by Catholic priests with regard to his public duties. He stressed that two Catholics had served as chief justice of the U.S. Supreme Court—Roger Brooke Taney and Edward Douglass White—without any question of "unwarranted religious influence" in their "official conduct," while thousands of Catholics had "risked and sacrificed their lives" in the U.S. military. Moving through Marshall's specific complaints, Smith's letter argued that encyclicals were not "articles of our faith" and that Smith, "a devout Catholic since childhood," was not even aware of them until he had read Marshall's letter. Smith argued that Marshall errantly thought "that Catholics must be all alike in mind and in heart, as though they had been poured into and taken out of the same mould." Quoting theologian John Ryan, Saint Paul archbishops John Ireland and Austin Dowling, and Cardinal James Gibbons, Smith's letter articulated a synthesis of Americanism and Catholicism in which all religions enjoyed equal religious liberty, freedom of conscience was sacrosanct, church and state were separated for the benefit of both, and Catholic ecclesiastics (including the pope) were not to interfere in the civil sphere. Smith's letter concluded with the "fervent prayer that never again in this land will any public servant be challenged because of the faith in which he has tried to walk humbly with his God."[51]

Public opinion, including newspaper editorials, overwhelmingly backed Smith's rejoinder to Marshall, holding that the governor had gotten the better of the exchange regarding Catholics and American public officeholding. For its part, the American Church hierarchy was pleased that anti-Catholic arguments had been effectively refuted amid rising anti-Catholic sentiment during the presidential campaign. Marshall himself believed that Smith and Duffy had misrepresented the Vatican's position on the relation of church and state. In a private exchange of letters with Marshall, Duffy argued that Marshall evinced a monolithic understanding of Catholicism and American Catholics, failing to understand the concept of the development of doctrine and differences of opinion within Catholicism and that the American Church hierarchy opposed "the union of Church and State." Historian Thomas J. Shelley argues that Duffy was in a sense "fortunate in the timing of his views" as the Vatican and American bishops sought to tamp down anxieties about "Catholic intolerance" raised during Smith's presidential campaign. Duffy also showed courage in continuing to express aspects of Americanist and modernist thought that had been condemned by the papacy but that had long marked Duffy's theological bent and interaction with American public culture. Duffy's views were similar to ones elaborated thirty years later by American theologian John Courtney Murray that would be incorporated into the Second Vatican Council's "Declaration on Religious Liberty."[52]

Alas, Smith and Duffy's effective response to Marshall's challenge to Catholic officeholding did not prevent Smith from decisively losing the 1928 election to Hoover, winning only 40.8 percent of the popular vote and forty electoral votes. Despite the strength of anti-Catholic sentiments in the region, the "Solid South's" decades-old allegiance to the Democratic Party meant that Smith carried six southern states as well as heavily Catholic Massachusetts and Rhode Island. Smith's Catholicism, his wet position on Prohibition, and his origins in urban immigrant America were significant factors in an election that illuminated increasing divides between rural and urban America and that indicated incipient party coalition shifts that would manifest fully in 1932 with Franklin Delano Roosevelt's defeat of Herbert Hoover in the wake of the Great Depression.[53]

The pastorate of Duffy's successor, Joseph McCaffrey, would stretch from 1932 until 1968, spanning social and cultural changes that the high-profile McCaffrey pugilistically characterized in an emerging white ethnic Catholic reactionary rhetorical and ideological style. While Francis Duffy had sought, like Edward McGlynn, to reconcile American culture's emphasis on individual conscience and separation of church and state with Catholic teaching, McCaffrey articulated a conservative stance on twentieth-century urban change rooted both in his Catholicism and in white-American-identified Irish American culture, particularly his connections to the New York City Police Department. McCaffrey had been born in New York City in 1890, and after studies at Fordham University and Dunwoodie Seminary was ordained in 1916. In World War I he served as chaplain with the Ninth Infantry, Second Division, and like Francis Duffy was decorated by the French and American governments for his service on the Western Front. Assigned to several parishes in northern Manhattan after the war, McCaffrey became chaplain of the New York City Police Department in 1924, a responsibility he would hold until 1954. After Duffy's death, McCaffrey also became chaplain of the 69th Regiment, and the cultures of Irish American military service and law enforcement were key to the civic values he expressed from the pulpit at Holy Cross and in public forums elsewhere in New York City.[54]

Like many white ethnic Catholic parishes in northeastern and Midwestern cities in the early to mid-twentieth century, Holy Cross was losing its traditional parishioners by the 1920s and 1930s as Irish Americans moved from Manhattan out to New York City's outer boroughs and its burgeoning suburbs. Historian Jay Dolan describes the period from 1920 to 1960 as simultaneously the pinnacle of American Catholic devotionalism and the era when white ethnic Catholic communities historically rooted in the urban core in ethnic parishes dispersed out to the suburbs. As historian Robert Orsi has noted, American Catholic devotions also decentered in the interwar period, away from shrines rooted in cathedrals and parishes in urban neighborhoods to devotions rooted not in local space but rather in time, with creative prayer regimens such as perpetual novenas facilitated through mail delivery and mass culture including radio, newspapers, and magazines. Notably, as Catholic culture shifted to mass media formats, Fr. Charles Coughlin, a suburban Detroit priest, came to national prominence in the mid-1930s with radio broadcasts that eventually challenged President Roosevelt's New Deal and took on an anti-Semitic tone. Joseph McCaffrey himself shared some ideological space with Coughlin in the 1930s, striking an isolationist tone in a 1936 memorial Mass for the 69th Regiment at Holy Cross Church in February 1936. In his sermon, McCaffrey railed against "the financial interests of this country" and the "warring nations of Europe," which he blamed for causing World War I and seeking to drag the United States into another one. In 1939, the Brooklyn chapter of Father Coughlin's American Citizens Committee wrote to McCaffrey congratulating him for his denunciation of radio station WNYC's refusal to broadcast the full Police Department Holy Name Communion Breakfast. The secretary of the Brooklyn chapter asserted that the decision of the city radio station to not run the full Catholic police breakfast revealed that Mayor Fiorello La Guardia was "a liberal. Moscow brand of liberalism, I suppose. Friends of Father Coughlin are behind you 100% in this fight for they appreciate what denial of free speech means. Thus in your fight for full time you have the moral support of all true Americans."[55]

Participating in the decentering of Catholic devotions as many of his working-class parishioners migrated out to the outer boroughs and sub-urbs but still came into Manhattan, in 1935 Fr. Joseph McCaffrey initi-ated what would become the parish's most popular ministry, one with significance far beyond Hell's Kitchen, the Perpetual Novena to Our Lady of the Miraculous Medal. With a live broadcast on Monday af-ternoons at one fifteen on radio station WHN, the Novena grew expo-nentially, eliciting massive numbers of listeners as well as worshippers who came to the church on West Forty-Second to participate in person. By 1942 the Novena attracted around twenty thousand participants to the church each Monday, with nine services that began at eleven ten in the morning and concluded at nine ten in the evening. A parishio-ner remembered of the era, "There were nine Novenas on Mondays, a sermon for each, so clergy disliked this, although there were many as-sistant priests at the time and they rotated so they only had to do it once a month." Seven years into the ministry, McCaffrey proudly noted with numerical precision that "more than 4,735,485 persons have made this Novena in this church." The pastor further explained that the radio broadcasts dramatically expanded the range of the devotion and the cir-cumstances in which the faithful, including the ill and disabled, could seek Marian intercession. "Countless others, in hospitals, in sanitariums, in sick rooms at home, have been enabled to participate in it." McCaf-frey asserted that three hundred churches in the metropolitan area had been thus inspired to initiate "similar devotions. And it has brought the conversion of more than 500 non-Catholics." The pastor exalted that thousands along Broadway had repeated the Novena's refrain, "O Mary, conceived without sin, pray for us who have recourse to thee," in the process converting the "Capital of Sin"—an appellation for Times Square as it increasingly became known as an entrepôt of commercialized sex—into a more godly locale.[56]

In his public prominence in the city, McCaffrey participated in the mid-twentieth-century Catholic deprecation of communism. While Catholic anticommunism flowed from Soviet hostility to Christianity and organized religion and conflicts over church and state in Mexico in the 1920s and Spain in the 1930s and the Cold War after 1945, McCaffrey's anticommunism took on a notably blunt edge in the context of the prominence of the American Communist Party–inspired left in New York City's politics and culture.[57] For example, in June 1937 McCaffrey spoke at a breakfast of Theta Kappa Phi, a fraternity of Catholic students who attended non-Catholic colleges and universities. Speeches at the breakfast, which followed Mass at Holy Cross, denounced "radical students" at City College whose "behavior" was "an insult to the taxpayers who are supporting that school."[58] In a sermon at Holy Cross in September 1936, McCaffrey made explicit the danger he saw of "communistic doctrines" being taught in secular schools, which in his view had infiltrated even the U.S. military "in our liberty-loving America." The Holy Cross pastor argued that the young could be saved from communism only through their education in Catholic schools and universities, which would inculcate in them strong Catholic and American values. Speaking of the Communist Party, McCaffrey asserted the ways in which it defied American capitalistic values, freedom of religion, and Catholic teaching on love and the family:

> Its propagandists deny the right to private property. They deny the sanctity of love and the stability of marriage and the home. They would substitute their doctrines of free love and the supremacy of the State. This philosophy would tell us, too, that man is to be denied the inalienable right to worship God according to the dictates of conscience, that there is no God; that churches ought to be destroyed and the priests and religious exterminated. . . . Sow your Moscows and you will reap your Spains. There is but one power the Communists fear, and that is the Catholic Church. They fear it because they fear the Catholic system of education, under which children are taught decency and morality, the doctrines of Jesus Christ.[59]

Seventeen years later, amid the Cold War, McCaffrey's anticommunism resonated just as ardently as he introduced Wisconsin senator Joseph McCarthy, a Catholic of Irish and German extraction, at the Police Department's Communion Breakfast at the Hotel Astor in 1953. McCarthy's demagogic anticommunism was popular among American Catholics. A May 1954 Gallup poll conducted during the Army-McCarthy hearings found that 56 percent of Catholics supported McCarthy, while the Republican senator's efforts to root out suspected communists enjoyed the support of 45 percent of Protestants. Introducing McCarthy to the Communion Breakfast, Msgr. McCaffrey lauded the Wisconsin senator as "one who has devoted time and talent and his life to the exposure and uprooting of Communists." The Holy Cross pastor asserted that McCarthy's mistakes "have been few" and that he had the appreciation of the Catholic policemen gathered at the breakfast. Extolling the values of New York City police officers, McCaffrey declared, "Senator, you need never investigate the loyalty of the New York City Police Department." This was too much for acerbic *New York Post* columnist Murray Kempton, a consistent McCarthy critic, who recalled McCarthy's hounding of witnesses in his investigation of the Army. Reflecting on McCaffrey's fulsome praise for McCarthy, Kempton argued that the relevant passage from the Gospel of St. Matthew was "Jesus Wept."[60]

Shifting sexual norms and their reshaping of Times Square's commercial landscape literally outside the doors of Holy Cross Church also became a prime focus for Msgr. McCaffrey. Trends toward a marked broadening of sexual expression from the 1920s and a significant narrowing of courts' definition of obscenity from the 1930s enhanced opportunities for overt commercialization of sexuality, combining along with the decline of the urban core to remake Times Square as a landscape of burlesque houses and pornographic book stores. In McCaffrey's view, the sexualization of Times Square was converting his parish into what a 1939 *Sunday Mirror* feature writer termed "the capital of the world's sin." Linking a Catholic insistence on marital sex for reproduction as the only acceptable sexual outlet with a concern for how the rampant commercialization of sex degraded the lived environment of his parishioners, McCaffrey waged a decades-long campaign against the sex industry in Times Square. He sought with some success, along with other religious leaders, to shut down burlesque houses on Forty-Second Street in the 1930s and 1940s and moved on to "lewd books" in the 1950s and 1960s. Seeking to turn back the direction of legal change, McCaffrey in a 1963 sermon at Holy Cross declared that "broad-minded" judges were responsible for the "flood of pornographic material" for sale within a short distance of his church. The cleric argued that pornographic publishers and booksellers should enjoy no right of free speech. In McCaffrey's view, America's Founding Fathers "did not anticipate giving free rein to the publication of pornographic literature when they established the principle of a free press." In a 1957 sermon, the monsignor noted that many parents had complained to him that their children were now easily able to obtain pornography in the neighborhood. Expressing a more general concern that he had about the rise of juvenile delinquency in New York City as well as a Catholic take on the relative hierarchy of vices for youth, McCaffrey held that it "is a lot worse to sell obscene literature to a 16-year-old boy than to sell him a glass of beer."[61]

McCaffrey's outspoken views on juvenile delinquency and on the surge in violent crime in New York City in the 1950s and especially the 1960s were shaped by his long relationship with the New York City Police Department, which largely employed Irish American Catholic men who had climbed by the second and third generations to lower-middle-class respectability in law enforcement careers. In 1942, according to one estimate, Catholics composed two-thirds of the Police Department, twelve out of eighteen thousand members, the majority of them Irish Americans.[62] From the late 1940s as well, the population of Hell's Kitchen diversified, with Puerto Ricans moving into the neighborhood as many Irish Americans left while migrations of blacks from the American South and the Caribbean darkened the racial complexion of the city at large. In this respect, McCaffrey's jeremiads against juvenile delinquency and rampant crime, while understandable in light of the increase in violent crime in the city, took on a racial context.[63] In September 1959, McCaffrey spoke at a funeral for a sixteen-year-old stabbed to death at a West Side playground; police had arrested several Puerto Rico–born youths in the crime. The Holy Cross pastor argued that all "known" gang members should be arrested and jailed. McCaffrey asserted that Mayor Robert Wagner's administration and its social workers had abetted the proliferation of juvenile delinquency and gang violence by "coddling" youth gang members. Articulating a reactionary rough justice crime control perspective shaped by decades of working closely with the police, the prelate denounced "the professional sob sisters, oversympathetic youth board consultants, and professional do-gooders who seem obsessed with the senseless theory that there is no such thing as a bad boy. This is like having a theory that there are no mad dogs." He urged that the police be given strengthened powers to deal with youth gangs and shortly after in an interview argued that the police should be allowed to use physical force on juvenile offenders, despite the complaints of "sob sisters" who "cried out 'brutality.'"[64]

In the late 1950s and 1960s the Times Square monsignor, whose tough-on-crime views were frequently reported in the New York newspapers, often spoke on what he viewed as the societal and legal causes of juvenile delinquency and how it must be countered by a robust and legally unhindered police force. Melding a crime control stance with Catholic family ideology in the Holy Cross Parish bulletin, McCaffrey argued that rather than "juvenile delinquency," the proper term was "juvenile criminality." "Anyone of any age who arms himself with a gun, a knife, a gasoline bomb, a garrison belt, or any such implement with the intention of attacking, murdering, or maiming another, is a criminal. . . . Most of these young criminals come from broken homes presided over by either drunken fathers or careless or immoral mothers who neither have no teach respect for authority."[65] In October 1965 the seventy-five-year-old pastor told the *New York Post* that city voters ought to reject any mayoral candidate who had not declared their opposition to a Civilian Review Board (this left William F. Buckley, running on the Conservative Party ticket, as the only acceptable candidate in a field that included John Lindsay and Abe Beame). McCaffrey argued that a review board would be devastating to police morale and would be used to portray the New York Police Department "as a force devoted to brutality." A defiant McCaffrey refused to back away from his position when the chancery asked him to respond to criticism that his "comment was quite evidently political and partisan."[66]

The seventy-eight-year-old monsignor retired in 1968, having pastored Holy Cross through four decades of vast social change. McCaffrey lamented upon his retirement that the sex industry in Times Square was "worse than ever." He had taken to joking that his church should be called "the shrine of the Parking Lots," as in recent years the "brick walkups and old-law tenements" of the old Hell's Kitchen had been torn down for "a dozen parking lots and garages."[67] Eight years earlier, as he had launched an effort to redecorate the church, McCaffrey lamented that respectable theaters on Forty-Second Street had given way to "nothing but crime, sex, and horror pictures. Parking lots and businesses have chased out practically all of the old parishioners."[68] McCaffrey's consistent jeremiad against alterations in the cultural fabric that white ethnic urban Catholics had inherited in the early twentieth century both participated in and anticipated a larger response to social change that would contribute to the consolidation of the New Right in the wake of the 1960s. Reacting against the sexual revolution and expanding notions of individual rights embodied in the liberalization of abortion laws and against movements for racial equality and integration, many white Catholics resisted what they saw as inimical social innovations and emphasized instead what they viewed as "moral, communal issues of identity and value," in Michael Novak's phrase.[69]

Since the late 1960s, Holy Cross Parish has experienced many trends characteristic of the American Catholic Church in the late twentieth century and early twenty-first. The parish saw the removal in the early 1990s of a copastor credibly accused of the sexual abuse of a teenage boy but in recent decades has also experienced lengthy pastorates of priests who have overseen key changes to better serve a flock that is increasingly diverse (and Latinx) but that is also shrinking and aging as Hell's Kitchen gentrifies and sizable numbers of baptized Catholics cease attending church regularly. In 2015 Holy Cross was merged with St. John the Baptist on West Thirtieth, which in 1852 was a German national parish whose suppression under interdict as lay trustees fought Archbishop John Hughes's demand for control made its rector, Fr. Joseph Anthony Lutz, available for Hughes to assign him as Holy Cross's first pastor.[70] Holy Cross's history spans the transformation of Irish American Catholicism in the northeastern United States from an immigrant church that served refugees from the Irish famine, exiles from a Catholic Ireland under British rule, to subsequent generations of Irish American Catholics and their diverse successors worshipping in urban parishes who have sought in varying ways to reconcile an evolving Catholic faith with a shifting American culture.

Epilogue

Catholicism, Regions, and American History

In 1999 a small group of students, faculty, and community members formed a Catholic student group, Radical Catholics for Justice and Peace, at the Evergreen State College in Olympia, Washington. The group never attracted more than a handful of student worshippers from among the college's several thousand enrolled students, perhaps because Evergreen students at large were indifferent to organized religion in general and Christianity and Catholicism in particular, even as they showed great curiosity in meaningful spiritual practices. Most of the small minority of practicing Catholic students on campus also seemed uninterested in the group, perhaps because they were embarrassed to publicly express their Catholicism in the campus setting or perhaps because the Rad Cats' liberation-theology-inspired approach did not appeal to them in an American Catholic era marked by the conservative restorationist papacies of John Paul II and Benedict XVI. The Rad Cats' relations with the Seattle Archdiocese and the local parish in Olympia, St. Michael's Church, were also fraught. Parish clergy were sometimes willing to celebrate Masses for the group, but at other times parish staff dismissed the group as overly radical and unworthy of parish support. Despite these problems and the difficulty of finding a way to be visibly Catholic in such a setting, the Rad Cats did persist for nearly a decade, with several highly committed student leaders who cosponsored social justice events with other campus groups, worked closely with Common Bread, a liberal Protestant student group also inspired by social justice, and held Masses on campus typically several times a year. Often the Masses were celebrated by Fr. Bill Bichsel, a septuagenarian Tacoma Jesuit deeply committed to liberation theology and activism, including ministry with the homeless at the Tacoma Catholic Worker and numerous nonviolent protests at U.S. military installations, for several of which he served federal jail sentences.[1]

The Rad Cats' nine-year existence in some ways embodied key aspects of the history of Catholic religiosity in the Pacific Northwest. As Patricia O'Connell Killen has perceptively argued, since its eighteenth-century settlement by European and Pacific Rim peoples, the Pacific Northwest has been characterized by "a cultural landscape of religious invisibility." Due to historical patterns of mobility and sparseness of population, the region has been unchurched, with relatively few belonging to organized religious bodies, has been religiously diverse but yet with no denomination approaching dominance, and has included large numbers of religiously indifferent persons and people uninterested in traditional churches, although many are "on spiritual quests." While the Catholic Church is the largest organized religious denomination in Washington, Oregon, and Idaho, it has never encompassed more than 10 percent of the region's population. As Killen notes, this makes the Pacific Northwest a region of "religious minorities," a locale where Catholics, such as the Rad Cats, have struggled mightily against invisibility, a challenging context that has provided "wide latitude for thought and action and demanded intense personal commitment on the part of those engaged in the project." These characteristics also make the Catholic Northwest in some respects quite unlike the Catholic South, Midwest, Southwest, and Northeast, analyzed at length in this book, underlining again the centrality and particularity of region in understanding the history of American Catholicism.[2]

Yet the themes of creative adaptation and uneven synthesis that have undergirded the history of Catholicism in the Pacific Northwest—and indeed more extremely and tenuously there than in any other region—are in fact evident throughout the histories of transnational, regional Catholic cultures analyzed in this book. Such a tension between the Catholic tradition rooted in Rome as well as in various Catholic immigrant homelands versus the desire or need to adapt to the American environment not only drove the Americanism controversies of the late nineteenth and early twentieth centuries but also informs ongoing aspects of the American Catholic experience. For example, the anti-abortion, pro-life emphasis of institutional American Catholic political engagement in the decades that followed the 1973 *Roe v. Wade* U.S. Supreme Court decision reflected not merely a persistence of Catholic understandings of sexuality and the family stemming from the nineteenth century even in the wake of the mid-twentieth-century sexual revolution but arguably, as importantly, a persistent communalistic emphasis even amid the extraordinary individualism of American life. The emphasis of the U.S. Catholic bishops on issues of "religious freedom," in recent years in alliance with evangelical Protestants and the Republican Party, reflects a strategic capture of a rhetoric of rights from liberals in light of a concern that an increasingly secularizing American society concerned with individual rights and sexual minorities may be overly dismissive of perspectives grounded in religious conviction.[3]

On the U.S. Supreme Court, where Catholics have composed a majority of justices since 2006, a similar uneasy tension exists between cultural Catholicism and American judicial and political ideologies that do not align easily with Catholic teaching. Conservative Catholic Supreme Court justices such as Antonin Scalia, Samuel Alito, Brett Kavanaugh, John Roberts, and, in a more complex case, Clarence Thomas may reflect the reactionary impulses and racial formations of mid- to late twentieth-century ethnic Catholics who came of age amid the urban crisis, suburbanization, and backlash against the racial egalitarianism and identity politics and regulatory state of the post–World War II era and Civil Rights Movement. The ideological legacy of Monsignor Joseph McCaffrey and his reaction against the postwar city resonates here. For conservative justices, Catholic piety (and not-so-tacit support from Catholic bishops in nomination battles) meshes well with judicial advocacy of restriction on abortion but less well with judicial support for the death penalty and efforts to disempower the regulatory state in favor of the free market; in addition, conservative justices' antistatism may align to an extent with historical American Catholic skepticism of the state. Justice Sonia Sotomayor, on the other hand, also illustrates the continuing paradoxes of "cultural Catholic" engagement with American public life. Born to parents in the Bronx who participated in the mid-twentieth-century Puerto Rican diaspora, Sotomayor in a sense represents the differing sensibility of Latinx Catholics arguably more alert to matters of economic and racial injustice in American society than some white ethnic Catholics. Yet the "Catholic justice" mantle fits awkwardly here as well, with Justice Sotomayor's positions on the death penalty and issues of racial equality and a more robust regulatory state aligning well with current Catholic social teaching but with issues of abortion law aligning less well, although Sotomayor's jurisprudence on abortion has arguably been at least somewhat more sympathetic to anti-abortion initiatives than that of other liberal justices.[4]

Catholic participation in U.S. electoral politics also continues to reflect the regionally inflected uneasy synthesis evident in the making of Catholic cultures and American society analyzed in this book. As John Tracy Ellis and others have noted, American Catholics have been wary since the early republic of commitment to particular political parties given the difficult fit between a transnational Catholic perspective and the American political ethos. But Catholics have been key components of party coalitions that include the antebellum and New Deal–era Democratic Parties (Irish and white ethnic Catholics) and the Republican Party beginning in the Reagan era (conservative white Catholics). In recent decades the Catholic swing vote in Midwestern and Mid-Atlantic states has been pivotal in American presidential contests and the overall Catholic vote has swayed between Democratic candidates and Republican ones. In 2004 exit poll data suggested that George W. Bush took the Catholic vote over John Kerry (a Catholic) by five points, 52 to 47 percent. In 2008 exit polls suggested that Barack Obama won the Catholic vote over John McCain by nine points, 54 to 45 percent, with white Catholics supporting McCain 52 to 47 percent and Latinos providing Obama's overall winning margin among Catholic voters. Yet Obama won the Catholic vote by only two points, 50 to 48 percent in 2012, as commanding margins among Hispanics offset a significant decline in support among white Catholics. In 2016 exit polls suggested that Donald Trump won the Catholic vote by seven points, 52 to 45 percent, prevailing among white Catholics 60 to 37 percent. Yet additional polling analysis suggested that Trump and Hillary Clinton more evenly split the Catholic vote, with Midwestern and northeastern white Catholics swinging decisively for Trump and Latinx Catholics in the West and the South voting overwhelmingly for Clinton. Dubuque County, Iowa, a redoubt of white Catholics descended from Irish and German Catholics, switched from support for Obama to Trump, emblematizing the crucial swing of blue-collar white Midwestern Catholics from the Obama coalition into the Trump camp. Clearly Catholic voters are no monolith, but the variability of white Catholic voters in particular and the growing numerical strength of the Latino vote suggest Catholic voters will continue to be of strategic importance, with Catholicism being the only major American religious denomination in the early twenty-first century in which believers are nearly evenly split between the two major political parties in their voting.[5]

Catholicism continues to have a vexed role in American public life, with, for example, conservative Catholic clerics in recent decades denying Holy Communion to Catholic Democratic presidential candidates in light of the Democratic Party's pro-choice position on abortion. In October 2019 Rev. Robert Morey denied Joe Biden Communion at St. Anthony Catholic Church in Florence, South Carolina. Similarly, in 2004 several conservative Catholic bishops said they would deny John Kerry Communion in their dioceses. The "wafer wars," in their conflation of Catholicism and American Catholic political officeholding, abandon the separation of church and state and freedom of conscience advocated by Fr. Francis Duffy and Al Smith in 1928 and by Democratic presidential candidate John F. Kennedy in his September 1960 speech before the Greater Houston Ministerial Alliance. Catholic Democrats have found themselves in an increasingly awkward position since 2016 in light of the broader polarization of political discourse, efforts in conservative and liberal state legislatures to restrict or expand access to abortion with the prospect of the potential reversal of *Roe v. Wade* in mind, and an insistence that Republicans and Democrats must embrace full-fledged pro-life or pro-choice positions respectively to conform to their party's orthodoxy. Only in Louisiana, the sole southern state with a large Catholic population, have pro-life Democrats (such as Governor John Bel Edwards) been able to retain their anti-abortion stance without strong opposition from within their party's base.[6]

Public opinion surveys in the 2010s found that the majority of American Catholics rejected Church positions on the prohibition of contraception, on the "religious liberty" of Catholic employers to refuse to offer contraception in health plans or services to married gay and lesbian couples, on the morality of homosexuality, and on bathrooms for transgendered people. While half of Catholics agreed that abortion was morally wrong, no consensus existed on other social issues among the American Catholic laity and an American Church hierarchy still dominated by clerics appointed by Popes John Paul II and Benedict XVI. Clearly, the relation of Catholicism and American identity is unsettled and continues to evolve, perhaps especially so in an era when Catholics still contribute a fifth of the population but with fallen-away Catholics and their descendants adding ranks to the rise of those of no formal religious affiliation to more than a quarter of the American population at the end of the 2010s.[7]

While American Catholicism continues to reflect an uneasy synthesis with American society, polity, and culture, region has been and remains central to American Catholic culture(s). As this book has argued, regional contexts are pivotal to understanding the development of American Catholicism. The ethnicity and national origin of particular Catholic groups and their connections to transnational Catholic homelands and their relations with the American Church hierarchy played out in vastly different regional landscapes that included varied ethnic compositions and population ratios with other religious groups including Protestants; Catholic visibility or invisibility; and urban and rural experiences of American individualistic capitalism, frontier expansion and settler colonialism, and racism. Catholics of Irish and English descent were a distinct minority within the Protestant-majority South, yet Catholics of French and African descent were a significant proportion of the population of New Orleans and southern Louisiana. Catholics from German, Irish, and Czech sources composed minority enclaves within the Lower Midwest, yet the Upper Midwest was densely Catholic, with Germans rather than Irish predominating in a Catholic population also composed of Gallic, Eastern European, and Southern European sources. Catholics have struggled for visibility in portions of the vast American West, no more so than in the Pacific Northwest, yet in the Southwest Mexican-descended and Native American Catholics have sustained some of the oldest Catholic parishes in what is now the United States despite American conquest, white settler colonialism, and colonialism within American Catholicism itself that denigrated Hispanic traditions in favor of Romanized and Americanized ones. The Northeast is the most densely U.S. Catholic region, with the Irish achieving an influential cultural dominance that strove to reconcile Catholicism and Americanism through radical and liberal approaches but also helped to shape American conservatism. New England's Catholicism is additionally composed of French Canadian and Southern European sources, while Mid-Atlantic Catholicism is similarly diverse with Latinx Caribbean

Catholics an increasingly important element since the mid-twentieth century. Mexican, Central American, and Andean Latinx Catholics have revitalized declining urban and rural parishes in all U.S. regions in recent years, while Asian Catholics including Filipinos, Vietnamese, and Koreans have elaborated the Catholic tapestry most notably in the Gulf South and in California and Hawaii in the Pacific region.[8] Meanwhile, as we have seen, priests and nuns from the Global South, including African nations such as Nigeria and Ghana, have helped to redress the shortfall in clergy amid a precipitous decline in Catholic religious vocations in the United States since the mid-twentieth century.[9]

Clearly "where" has mattered tremendously in American Catholicism. So has "who." Despite the Church's claims to universalism, this book has argued that ethnicity and national origin have mattered a great deal in American Catholicism, as have race and racism. Irish Catholics in nineteenth-century New York City attended territorial parishes that were homogenous by ethnicity, while national parishes ensured that Germans in the Midwest and Northeast could maintain their German-language-identified Catholic culture, a pattern that was sustained for subsequent Catholic immigrant groups arriving from Southern and Eastern Europe into the early twentieth century (although not for Puerto Rican Catholics who arrived in New York City in the mid-twentieth century and found themselves worshipping in Spanish-language Masses in the basements of existing, declining parishes).[10] Yet national parishes for African American Catholics in places such as New Orleans and New York City became a means to racially segregate Catholic worship in cities that had experienced earlier traditions of integrated worship of white and black Catholics (most notably, as we saw, in the Gallic Catholicism of nineteenth-century New Orleans). Even as Catholics of Mexican descent in Los Angeles found ways to sustain a Mexican Catholic community at La Placita, white Angelenos fixated on a romantic Spanish mission past and denied, downplayed, or cast a patronizing if fascinated Anglo gaze on the racially mixed Mexican elements of the Plaza Church's Catholic devotions. Class similarly has been an important element in American Catholicism, as a largely working-class "Immigrant Church" in the nineteenth century became a predominantly middle-class Church in the twentieth century, the descendants of European Catholic immigrants moving out to suburbs and their descendants eventually sharing dioceses with working-class Latinx immigrants who have renewed urban and rural parishes in recent decades.[11] Gender has also mattered immensely, from the male hierarchy that has undergirded the Church's organization and arguably provided the conditions for clerical sexual abuse and its concealment to the ways in which Catholic women religious found vocations outside of marriage and the home that undercut nineteenth-century Protestant notions confining women to the domestic sphere and to women seers in Wisconsin whose visions of Mary have defied the local male Church hierarchy's exclusive claims to authority over Catholic orthodox religiosity.

In short, this book has argued that in order to understand the history of American Catholicism properly we must understand the various kinds of Catholics who have made it and the varied American places in which they have forged an American Catholicism that has never stopped at water's edge.

ACKNOWLEDGMENTS

This book has had a lengthy gestation, and a number of people helped to make it possible. The late Fr. John P. Boyle, Professor of Religion at the University of Iowa and a distinguished theologian, was a significant mentor in my graduate school days. We had many rich conversations about American Catholic history, including that of the Midwest and other regions and regarding ethnic Catholicism. Fr. Boyle was also a rich model of the engagement of the Catholic intellectual with American society and the academy. He indeed was a historical actor within the mid- to late twentieth-century controversies over academic freedom at Catholic universities in the United States. In 1985, Fr. Boyle withdrew his candidacy to become dean of the Catholic University of America's School of Religious Studies after Washington archbishop James Hickey objected to aspects of his 1977 book, *The Sterilization Crisis: A New Crisis for the Catholic Hospital?* I learned much from conversations with Fr. Boyle, influences that I suspect helped to shape what years later became the intellectual agenda of this book.

In 1989–90 as a sophomore at Washington University in St. Louis, I took Rowland Berthoff's two-semester sequence on American social history and vividly recall his lecture on Peter Paul Cahensly and the debates among American Catholics in the late nineteenth century over "Americanization" versus the preservation of immigrant Catholic cultures. Professor Berthoff was my undergraduate mentor, and I learned a tremendous amount from his extraordinary curiosity and brilliant synthesis of transatlantic and American histories, work he had embarked on long before the vogue for transnational history. This book is indebted in at least a small way to Professor Berthoff's lecture on Peter Paul Cahensly but also in a large way to how he encouraged me as a student and offered an inspiring model of an American historian who read and thought capaciously.

Jennifer Hammer at New York University Press has been a superlative editor, highly supportive and nurturing of the book from the very beginning. I am also grateful to a number of other members of the NYU Press staff, including Ellen Chodosh, Amy Klopfenstein, Veronica Knutson, Martin Coleman, and Joseph Dahm, for their fine assistance with the publication process. Several anonymous readers for the press offered valuable suggestions. Msgr. Thomas J. Shelley, Emeritus Professor of Church History at Fordham University, was quite supportive at an early stage and particularly helpful with identifying useful sources on New York Catholic history. Michael Pasquier, Jaak Seynaeve Professor of Christian Studies at Louisiana State University, offered helpful suggestions on portions of the draft Louisiana chapter, as did Anthony Burke Smith of the University of Dayton. Mario T. García, Professor of Chicana/o Studies and History at the University of California, Santa Barbara, offered encouragement as I worked on the La Placita chapter; his important work on Fr. Luis Olivares and Chicana/o Catholic activism was foundational to the latter portions of that chapter. A number of archivists and church staff members assisted with the research, including Ed Reigadas at Holy Cross on West Forty-Second in Manhattan, Tyla Cole at the Diocese of Davenport, Rachel Santos at St. Mary's in Iowa City, and the staffs of the Archives of the Archdioceses of New York and New Orleans and of the special collections of the New York State Library. Special mention must be made of Jack Belsom, whose encyclopedic knowledge of New Orleans Catholicism was invaluable as I was conducting research and writing. I am grateful to Fr. Raphael Ezeh, MSP, for his assistance with the research on the history of Our Lady of Lourdes Parish, New Orleans, and to the late Judith K. Schafer of Tulane University for her suggestions and reading of a draft version of the New Orleans chapter. Sister Marie Vittetoe, CHM, offered key insights into Iowa Catholic history. Fr. Steven Avella, a historian at Marquette University, generously offered advice on research on Wisconsin Marian apparitions, as did Thomas A. Kselman, Professor Emeritus of History at Notre Dame. The late Fr. Peter Colapietro offered an extraordinary example of a New York City Catholic parish pastor and was highly supportive of this project. Also at Holy Cross Parish, Fr. Francis Gasparik, OFM Cap., and Fr. Michael Marigliano, OFM Cap., offered kind aid.

Alas, despite considerable efforts, I was unable to gain access to any of La Placita's materials in the Archdiocese of Los Angeles's archives.

While this is sadly not an unfamiliar situation for historians of American Catholicism, I do hope that in the future scholars will receive a more professional and collegial reception from this and other diocesan archives. Happily, there are indications that this situation is beginning to change.

I am grateful to the Cushwa Center for the Study of American Catholicism at the University of Notre Dame, which provided funding to travel to South Bend to use the University Archives and the collections of the Hesburgh Libraries, where archivists and librarians provided excellent support. *Louisiana History* and the *Annals of Iowa* published early iterations of portions of what became chapters of this book. I am grateful for permission to republish "The Strange Career of New Orleans Catholicism: Race at Our Lady of Lourdes Parish, 1905–2006," *Louisiana History* 58, no. 1 (Winter 2017): 59–92, and "The Making of a Midwestern Catholicism: Identities, Ethnicity, and Catholic Culture in Iowa City, 1840–1940," *Annals of Iowa* 76, no. 3 (Summer 2017): 201–26.

John Amodeo, Willie Shapiro, David Enos, Coleen Maddy, Dennis Downey, Jason Kennedy Duncan, Rob Hosken, and my colleagues Sara McDougall, Edward Paulino, and David Munns assisted in a variety of ways. Any errors herein are my own.

This book is dedicated in memoriam to Daniel Golebiewski. As an undergraduate Daniel, a son of Białystok, Poland, Greenpoint, Brooklyn, and Maspeth, Queens, took my U.S. history survey and global lynching and modern Catholicism courses at the John Jay College of Criminal Justice. One day he came into my office and asked whether I might have a need for a research assistant. Daniel offered superb research assistance for the New Orleans chapter, finding articles on Our Lady of Lourdes Parish in historical New Orleans newspapers. Alas, I was never able to give him the assignment he most wanted and which he requested several times, which was to read Polish-language Catholic newspapers from the American Rust Belt in the late nineteenth and early twentieth centuries. Daniel went on to earn an MA in Human Rights from Columbia University and at the time of his tragic passing from Wilson's disease in January 2020 was a PhD candidate in Political Science at the CUNY Graduate Center. Daniel would have become a brilliant and accomplished scholar, and I am grateful for the exemplary aid he provided in the research for this book.

NOTES

Manuscript collections frequently cited in these notes have been identified by the following abbreviations:

AANO Archives of the Archdiocese of New Orleans
AANY Archives of the Archdiocese of New York

INTRODUCTION

1 See, for example, John Tracy Ellis, *American Catholicism*, 2nd ed. (Chicago: University of Chicago Press, 1969); James Hennessey, *American Catholics: A History of the Roman Catholic Community in the United States* (New York: Oxford University Press, 1983); Jay P. Dolan, *The American Catholic Experience: A History from Colonial Times to the Present* (Garden City, NY: Doubleday, 1985); Jay P. Dolan, *In Search of an American Catholicism: A History of Religion and Culture in Tension* (New York: Oxford University Press, 2003); Charles R. Morris, *American Catholic: The Saints and Sinners Who Built America's Most Powerful Church* (New York: Times Books, 1997); John T. McGreevy, *Catholicism and American Freedom: A History* (New York: Norton, 2003); Patrick W. Carey, *Catholics in America: A History* (Westport, CT: Praeger, 2004); James M. O'Toole, *The Faithful* (Cambridge, MA: Harvard University Press, 2008); James T. Fisher, *Communion of Immigrants: A History of Catholics in America* (New York: Oxford University Press, 2008); Mark Massa and Catharine Osborne, eds., *American Catholic History: A Documentary Reader*, 2nd ed. (New York: New York University Press, 2017); Jon Gjerde, *Catholicism and the Shaping of Nineteenth-Century America*, ed. S. Deborah Kang (New York: Cambridge University Press, 2012); John T. McGreevy, *American Jesuits and the World: How an Embattled Religious Order Made Modern Catholicism Global* (Princeton, NJ: Princeton University Press, 2016). Hennessey, Dolan, Carey, O'Toole, Fisher, McGreevy, Gjerde, and Massa and Osborne, for instance, are commendably attentive to region, ethnicity, and transnational connections, but much of the U.S. Catholic studies literature has tended to represent the urban northeastern and Mid-Atlantic European Catholic immigrant experience (with occasional detours into the urban Catholic Midwest) as somehow representative of the entirety of the American Catholic milieu. While not ignored entirely, the lengthy history of Mexican American Catholicism in the American Southwest receives marginal treatment in many of these American Catholic

histories. The African American Catholic experience also sits uncomfortably and has been marginalized in models of American Catholic history predicated on European Catholic immigration and American assimilation. For this crucial point, see Timothy Matovina, *Latino Catholicism: Transformations in America's Largest Church* (Princeton, NJ: Princeton University Press, 2011), viii, 3–6, 46.

2 For arguments for a less nationalistic and more transnational history of American Catholicism, particularly in light of the centrality of international relationships to the structure of Catholicism, see Peter R. D'Agostino, *Rome in America: Transnational Catholic Ideology from the Risorgimento to Fascism* (Chapel Hill: University of North Carolina Press, 2004); John T. McGreevy, "Bronx Miracle," *American Quarterly* 52, no. 3 (September 2000): 412–13, 438n19. For an essential interpretation of German Catholics in the Midwest that emphasizes transatlantic connections along with diasporic identity formation, see Kathleen Neils Conzen, "Immigrant Religion and the Republic: German Catholics in Nineteenth-Century America," *German Historical Institute Bulletin* 35 (Fall 2004): 43–56.

3 Jeffrey Marlett, "'There Is a Church West of Buffalo!' Catholic Studies and Regional Identity," *American Catholic Studies Newsletter* 31, no. 2 (Fall 2004): 1–10; Ellis, *American Catholicism*, 89–93, 102–3, 299–300 (for quotation). For example, Ellis addresses southern Catholicism briefly in the contexts of slavery, the Civil War, and the failure to seek African American converts in the nineteenth century. For a crucial argument for more engagement of U.S. Catholic historians with region, see Michael J. McNally, "The Universal in the Particular: The New Regional History and Catholicism in the United States." *U.S. Catholic Historian* 18, no. 3 (2000): 1–12. For a critique of the dearth of scholarship on U.S. regional and southern Catholic cultures, see Michael Pasquier, "Medugorje in the American South: Our Lady of Tickfaw and the Politics of Devotion," *U.S. Catholic Historian* 24, no. 4 (Fall 2006): 131n14. For an argument that Catholic historians have largely ignored the American South, see James M. Woods, *A History of the Catholic Church in the American South, 1513–1900* (Gainesville: University Press of Florida, 2011), xiii. For the nineteenth-century Catholicism shaped by French-speaking priests in the trans-Appalachian West, see Michael Pasquier, *Fathers on the Frontier: French Missionaries and the Roman Catholic Priesthood in the United States, 1789–1870* (New York: Oxford University Press, 2010). For important work on the Catholic Midwest and West, see Thomas W. Spalding, "Frontier Catholicism," *Catholic Historical Review* 77, no. 3 (1991): 470–84; Jeffrey D. Marlett, *Saving the Heartland: Catholic Missionaries in Rural America, 1920–1960* (DeKalb: Northern University Illinois Press, 2002); Anne M. Butler, *Across God's Frontiers: Catholic Sisters in the American West, 1850–1920* (Chapel Hill: University of North Carolina Press, 2012). Useful overviews of the regional dimensions of U.S. Catholicism can be found in the two-volume series "Religious Geography: The Significance of Regions and the Power of Places" in the *U.S. Catholic Historian* 18, nos. 3–4 (Summer and Fall 2000). Mark Silk and Andrew Walsh's Religion by Region series offers essential analy-

sis of the religious landscape of particular American regions, including chapters surveying regional Catholic cultures. Jan Shipps and Mark Silk, eds., *Religion and Public Life in the Mountain West: Sacred Landscapes in Transition* (Walnut Creek, CA: AltaMira Press, 2004); Patricia O'Connell Killen and Mark Silk, eds., *Religion and Public Life in the Pacific Northwest: The None Zone* (Walnut Creek, CA: AltaMira Press, 2004); Andrew Walsh and Mark Silk, eds., *Religion and Public Life in New England: Steady Habits, Changing Slowly* (Walnut Creek, CA: AltaMira Press, 2004); Philip Barlow and Mark Silk, eds., *Religion and Public Life in the Midwest: America's Common Denominator?* (Walnut Creek, CA: AltaMira Press, 2004); Charles Reagan Wilson and Mark Silk, eds., *Religion and Public Life in the South: In the Evangelical Mode* (Walnut Creek, CA: AltaMira Press, 2005); Wade Clark Roof and Mark Silk, eds., *Religion and Public Life in the Pacific Region: Fluid Identities* (Walnut Creek, CA: AltaMira Press, 2005); Randall Balmer and Mark Silk, eds., *Religion and Public Life in the Middle Atlantic Region: The Fount of Diversity* (Walnut Creek, CA: AltaMira Press, 2006); Mark Silk and Andrew Walsh, eds., *One Nation, Divisible: How Regional Religious Differences Shape American Politics* (Lanham, MD: Rowman & Littlefield, 2008).

4 Hennessey, *American Catholics*; Dolan, *American Catholic Experience*; Dolan, *In Search of an American Catholicism*; Carey, *Catholics in America*; O'Toole, *Faithful*; Fisher, *Communion of Immigrants*.

5 For analysis of the experience of Catholics in the predominantly Protestant antebellum South, see Randall M. Miller and Jon Wakelyn, eds., *Catholics in the Old South: Essays on Church and Culture* (Mercer, GA: Mercer University Press, 1983; repr., 1999), including, for the "cultural captivity" thesis, Miller, "A Church in Cultural Captivity: Some Speculations on Catholic Identity in the Old South," 11–52. For southwest Louisiana, see Clifford J. Clarke, "Religion and Regional Culture: The Changing Pattern of Religious Affiliation in the Cajun Region of Southwest Louisiana," *Journal for the Scientific Study of Religion* 24, no. 4 (December 1985): 384–95. John T. Gillard, *Colored Catholics in the United States* (Baltimore: Josephite Press, 1941), 30, includes statistics asserting that 38.7 percent of all black Catholics in the United States in 1940 lived in Louisiana. For Irish Catholics in the South, see Dennis Clark, "The South's Irish Catholics: A Case of Cultural Confinement," in Miller and Wakelyn, *Catholics in the Old South*, 195–209. For a recent comprehensive survey of the history of U.S. southern Catholicism, including Louisiana and the Gulf Coast, see Woods, *History of the Catholic Church*. For the Maryland tradition, see H. S. Spalding, *Catholic Colonial Maryland: A Sketch* (Milwaukee: Bruce, 1931); Thomas W. Spalding, *The Premier See: A History of the Archdiocese of Baltimore, 1789–1989* (Baltimore: Johns Hopkins University Press, 1989); Thomas Murphy, *Jesuit Slaveholding in Maryland, 1717–1838* (New York: Routledge, 2001); Robert Emmett Curran, *Shaping American Catholicism: Maryland and New York, 1805–1915* (Washington, DC: Catholic University Press, 2012); Antoinette Patricia Sutto, *Loyal Protestants and Dangerous Papists: Maryland and*

the Politics of Religion in the English Atlantic, 1630–1690 (Charlottesville: University of Virginia Press, 2015). For the "Immigrant Church" of the late nineteenth and early twentieth centuries, see O'Toole, *Faithful*, 94–144.

6 Matovina, *Latino Catholicism*, 3–16. Useful overviews of Catholic history in the American West can be found in Steven M. Avella, "Catholicism on the Pacific: Building a Regional Scaffolding," *U.S. Catholic Historian* 31, no. 2 (2013): 1–24; Roberto R. Treviño and Richard V. Francaviglia, *Catholicism in the American West: A Rosary of Hidden Voices* (College Station: Texas A&M University Press, 2007); Jeffrey M. Burns, "Building the Best: A History of Catholic Parish Life in the Pacific States" and Carol L. Jensen, "Deserts, Diversity, and Self-Determination: A History of the Catholic Parish in the Intermountain West," both in *The American Catholic Parish: A History from 1850 to the Present*, ed. Jay P. Dolan (Mahwah, NJ: Paulist Press, 1987), 10–276. For an important treatment of urban Catholicism in California, see Steven M. Avella, *Sacramento and the Catholic Church: Shaping a Capital City* (Reno: University of Nevada Press, 2008).

7 "In New Orleans, More Quietly Settled, Decades-Old Catholic Church Sex Abuse Cases Surface," *New Orleans Advocate*, September 20, 2018, www.theadvocate. com; "Here Are the 57 Clergy 'Credibly Accused' of Abuse in the Archdiocese of New Orleans," *New Orleans Times-Picayune*, November 2, 2018, www.nola.com. For children of color and clerical sexual abuse, see "Church Offers Little Outreach to Minority Victims of Priests," Associated Press, January 4, 2020.

8 John Jay College of Criminal Justice, "The Nature and Scope of Sexual Abuse of Minors by Catholic Priests and Deacons in the United States, 1950–2002" (Washington, DC: United States Conference of Catholic Bishops, 2004). Brett Grainger, ed., "Forum: Catholic Sex Abuse and the Study of Religion" (contributions by Matthew Cressler, Brian Clites, Susan B. Ridgely, Jeremy V. Cruz, Jack Lee Downey, Julie Byrne, and Kathryn Lofton), *American Catholic Studies* 30, no. 2 (Summer 2019): 1–29. For an overview of the history of American sexuality, see John D'Emilio and Estelle B. Freedman, *Intimate Matters: A History of Sexuality in America*, 2nd ed. (Chicago: University of Chicago Press, 1997).

9 Leslie Woodcock Tentler, "On the Margins: The State of American Catholic History," *American Quarterly* 45, no. 1 (1993): 104–27. For the inadequacy of a "historiography without gods," see Robert A. Orsi, *History and Presence* (Cambridge, MA: Belknap, 2016), esp. 62–65. In 2018–19, the Pew Research Center found that 43 percent of Americans identified with various Protestant denominations, and 20 percent considered themselves Catholic. Of Americans, 17 percent described their religion as "nothing in particular," while 5 percent described themselves as agnostic and 4 percent as atheist. In 2009, the "nones" had tallied 12 percent, agnostics 3 percent, and atheists 2 percent, while Protestants and Catholics had counted 51 percent and 23 percent, respectively. Pew Research Center, "In U.S., Decline of Christianity Continues at Rapid Pace" (October 17, 2019), www.pewforum.org.

1. THE STRANGE CAREER OF NEW ORLEANS CATHOLICISM

1 "Everett Williams, New Orleans' First Black Superintendent of Schools, Dies at 82," *New Orleans Times-Picayune*, July 30, 2013. The definitive history of Catholicism in New Orleans and in Louisiana remains Roger Baudier, *The Catholic Church in Louisiana* (New Orleans: N.P., 1939). For the historical context of the development of the cult of Our Lady of Prompt Succor, see Michael Pasquier, "Our Lady of Prompt Succor: The Search for an American Marian Cult in New Orleans," in *Saints and Their Cults in the Atlantic World*, ed. Margaret Cormack (Columbia: University of South Carolina Press, 2006), 128–49. This paragraph is influenced by my observation of and participation as a worshipper in around ten daily Masses at Our Lady of Lourdes in July 2005.

2 Coleman Warner, "Freret's Century: Growth, Identity, and Loss in a New Orleans Neighborhood," *Louisiana History* 42, no. 3 (Summer 2001): 343. For the marginal experience of Irish Catholics in nineteenth-century New Orleans in the context of French Catholic supremacy and the forces that ended Francophone dominance after World War I, see Michael Doorley, "Irish Catholics and French Creoles: Ethnic Struggles within the Catholic Church in New Orleans, 1835–1920," *Catholic Historical Review* 87, no. 1 (January 2001): 34–54. Randall M. Miller unpersuasively asserts that Irish Catholics had become "the dominant element" in New Orleans Catholicism by the 1850s. Randall M. Miller, "A Church in Cultural Captivity: Some Speculations on Catholic Identity in the Old South," in *Catholics in the Old South: Essays on Church and Culture*, ed. Randall M. Miller and Jon Wakelyn (Mercer, GA: Mercer University Press, 1983; repr., 1999), 36–37. For the persistence of the French language in south Louisiana Catholicism into the twentieth century, see Sylvie Dubois, Emilie Gagnet Leumas, and Malcolm Richardson, *Speaking French in Louisiana, 1720–1955: Linguistic Practices of the Catholic Church* (Baton Rouge: Louisiana State University Press, 2018). James Bennett offers the most comprehensive and persuasive treatment of the origins of racial segregation in New Orleans Catholicism as well as a comparison with Crescent City Methodism in *Religion and the Rise of Jim Crow in New Orleans* (Princeton, NJ: Princeton University Press, 2005). For important interpretations of the history of American Catholicism, see Jay P. Dolan, *The American Catholic Experience: A History from Colonial Times to the Present* (Garden City, NY: Doubleday, 1985); Dolan, *In Search of an American Catholicism: A History of Religion and Culture in Tension* (New York: Oxford University Press, 2003); John T. McGreevy, *Catholicism and American Freedom: A History* (New York: W.W. Norton, 2003). For Catholics and race in northern U.S. cities, see John T. McGreevy, *Parish Boundaries: The Catholic Encounter with Race in the Twentieth-Century Urban North* (Chicago: University of Chicago Press, 1996); Timothy B. Neary, *Crossing Racial Boundaries: Race, Sports, and Catholic Youth in Chicago, 1914–1954* (Chicago: University of Chicago Press, 2016); Karen J. Johnson, *One in Christ: Chicago Catholics and the Quest for Interracial Justice* (New York: Oxford University Press, 2018). For

African American Catholics in the twentieth-century urban North, see Matthew
J. Cressler, *Authentically Black and Truly Catholic: The Rise of Black Catholicism in
the Great Migration* (New York: New York University Press, 2017).

3 Henry C. Bezou, *Lourdes on Napoleon Avenue* (New Orleans: Laborde, 1980),
3–7; "Guide to the News, City and Suburban," *New Orleans Daily Picayune*, April
16, 1905, 2; "The New Catholic Church," *New Orleans Daily Picayune*, April 23,
1905, 43; "Fifteen Choice Building Lots," *New Orleans Daily Picayune*, May 22,
1905, 2; "Our Lady of Lourdes," *New Orleans Daily Picayune*, September 10, 1905,
7. Lourdes was apparently the only parish established during Chapelle's tenure as
archbishop, 1898–1905. Chapelle, a theological conservative, reversed a number
of the initiatives of his more liberal, Dutch-born predecessor, Francis Janssens.
During his tenure as prelate in New Orleans, Chapelle also served as apostolic
delegate to Cuba and Puerto Rico, which may have distracted him from New
Orleans matters, including parish building. Bennett, *Religion and the Rise of Jim
Crow*, 190–91, 286n54.

4 Bezou, *Lourdes on Napoleon Avenue*, 3–9.

5 Richard Campanella, "An Ethnic Geography of New Orleans," *Journal of American History* 94, no. 3 (December 2007): 704–5; Paul F. Lachance, "The 1809 Immigration of Saint-Domingue Refugees to New Orleans: Reception, Integration,
and Impact," *Louisiana History* 29, no. 2 (Spring 1988): 109–41, esp. 112, 128. For
an argument for the complexity of Creole and American residence patterns in antebellum New Orleans, see Arnold Hirsch and Joseph Logsdon, eds., *Creole New
Orleans: Race and Americanization* (Baton Rouge: Louisiana University Press,
1992), 154–56. For a definitive history of early New Orleans, see Lawrence N.
Powell, *The Accidental City: Improvising New Orleans* (Cambridge, MA: Harvard
University Press, 2012).

6 Campanella, "Ethnic Geography of New Orleans," 708–9; Doorley, "Irish
Catholics and French Creoles," 45; Gilles Vandal, *The New Orleans Riot of 1866:
Anatomy of a Tragedy* (Lafayette: Center for Louisiana Studies, 1984); John B.
Alberts, "Black Catholic Schools: The Josephite Parishes of New Orleans during
the Jim Crow Era," *U.S. Catholic Historian* 12, no. 1 (Winter 1994): 77–98.

7 Warner, "Freret's Century," 327–32.

8 Ibid., 338; Bezou, *Lourdes on Napoleon Avenue*, 32.

9 Warner, "Freret's Century," 327–35.

10 Ibid., 330.

11 Ibid., 331.

12 Ibid., 337–38.

13 Caryn Cossé Bell, "French Religious Culture in Afro-Creole New Orleans, 1718–
1877," *U.S. Catholic Historian* 17, no. 2 (Spring 1999): 1–16; Emily Clark and Virginia Meacham Gould, "The Feminine Face of Afro-Catholicism in New Orleans,
1727–1852," *William and Mary Quarterly* 59, no. 2 (April 2002): 409–48; Stephen J.
Ochs, "A Patriot, a Priest, and a Prelate: Black Catholic Activism in Civil War New

Orleans," *U.S. Catholic Historian* 12, no. 1 (Winter 1994): 49–75; Doorley, "Irish Catholics and French Creoles," 37, 43, 48, 52.

14 R. Po-Chia Hsia, *The World of Catholic Renewal 1540–1770* (New York: Cambridge University Press, 2005), 37–42; Clark and Gould, "Feminine Face of Afro-Catholicism"; Bennett, *Religion and the Rise of Jim Crow*, 138–40.

15 Clark and Gould, "Feminine Face of Afro-Catholicism," 421.

16 Hsia, *World of Catholic Renewal*, 29–31; Clark and Gould, "Feminine Face of Afro-Catholicism," 416–17, 423. For the broader context of transatlantic slavery and Catholicism, particularly in terms of sainthood and canonization, see Katie Walker Grimes, *Fugitive Saints: Catholicism and the Politics of Slavery* (Minneapolis: Fortress Press, 2017).

17 Clark and Gould, "Feminine Face of Afro-Catholicism," 438–41.

18 Ibid., 412; Ochs, "A Patriot, a Priest, and a Prelate," 56–58.

19 Bennett, *Religion and the Rise of Jim Crow*, 144, 218–19; Ochs, "A Patriot, a Priest, and a Prelate," 58.

20 Bell, "French Religious Culture," 1; Ochs, "A Patriot, a Priest, and a Prelate," 57. For the perspectives of American Catholics on antebellum slavery, see McGreevy, *Catholicism and American Freedom*, 43–66.

21 Bell, "French Religious Culture," 7–9.

22 Ibid., 1–3.

23 Ibid., 13–14. The definitive history of black Creole spiritualism in New Orleans is Emily Suzanne Clark, *A Luminous Brotherhood: Afro-Creole Spiritualism in Nineteenth-Century New Orleans* (Chapel Hill: University of North Carolina Press, 2016).

24 Ochs, "A Patriot, a Priest, and a Prelate," 49.

25 Ibid., esp. 49–50, 72–75; Alberts, "Black Catholic Schools," 79.

26 Alberts, "Black Catholic Schools," 78–84; Bennett, *Religion and the Rise of Jim Crow*, 148–49, 162–78; Bambra Pitman, "Culture, Caste, and Conflict in New Orleans Catholicism: Archbishop Janssens and the Color Line," *Louisiana History* 49, no. 4 (Fall 2008): 423–62; Doorley, "Irish Catholics and French Creoles," 51.

27 Quoted in Pitman, "Culture, Caste, and Conflict," 449.

28 Quoted in ibid., 451.

29 Ibid., 451.

30 Ibid., 457; Alberts, "Black Catholic Schools," 83–85; Bennett, *Religion and the Rise of Jim Crow*, 178–92; Ronald L. Sharps, "Black Catholics in the United States: A Historical Chronology," *U.S. Catholic Historian* 12, no. 1 (1994): 119–41; "Pope Francis Elevates Augustus Tolton to 'Venerable,'" *Chicago Catholic*, June 19, 2019.

31 Bezou, *Lourdes on Napoleon Avenue*, 3–9; Alberts, "Black Catholic Schools," 83–85. For rising racial proscription, white violence, and African American resistance during the onset of Jim Crow in Louisiana, see William Ivy Hair, *Carnival of Fury: Robert Charles and the New Orleans Race Riot of 1900* (Baton Rouge: Louisiana State University Press, 1976).

32 Baudier, *Catholic Church in Louisiana*, 496, 517, 519, 529; Alberts, "Black Catholic Schools," 85–94; Bennett, *Religion and the Rise of Jim Crow*, 148, 199, 226–27. Alberts gives the founding of Blessed Sacrament in 1915, while Baudier lists 1918. In 1925, the archdiocese established a Teacher's Training College and College of Liberal Arts that became Xavier University, finishing out a "a full system of segregated black education" that Alberts, 91, describes as "unique in the world." The segregation of southern Louisiana Catholicism is treated in Dolores Egger Labbé, *Jim Crow Comes to Church: The Establishment of Segregated Catholic Parishes in South Louisiana* (Lafayette: University of Southwestern Louisiana, 1971; repr., Arno Press, 1978). For overviews of African American Catholicism in the nineteenth and early twentieth centuries, see John T. Gillard, *Colored Catholics in the United States* (Baltimore: Josephite Press, 1941); Cyprian Davis, *The History of Black Catholics in the United States* (New York: Crossroad, 1995), 163–237; Cyprian Davis, "African American Catholics," in *The Encyclopedia of American Catholic History*, ed. Michael Glazier and Thomas J. Shelley (Collegeville, MN: Liturgical Press, 1997), 6–13.

33 Baudier, *Catholic Church in Louisiana*, 496, 517, 519, 529; Alberts, "Black Catholic Schools," 85–94; Bennett, *Religion and the Rise of Jim Crow*, 192–228. For the racism and segregation encountered by African American women religious in the nineteenth and twentieth centuries, see Shannen Dee Williams, "Forgotten Habits, Lost Vocations: Black Nuns, Contested Memories, and the 19th Century Struggle to Desegregate U.S. Catholic Religious Life," *Journal of African American History* 101, no. 3 (Summer 2016): 231–60.

34 Bezou, *Lourdes on Napoleon Avenue*, 1–16; "Twelfth Ward Meeting," *New Orleans Daily Picayune*, November 17, 1911, 3; "Bowen Explains Campaign Costs Are Economical," New Orleans Times-Picayune, August 25, 1922, 7; Walter Greaves Cohan and Jack B. McGuire, *Louisiana Governors: Rulers, Rascals, and Reformers* (Jackson: University Press of Mississippi, 2008), 143. For Harry McEnerny and the rise of sports writing in New Orleans, see Dale A. Somers, *The Rise of Sports in New Orleans: 1850–1900* (Baton Rouge: Louisiana University Press, 1972), 279.

35 Bennett, *Religion and the Rise of Jim Crow*, 168–71, 194, 287n4.

36 Roger Baudier, *Our Lady of Lourdes Parish* (New Orleans: Archdiocese of New Orleans, 1957), 29; "Model Catholic School Shows Father Kavanagh's Success," *New Orleans Daily Picayune*, June 22, 1910, 6; Hodding Carter, *The Past as Prelude: New Orleans, 1718–1968* (Gretna, LA: Pelican, 1968), 138; Bezou, *Lourdes on Napoleon Avenue*, 17 (quote is from 17).

37 Bezou, *Lourdes on Napoleon Avenue*, 14–15, 18; James T. Moore, *Acts of Faith: The Catholic Church in Texas, 1900–1950* (College Station: Texas A&M University, 2002), 99.

38 Bezou, *Lourdes on Napoleon Avenue*, 21–22.

39 Baudier, *Our Lady of Lourdes Parish*, 26; Bezou, *Lourdes on Napoleon Avenue*, 31–32. For the influence of mass culture, including advertising, on Catholic devotional culture in the middle decades of the twentieth century, see Robert Orsi,

"The Center Out There, in Here, and Everywhere Else: The Nature of Pilgrimage to the Shrine of Saint Jude, 1929–1965," *Journal of Social History* 25, no. 2 (Winter 1991): 213–32.

40 Bezou, *Lourdes on Napoleon Avenue*, 6, 23–24.

41 Baudier, *Our Lady of Lourdes Parish*, 25–26; Bezou, *Lourdes on Napoleon Avenue*, 10, 18; James F. Donovan, *Parish of Our Lady of Lourdes* (New Orleans, 1928), 12; "Our Lady of Lourdes," *New Orleans Daily Picayune*, October 23, 1905, 5; "Passionist Leaders to Begin Mission To-day at Our Lady of Lourdes," *New Orleans Daily Picayune*, March 4, 1906, 30.

42 Bezou, *Lourdes on Napoleon Avenue*, 6. For a succinct discussion of the transatlantic formation and elaboration of the Lourdes devotion, see John T. McGreevy, "Bronx Miracle," *American Quarterly* 52, no. 3 (September 2000): 413–21. For the French context of the development of the Lourdes devotion, see Thomas A. Kselman, *Miracles and Prophecies in Nineteenth-Century France* (New Brunswick, NJ: Rutgers University Press, 1983). For analysis of Marian apparitions, including Lourdes, in the nineteenth and twentieth centuries, see Sandra L. Zimdars-Swartz, *Encountering Mary: From La Salette to Medjugorje* (Princeton, NJ: Princeton University Press, 1991).

43 McGreevy, "Bronx Miracle," 415–18; the Perché quotations are from 416, 418.

44 Ibid., 417–18.

45 Baudier, *Our Lady of Lourdes Parish*, 28; Bezou, *Lourdes on Napoleon Avenue*, 13–14; Donovan, *Parish of Our Lady of Lourdes*, 17–20; McGreevy, "Bronx Miracle," 417–18; quotations from "Famous Lourdes Grotto Reproduced Here at the Church on Napoleon Avenue," *New Orleans Daily Picayune*, July 19, 1908, 7.

46 Baudier, *Our Lady of Lourdes Parish*, 31; Bezou, *Lourdes on Napoleon Avenue*, 25–31; Donovan, *Parish of Our Lady of Lourdes*, 24–30; Doorley, "Irish Catholics and French Creoles," 53–54; quotation is from Bezou, 25. The new Lourdes Church was designed by architectural firm J. H. Petty, which had recently designed Notre Dame Seminary, built by Archbishop John William Shaw as he sought to recruit a native-born clergy, sixteen years after Archbishop Chapelle had closed the Bouligny Seminary.

47 Bezou, *Lourdes on Napoleon Avenue*, 35–37.

48 Ibid., 30–31; Baudier, *Our Lady of Lourdes Parish*, 37, 42. William J. Guste would serve as parish trustee until his death in 1958. His sons William J. "Billy" Guste Jr. and Monsignor Robert Guste would serve, respectively, as attorney general of Louisiana (1972–92) and administrator of Our Lady of Lourdes Parish (1997–2000). Obituaries of Msgr. Robert Guste and William J. Guste Jr., *New Orleans Times-Picayune*, August 5, 2010, July 25, 2013.

49 Bezou, *Lourdes on Napoleon Avenue*, 30–31.

50 "Rev. Wickham, Noted Radio Speaker, to Preach in N.O.," (New Orleans) *Catholic Action of the South*, January 21, 1933, 8. On shifts in notions of femininity in the early decades of the twentieth century, see Martha H. Patterson, *Beyond the Gibson Girl, Reimagining the American New World, 1895–1915* (Champaign: University

of Illinois Press, 2005) and John D'Emilio and Estelle B. Freedman, *Intimate Matters: A History of Sexuality in America*, 2nd ed. (Chicago: University of Chicago Press, 1999), 171–282.

51 Bezou, *Lourdes on Napoleon Avenue*, 37–38; Baudier, *Our Lady of Lourdes Parish*, 33.

52 Bezou, *Lourdes on Napoleon Avenue*, 38.

53 Ibid., 38–41; "Msgr. Kavanagh, Lourdes Pastor, Called by Death," (New Orleans) *Catholic Action of the South*, July 26, 1934, 2.

54 "Monsignor Kavanagh," (New Orleans) *Catholic Action of the South*, August 2, 1934, 2.

55 Bezou, *Lourdes on Napoleon Avenue*, 41; "Bless Monument to Msgr. Kavanagh Sunday Afternoon," (New Orleans) *Catholic Action of the South*, April 13, 1935, 2; "Monsignor Kavanagh's Monument Blessed by Bishop Laval," (New Orleans) *Catholic Action of the South*, April 25, 1935, 6.

56 Bezou, *Lourdes on Napoleon Avenue*, 41–43; Baudier, *Our Lady of Lourdes Parish*, 34.

57 Justin D. Poché, "Religion, Race, and Rights in Catholic Louisiana, 1938–1970" (Ph.D. diss., University of Notre Dame, 2007), 75–77; Bezou, *Lourdes on Napoleon Avenue*, 42–44; Richard White, *Kingfish: The Reign of Huey P. Long* (New York: Random House, 2006), 188–204.

58 Poché, "Religion, Race, and Rights," 73–75. For Huey Long's political career and his relationship to black Louisianans, see T. Harry Williams, *Huey Long* (1969; repr., New York: Vintage, 1981); William Ivy Hair, *The Kingfish and His Realm: The Life and Times of Huey P. Long* (Baton Rouge: Louisiana State University Press, 1991); Adam Fairclough, *Race and Democracy: The Civil Rights Struggle In Louisiana* (Athens: University of Georgia Press, 1995), 44–45.

59 Poché, "Religion, Race, and Rights," 75–77; Bezou, *Lourdes on Napoleon Avenue*, 44; "C.P.A. Will Aid Crusade to Help Mexican Church," (New Orleans) *Catholic Action of the South*, May 30, 1935, 9. For the *Catholic Action of the South* in the larger context of the history of the Catholic press in New Orleans, see Elisabeth Joan Doyle, "Mightier Than the Sword: The Catholic Press in Louisiana," in *Cross, Crucible, and Crozier: A Volume Celebrating the Bicentennial of a Catholic Diocese in Louisiana*, ed. Glenn R. Conrad (New Orleans: Archdiocese of New Orleans, 1993), 255–57. For the "Catholic Action" impulse in American Catholicism, a Catholic response to the Protestant "social gospel" in the early to middle years of the twentieth century, see James M. O'Toole, *The Faithful: A History of Catholics in America* (Cambridge, MA: Harvard University Press, 2008), 145–98. For the Catholic Legion of Decency and the relationship of Catholicism to American popular culture, including the motion picture industry, from the 1930s through the 1950s, see James T. Fisher, "Catholicism as American Popular Culture," in *American Catholics, American Culture: Tradition and Resistance, Vol. 2: American Catholics in the Public Square*, ed. Margaret O'Brien Steinfels (New York: Rowman & Littlefield, 2004), 104–5, and Una Cadegan, "Guardians of Democracy or

Cultural Storm Troopers? American Catholics and the Control of Popular Media, 1934–66," *Catholic Historical Review* 87, no. 2 (April 2001): 252–82.

60 Bezou, *Lourdes on Napoleon Avenue*, 44. In a 1940 Parochial Visitation Report, Wynhoven merely referred to the nearby black territorial parish, "Holy Ghost Church on boundary, Louisiana Ave.," when asked what provision Lourdes was making for "Catholic Negroes" living in the parish. Archdiocese of New Orleans Parochial Visitation Report, Our Lady of Lourdes Parish, June 20, 1940, Our Lady of Lourdes Parish File (subsequently OLOLPF), Archives of the Archdiocese of New Orleans (henceforth AANO).

61 Bezou, *Lourdes on Napoleon Avenue*, 54–55; Baudier, *Our Lady of Lourdes Parish*, 36; Claire L. Vasterling, "A History of Our Lady of Lourdes School Auxiliary," October 23, 1959, OLOLPF, AANO.

62 Poché, "Religion, Race, and Rights," 76–78.

63 Bezou, *Lourdes on Napoleon Avenue*, 54–55; Baudier, *Our Lady of Lourdes Parish*, 36; Beverly Jacques Anderson, *Cherished Memories: Snapshots of Life and Lessons from a 1950s New Orleans Creole Village* (Bloomington, IN: iUniverse, 2011), 81.

64 "Louis Philip Caillouet" and "Lucien Joseph Caillouet," in Louisiana Historical Association, "Louisiana Dictionary of Biography," http://lahistory.org; Bezou, *Lourdes on Napoleon Avenue*, 59–60; Baudier, *Our Lady of Lourdes Parish*, 38–39.

65 For interpretations of American Catholicism in the mid-twentieth century see Dolan, *In Search of an American Catholicism*, 180–89; Anthony Burke Smith, *The Look of Catholics: Portrayals in Popular Culture from the Great Depression to the Cold War* (Lawrence: University Press of Kansas, 2010); James T. Fisher, *Communion of Immigrants: A History of Catholics in America* (New York: Oxford University Press, 2008), 114–33; McGreevy, *Catholicism and American Freedom*, 166–88.

66 Baudier, *Our Lady of Lourdes Parish*, 40–41. For an argument that air conditioning accomplished a wide-ranging transformation of southern culture that eroded its distinctiveness, see Raymond Arsenault, "The End of the Long Hot Summer: The Air Conditioner and Southern Culture," *Journal of Southern History* 50, no. 4 (November 1984): 597–628. Arsenault, 628, holds that "General Electric has proved a more devastating invader than General Sherman."

67 Baudier, *Our Lady of Lourdes Parish*, 11–18, 40–41; Bezou, *Lourdes on Napoleon Avenue*, 62–66.

68 Archdiocese of New Orleans Parochial Visitation Report, Our Lady of Lourdes Parish, January 26, 1959, OLOLPF, AANO, 10.

69 Ibid.

70 Ibid.; Diane T. Manning and Perry Rogers, "Desegregation of the New Orleans Parochial Schools," *Journal of Negro Education* 71, nos. 1–2 (Winter/Spring 2002): 32–33; author's interview with Olympia and Harold Boucree, New Orleans, October 16, 2010; Warner, "Freret's Century," 343.

71 Warner, "Freret's Century," 339–49; author's interview with Olympia and Harold Boucree. For a historical overview of black Creoles and New Orleans political culture, see Arnold R. Hirsch, "Fade to Black: Hurricane Katrina and the Disappear-

ance of Creole New Orleans," *Journal of American History* 94, no. 3 (December 2007): 752–61. For the larger context of black Catholicism in the United States in the middle decades of the twentieth century, see Davis, *History of Black Catholics,* 238–59.

72 Warner, "Freret's Century," 339–49.

73 Manning and Rogers, "Desegregation of the New Orleans Parochial Schools," 31–41.

74 Ibid., 31–41. For the desegregation of parochial schools in the Catholic urban North, see McGreevy, *Parish Boundaries.* For Leander Perez and the context of his political career, see Glen Jeansonne, *Leander Perez: Boss of the Delta* (Jackson: University Press of Mississippi, 2006). For Catholic dioceses and desegregation across the South, see Mark Newman, *Desegregating Dixie: The Catholic Church in the South and Desegregation, 1945–1992* (Jackson: University Press of Mississippi, 2018).

75 Warner, "Freret's Century," 349–57; Arnold R. Hirsch, "Simply a Matter of Black and White: The Transformation of Race and Politics in Twentieth-Century New Orleans," in Hirsch and Logsdon, *Creole New Orleans,* 263–93. The Freret business district reversed the late twentieth-century trends in the years since Katrina, seeing significant revitalization as a newly fashionable commercial district. For a sanguine view that post-Katrina redevelopment of Freret has benefitted both white newcomers and long-term African American residents, albeit with tensions, see "The Redevelopment of Freret Street," *New Orleans Gambit,* August 13, 2013, www.bestofneworleans.com.

76 Bezou, *Lourdes on Napoleon Avenue,* 75–77.

77 Ibid., 77.

78 Author's interview with Olympia and Harold Boucree.

79 Bezou, *Lourdes on Napoleon Avenue,* 75. For the social experience of the convergence of Vatican II and the Civil Rights Movement in Catholic parishes in the northern United States, see John T. McGreevy, "Racial Justice and the People of God: The Second Vatican Council, the Civil Rights Movement, and American Catholics," *Religion and American Culture* 4, no. 2 (Summer 1994): 221–54, and McGreevy, *Parish Boundaries.*

80 Bezou, *Lourdes on Napoleon Avenue,* 77–83, 86; author's interview with Olympia and Harold Boucree.

81 "In New Orleans, More Quietly Settled, Decades-Old Catholic Church Sex Abuse Cases Surface," *New Orleans Advocate,* September 20, 2018, www.theadvocate. com; "Here Are the 57 Clergy 'Credibly Accused' of Abuse in the Archdiocese of New Orleans," *New Orleans Times-Picayune,* November 2, 2018, www.nola. com. Three additional clerics "credibly accused" of sexual abuse, James Benedict, John Thomann, and Lawrence Hecker, served as assistant priests at Lourdes in the 1940s, 1950s, and 1960s, respectively, in each case within a decade of their reported abuse. "Five Pastors; Two Assistants Named to Positions in Orleans Archdiocese," *Clarion Herald,* August 1, 1963.

82 Obituary for Bishop Harold R. Perry, *New York Times*, July 19, 1991; Bezou, *Lourdes on Napoleon Avenue*, 33; Earl F. Niehaus, "Black and Catholic: A Generation of Change," in Conrad, *Cross, Crucible, and Crozier*, 186.

83 Author's interview with Olympia and Harold Boucree; Cecilia A. Moore, "Conversion Narratives: The Dual Experiences and Voices of African American Catholic Converts," *U.S. Catholic Historian* 28, no. 1 (Winter 2010): 32.

84 Bezou, *Lourdes on Napoleon Avenue*, 87. Later admitted to the Franciscan order, Fernand Cheri was appointed auxiliary bishop of New Orleans in January 2015. "Cheri Returns as Auxiliary Bishop," *New Orleans Advocate*, January 13, 2015, 1B.

85 In 1989 a black Catholic priest in Washington, D.C., the Rev. George Augustus Stallings Jr., formed a breakaway black Catholic church, the African American Catholic Congregation (Imani Temple); Stallings was excommunicated the following year. Ronald L. Sharp, "Black Catholic Gifts of Faith," *U.S. Catholic Historian* 15, no. 4 (Fall 1997): 29–30, offers a useful overview of the historical development of African American Catholic cultural expression. For the post–Vatican II emergence of an African American Catholic liturgical style, see Matthew J. Cressler, "Black Power, Vatican II, and the Emergence of Black Catholic Liturgies," *U.S. Catholic Historian* 32, no. 4 (Fall 2014): 99–119, and Cressler, *Authentically Black and Truly Catholic*. For key overviews of African American Catholic religiosity, including liturgical practice, see Cyprian Davis and Diana L. Hayes, *Taking Down Our Harps: Black Catholics in the United States* (Maryknoll, NY: Orbis Books, 1998); M. Shawn Copeland, ed., *Uncommon Faithfulness: The Black Catholic Experience* (Maryknoll, NY: Orbis Books, 2009); Diana L. Hayes and Cecilia A. Moore, "We Have Been Believers: Black Catholic Studies," in *The Catholic Studies Reader*, ed. James T. Fisher and Margaret M. McGuinness (New York: Fordham University Press, 2011), 259–81.

86 Bezou, *Lourdes on Napoleon Avenue*, 92; "Our Lady of Lourdes Plans Anniversary Celebration," *New Orleans Times-Picayune*, October 11, 1980, 10.

87 "Lourdes School," *New Orleans Times-Picayune*, March 10, 1979.

88 "Pastors over the Past 100 Years," OLOLPF, AANO; author's interview with Olympia and Harold Boucree. For historical overview of the development of the Vietnamese Catholic community in eastern New Orleans that took root after the flight of Vietnamese Catholics from Vietnam following the fall of Saigon in 1975, see Carl L. Bankston III, "Vietnamese-American Catholicism: Transplanted and Flourishing," *U.S. Catholic Historian* 18, no. 1 (Winter 2000): esp. 45–51.

89 "Pastors over the Past 100 Years," OLOLPF, AANO; "One Voice, Many Faces: Part 7-Black and Catholic," *Chicago Catholic Examiner*, December 28, 2012; "Missionary Society of St. Paul," www.mspfathers.org; "Daughters of Divine Love Congregation," www.daughtersofdivinelovedev.org; Philip Jenkins, *The Next Christendom: The Coming of Global Christianity* (New York: Oxford University Press, 2002).

90 Author's email interview with Fr. Raphael Ezeh, September 2010.

91 "Hurricane Katrina Flooding Compared to a 500-Year Storm Today," *New Orleans Times-Picayune*, August 16, 2013; Campanella, "Ethnic Geography of New Orleans," 711–15.

92 "The Deadly Choices at Memorial," *New York Times*, August 25, 2009.

93 Author's email correspondence with Fr. Raphael Ezeh, September 2005.

94 Ibid.

95 Author's email correspondence with Fr. Raphael Ezeh, October–December 2005; author's interview with Olympia and Harold Boucree.

96 Author's email correspondence with Fr. Raphael Ezeh, February–March 2006; author's email interview with Jill Benoit, September 20, 2010.

97 "New Orleans Archdiocese to Close 25 Church Parishes," *Baton Rouge Advocate*, April 10, 2008; "Archdiocese Finalizes Additional Parish Mergers," *Clarion Herald*, August 9, 2008.

98 In an effort that crossed historical racial boundaries in Crescent City Catholicism, parishioners at St. Henry devised a plan to share space with four parishes, including Blessed Sacrament, an African American parish that was slated for closure and merger with St. Joan of Arc, another African American parish some distance away in Carrollton. Archbishop Hughes displayed little interest in the plan, and St. Henry and Our Lady of Good Counsel were closed and merged with St. Stephen. Although neither church would regain parish status, parishioners' protests ultimately proved partially successful. Under Hughes' successor, Gregory Aymond, daily Masses were resumed at St. Henry and Our Lady of Good Counsel became a center for Charismatic Catholics, hosting several Masses a week. "New Orleans Police Remove Parishioners Occupying Closed Uptown Churches," *New Orleans Times-Picayune*, January 6, 2009; "Shuttered Uptown Catholic Church Reopens as Charismatic Community Center," *New Orleans Times-Picayune*, December 11, 2011; "The Mass Is Ended," *New Orleans Gambit*, September 16, 2008. On the "vigiling" movement that arose in Boston after Cardinal Bernard Law announced the closure of eighty-three churches, see Kathleen Kautzer, *The Underground Church: Nonviolent Resistance to the Vatican Empire* (Boston: Brill Books, 2012), 186–87.

99 Trushna Parekh, "Of Armed Guards and Kente Cloth: Afro-Creole Catholics and the Battle for St. Augustine Parish in Post-Katrina New Orleans," *American Quarterly* 61, no. 3 (September 2009): 557–81; "The Mass Is Ended," *New Orleans Gambit*, September 16, 2008; Donald E. DeVore, "Water in Sacred Places: Rebuilding New Orleans Black Churches as Sites of Community Empowerment," *Journal of American History* 94, no. 3 (December 2007): 762–69.

100 "Archbishop Hughes' Tenure Was Stormiest in Recent N.O. History," *New Orleans Times-Picayune*, June 13, 2009; "The Mass Is Ended," *New Orleans Gambit*, September 16, 2008.

101 "Church Closings in New Orleans Reflect a National Trend," *National Catholic Reporter*, April 29, 2008.

102 Author's email interview with Jill Benoit.

103 Author's interview with Olympia and Harold Boucree.

104 Author's email interview with Sadie White, August 7, 2010.

105 Ibid.

106 Author's interview with Olympia and Harold Boucree.

107 Author's email interview with Jill Benoit.

108 "Three Parishes form a Blessed Trinity," *Clarion Herald*, August 9, 2008, 1–8.

109 Author's interview with Olympia and Harold Boucree; Archdiocese of New Orleans, "Holy Rosary Academy and School to Re-locate for the Upcoming School Year," www.archno.org; "The Redevelopment of Freret Street," *New Orleans Gambit*, August 13, 2013.

110 "Empty Churches Breed Concern," *New Orleans Times-Picayune*, April 9, 2008; "Three Parishes form a Blessed Trinity," *Clarion Herald*, August 9, 2008, 1–8; "With Love, from Slidell to Zanzibar," *Clarion Herald*, October 1, 2013, http://clarionherald.info; Jenkins, *Next Christendom*; Paul Gifford, "Some Recent Developments in African Christianity," *African Affairs* 93, no. 373 (October 1994): 513–34; Paul Gifford, *Christianity, Development, and Modernity in Africa* (New York: Oxford University Press, 2016), esp. 69–144. Archbishop Alfred Hughes acknowledged African American Catholic perspectives with a 2006 pastoral letter that asked white Catholics to recognize a significant historical legacy of white privilege and contemporary structural inequities in the region. In 2011 Hughes's successor, Archbishop Gregory Aymond, initiated a campaign requesting all parishes to pray weekly for an end to "murder, violence, and racism." "Archbishop Hughes' Tenure Was Stormiest in Recent N.O. History," *New Orleans Times-Picayune*, June 13, 2009; Archdiocese of New Orleans, "Archbishop Aymond Officially Announces Start of the 'New Battle of New Orleans' Prayer Campaign" (March 9, 2011), www.archno.org. In early 2015, the pastor of Blessed Trinity Parish, Fr. Dennis Hayes III, reported plans to remove the stained glass windows from Lourdes Church and to sell the unused church and rectory buildings. *Blessed Trinity Catholic Church Bulletin*, January 11, 2015. In June 2016, the archdiocese sold the property to the New Orleans Opera Association. Curbed New Orleans, "Our Lady of Lourdes Church Uptown Sells for $1.3M" (June 1, 2016), http://nola.curbed.com. This paragraph is influenced by my observation of and participation as worshipper in around a dozen Masses at Blessed Trinity between 2009 and 2019.

2. THE MAKING OF A MIDWESTERN CATHOLICISM

1 "History of Saint Mary's Church," www.icstmary.org; Joseph Fuhrmann, *Souvenir of the Diamond Jubilee of St. Mary's Church, Iowa City, Iowa* (Iowa City, 1916), 23, 28. The author sought to access archival records at the Diocese of Davenport but was informed that no relevant parish records existed for the period under consideration; the author is grateful to Tyla Cole for her assistance. An effort to search archival materials at Iowa City parishes yielded only sacramental records; the author thanks Rachel Santos at St. Mary's Church for her aid. Fortunately, numerous extant primary sources, including newspaper sources and published

clergy's correspondence, as well as Joseph Fuhrmann's richly detailed if randomly organized 1916 St. Mary's parish history—which often quotes primary sources verbatim, often without attribution—enable the reconstruction of Iowa City's nineteenth-century ethnic Catholicism.

2 For an important theoretical discussion of the dynamics of diasporic religious identity, see Jonathan Z. Smith, *Map Is Not Territory: Studies in the Histories of Religions* (Leiden: E.J. Brill, 1978), xiv.

3 Looking across the Midwest, Philip Barlow finds that Catholics, Lutherans, and United Methodists claimed the largest numbers of religious adherents in 2000, at 39 percent, 14 percent, and 7 percent, respectively, with Methodists prevalent in the Lower Midwest and with a "Lutheran and Catholic-Lutheran zone in the region's upper reaches." Phillip L. Barlow, "A Demographic Portrait: America Writ Small?," in *Religion and Public Life in the Midwest: America's Common Denominator?*, ed. Philip Barlow and Mark Silk (Lanham, MD: Rowman AltaMira, 2004), 21–47. For a discussion of the factors shaping the historical geography of Iowa Catholicism, see Madeleine M. Schmidt, *Seasons of Growth: History of the Diocese of Davenport, 1881–1981* (Davenport, IA: Diocese of Davenport, 1981), 98–105. For an overview of religiosity in nineteenth-century Iowa, including the efforts of Catholics, Methodists, Congregationalists, Presbyterians, Quakers, and Jews, see Dorothy Schwieder, *Iowa: The Middle Land* (Ames: Iowa State University Press, 1996), 109–18. For analysis of the experiences of Irish women religious and Catholicism more generally on the nineteenth-century Iowa frontier, see Helen Marie Burns, "Active Religious Women on the Iowa Frontier: A Study in Continuity and Discontinuity" (Ph.D. diss., University of Iowa, 2001). For institutional Catholicism in the Diocese of Des Moines, see Steven M. Avella, *The Catholic Church in Southwest Iowa* (Collegeville, MN: Liturgical Press, 2018). A useful overview of the development of Catholicism in the urban and rural Midwest can be found in Stephen J. Shaw, "The Cities and the Plains, a Home for God's People: A History of the Catholic Parish in the Midwest," in *The American Catholic Parish: A History from 1850 to the Present, Vol. 2: The Pacific, Intermountain West, and Midwest States*, ed. Jay P. Dolan (New York: Paulist, 1987), 277–401. For a more recent overview, see Jay P. Dolan, "Catholics in the Midwest: Final Revised Draft," www3.nd.edu, and Dolan, "A Different Breed of Catholics," in Barlow and Silk, *Religion and Public Life in the Midwest*, 109–34. Besides the works cited above, American Catholic studies has largely neglected the Midwest, with the important exception of scholarship on the urban Rust Belt's multiethnic Catholicism. See, for example, John T. McGreevy, *Parish Boundaries: The Catholic Encounter with Race in the Twentieth-Century Urban North* (Chicago: University of Chicago Press, 1996); Robert Orsi, "The Center Out There, in Here, and Everywhere Else: The Nature of Pilgrimage to the Shrine of Saint Jude, 1929–1965," *Journal of Social History* 25, no. 2 (Winter 1991): 213–32; Matthew J. Cressler, *Authentically Black and Truly Catholic: The Rise of Black Catholicism in the Great Migration* (New York: New York University Press, 2017); Steven M. Avella, *This Confident Church:*

Chicago Catholicism, 1940–1965 (South Bend, IN: University of Notre Dame Press, 1992); Steven M. Avella, *In the Richness of the Earth: A History of the Archdiocese of Milwaukee, 1843–1958* (Milwaukee: Marquette University Press, 2002); Leslie Woodcock Tentler, *Seasons of Grace: A History of the Catholic Archdiocese of Detroit* (Detroit: Wayne State University Press, 1990). For the Catholic experience in a predominantly Protestant portion of the rural Upper Midwest in the early twentieth century, see Leslie Woodcock Tentler, "'A Model Rural Parish': Priests and People in the Michigan 'Thumb,' 1923–1928," *Catholic Historical Review* 78, no. 3 (July 1992): 413–30.

4   Kathleen Neils Conzen, "German Catholics in America," in *The Encyclopedia of American Catholic History*, ed. Michael Glazier and Thomas J. Shelley (Collegeville, MN: Liturgical Press, 1997), 582; Iowa State Data Center, "Total Population for Iowa's Incorporated Places; 1850–2000," www.iowadatacenter.org.

5   For historical analysis of the experience of Catholics in the Protestant majority South, see Randall M. Miller and Jon Wakelyn, eds., *Catholics in the Old South: Essays on Church and Culture* (Mercer, GA: Mercer University Press, 1983; repr., 1999); James M. Woods, *A History of the Catholic Church in the American South, 1513–1900* (Gainesville: University Press of Florida, 2011).

6   Mary Nona McGreal, *Samuel Mazzuchelli: American Dominican* (Notre Dame, IN: Ave Maria Press, 2005), 9–175. McGreal offers a comprehensive, scholarly, and highly sympathetic treatment of Mazzuchelli's life. For Mazzuchelli's missions among Natives, his disputes over funding with federal Indian agents that favored Protestants, and his opposition to treaty violations and Indian removal, see McGreal, *Samuel Mazzuchelli*, 93, 96, 99, 168–69; Kenneth E. Colton, "Father Mazzuchelli's Iowa Mission," *Annals of Iowa* 21, no. 4 (1938): 310, 313–14.

7   B. C. Lenehan, "Right Rev. Mathias Loras, D.D., First Bishop of Dubuque," *Annals of Iowa* 3, no. 8 (January 1899): 577–84. Michael Pasquier, *Fathers on the Frontier: French Missionaries and the Roman Catholic Priesthood in the United States, 1789–1870* (New York: Oxford University Press, 2010). Pasquier's analytically rich treatment of French missionary priests in the nineteenth-century trans-Appalachian West provides essential context for understanding clerics such as Mathias Loras.

8   Samuel Mazzuchelli, *The Memoirs of Father Samuel Mazzuchelli, O.P.,* trans. Mary Benedicta Kennedy (Chicago: W. F. Hall, 1915), also available at www.fathermazzuchellisociety.org; all quotations are from chaps. 33 and 34. Fuhrmann, *Souvenir of the Diamond Jubilee*, 8–11; McGreal, *Samuel Mazzuchelli*, 188. For Mazzuchelli's attempt to synthesize Catholicism and American republicanism, see Mary Nona McGreal, "Samuel Mazzuchelli: Participant in Frontier Democracy," *Records of the American Catholic Historical Society of Philadelphia* 87, no. 1 (1976): 99–114, and McGreal, *Samuel Mazzuchelli*, 305–19. For an overview of efforts among Catholics in the early American republic, such as Baltimore Bishop John Carroll, to reconcile Catholicism with republicanism and other Enlightenment values, see Jay P. Dolan, "The Search for an American Catholicism," *Catholic Historical Review* 82, no. 2 (April 1996): 174–78; Jay P. Dolan, *In Search of an American Catholicism: A*

History of Religion and Culture in Tension (New York: Oxford University Press, 2002), 13–45; Michael Breidenbach, "Conciliarism and the American Founding," *William and Mary Quarterly* 73, no. 3 (July 2016): 467–500; James M. O'Toole, *The Faithful* (Cambridge, MA: Harvard University Press, 2008), 35–37. Mazzuchelli's synthesis of "Catholicity" and American republicanism, which he sometimes defended against anti-Catholic polemicists around the Old Northwest, may have reflected a more optimistic, Enlightenment-inflected view of the potential for an American Catholicism than would be found among ultramontane Catholic thinkers in the United States later in the antebellum period. For the ultramontane revival in the United States, see John T. McGreevy, *Catholicism and American Freedom: A History* (New York: Norton, 2003), 27–30.

9 Pasquier, *Fathers on the Frontier*, 11–18; McGreevy, *Catholicism and American Freedom*, 27–30; Mark G. McGowan, *The Waning of the Green: Catholics, the Irish, and Identity in Toronto, 1887–1922* (Montreal: McGill-Queen's University Press, 1999), 91–93.

10 McGreal, *Samuel Mazzuchelli*, 175–81; Fuhrmann, *Souvenir of the Diamond Jubilee*, 11–15. For the letter in which Pelamourgues criticized Loras for building too many churches in new settlements with small numbers of Catholics, see Schmidt, *Seasons of Growth*, 53.

11 Fuhrmann, *Souvenir of the Diamond Jubilee*, 15–19. Emmett Larkin, "The Devotional Revolution in Ireland, 1850–1875," *American Historical Review* 77, no. 3 (June 1972): 625–52, remains a seminal statement of the reshaping of Irish Catholicism in the pivotal years that encompassed the famine and the diasporic exodus to elsewhere in Great Britain, North America, and Australia.

12 For the exchanges between Rev. Bushnell and Rev. Poyet, see "For the Iowa Republican," *Iowa City Republican*, April 24, 1850, 2; "Communications. For the Iowa Republican," *Iowa City Republican*, May 8, 1850, 2–3; "Communications. For the Iowa Republican," *Iowa City Republican*, May 22, 1850, 2. For anti-Catholicism and sectarian debates in American political discourse in the nineteenth century, see Jon Gjerde, *Catholicism and the Shaping of Nineteenth-Century America*, ed. S. Deborah Kang (New York: Cambridge University Press, 2012); Jenny Franchot, *Roads to Rome: The Antebellum Protestant Encounter with Catholicism* (Berkeley: University of California Press, 1992).

13 Schmidt, *Seasons of Growth*, 77.

14 Fuhrmann, *Souvenir of the Diamond Jubilee*, 19–20; Theodosius Plassmeyer, "The Early Church in Iowa City," *Iowa Catholic Historical Review* 9 (February 1936): 31. For Franz Xavier Weninger, see Conzen, "German Catholics in America," 576. Sources variously list Fr. Mathias Michels as "Mathias Michael."

15 Larkin, "Devotional Revolution in Ireland"; David W. Miller, "Irish Catholicism and the Great Famine," *Journal of Social History* 9, no. 1 (Fall 1975): 81–98; Michael P. Carroll, "Re-thinking Popular Catholicism in Pre-famine Ireland," *Journal for the Scientific Study of Religion* 34, no. 3 (1995): 354–65; Jay P. Dolan, *The Irish Americans: A History* (New York: Bloomsburg, 2010); Jay P. Dolan, "Immigrants

in the City: New York's Irish and German Catholics," *Church History* 41, no. 3 (September 1972): 354–68, esp. 364; Shaw, "Cities and the Plains," 305–7; Lawrence J. McCaffrey, "Irish Textures in American Catholicism," *Catholic Historical Review* 78, no. 1 (January 1992): 1. For conflict between Irish and Germans in antebellum New York City and the creation of national parishes identified with ethnic communities that spoke foreign languages as a way to avert such conflict, see Dolan, "Immigrants in the City," 360, 362, and Jay P. Dolan, *The Immigrant Church: New York's Irish and German Catholics, 1815–1865* (1975; repr., Notre Dame, IN: University of Notre Dame Press, 1983), 87–98.

16 Shaw, "Cities and the Plains," 306–15; Emmet H. Rothan, *The German Catholic Immigrant in the United States* (Washington, DC: Catholic University Press, 1946); Colman J. Barry, OSB, *The Catholic Church and German Americans* (Milwaukee: Bruce, 1953); Conzen, "German Catholics in America," 571–83; 578 (quotation); Kathleen Neils Conzen, "Immigrant Religion in the Public Sphere: The German Catholic Milieu in America," in *German-American Immigration and Ethnicity in Comparative Perspective*, ed. Wolfgang Helbich and Walter Kamphoefner (Madison, WI: Max Kade Institute, 2004), 69–116. Rothan, *German Catholic Immigrant*, 66–69, treats early German Catholic settlement in Iowa. Rothan finds eighteen German Catholic churches with priests in residence in Iowa by 1860. For an interesting comparison of the histories of German Catholic parishes in Baltimore and rural Kansas, see Thomas W. Spalding, "German Parishes East and West." *U.S. Catholic Historian* 14, no. 2 (Spring 1996): 37–52. The Weltanschauung of German Catholic immigrants in the nineteenth-century United States is vividly displayed in the letters they wrote back to family and friends in Germany. I am grateful to Alina Zeller for assisting me in accessing the Emigrant Letter Collection at the Gotha Research Library, Gotha, Germany.

17 Joseph Cada, *Czech-American Catholics, 1850–1920* (Lisle, IL: Center for Slav Culture, 1964), 9–10.

18 *Book II of Baptisms, 1860–1878* (St. Mary Church, Iowa City, 1878).

19 Plassmeyer, "Early Church in Iowa City," 21–23; William Henry Perrin, ed., *History of Effingham County* (Chicago: O. L. Baskin, 1883), 255. Bishop Clement Smyth, a Trappist, was born in County Clare in 1810 and came to Iowa with the founding of New Melleray Abbey in Dubuque County in 1849. Schmidt, *Seasons of Growth*, 91–92. Sources variously list Adolph Spocek as "Adolph Spacek."

20 Letter of Fr. Capistran Zwinge to Fr. Commissary Mathias, June 13, 1864, translated from German and quoted in Plassmeyer, "Early Church in Iowa City," 24–25.

21 Letter of Fr. Capistran Zwinge to Fr. Commissary Mathias, June 1, 1865, translated from German and quoted in Plassmeyer, "Early Church in Iowa City," 31–32.

22 Ibid.

23 Plassmeyer, "Early Church in Iowa City," 34–37.

24 Letter of June 24, 1865, translated from German and quoted in Plassmeyer, "Early Church in Iowa City," 34.

25 Fuhrmann, *Souvenir of the Diamond Jubilee*, 23, 86; Plassmeyer, "Early Church in Iowa City," 21–37.

26 Fuhrmann, *Souvenir of the Diamond Jubilee*, 26–30; Francis R. Lalor, *Celebrating Thanks! A History of Saint Mary's Parish on Its Sesquicentennial Anniversary, 1841–1991* (Iowa City: St. Mary's Parish, 1993), 11–12. The impulse to ethnic separatism/segregation was hardly limited to Catholics in Iowa City, although it had different contexts in Protestant churches with a less constrained sense of lay initiative and a less elaborated church hierarchy. In the late nineteenth century, Iowa City was home to German Lutheran and German Methodist congregations, in addition to English-speaking ones, and to two Methodist Episcopal congregations, one for whites and one for African Americans. "Churches," *Iowa City Citizen*, August 26, 1892, 2.

27 Kenneth Patrick Michael Donnelly, *St. Patrick's Church, Iowa City, Iowa, 1872–1972* (Iowa City, 1972), 1–22; "Tribute to Loved Priest," *Iowa City Daily Press*, December 9, 1904, 2; "Iowa City. St. Patrick's. The Rev. P.J. O'Reilly, Pastor," *Catholic Messenger*, February 3, 1938, 28. Fuhrmann, *Souvenir of the Diamond Jubilee*, 67–76; Dolan, *Irish Americans*. For the history of St. Agatha's Seminary, see "Historic Iowa City Women's Seminary Paves the Way Toward Equal Access to Education," *Little Village*, December 6, 2016.

28 *Centennial, St. Wenceslaus Church Iowa City Iowa, 1893–1993* (Iowa City: Sutherland, 1993); *The Catholic Church in the United States of America: Undertaken to Celebrate the Jubilee of His Holiness, Pope Pius X* (New York: Catholic Editing, 1914), 607; "Those Who Assisted in the Work," *Iowa City Daily Citizen*, June 24, 1893, 5; "A New Bethel" (quotation), *Iowa City Daily Citizen*, June 26, 1893, 3; "The Local News," *Iowa City State Press*, September 5, 1903, 4; "The Debt Wiped Out," *Iowa Catholic Messenger*, February 27, 1897, 5; Cada, *Czech-American Catholics*.

29 For a succinct treatment of the political and religious contexts for the Kulturkampf, see Steven Ozment, *A Mighty Fortress: A New History of the German People* (New York: HarperCollins, 2004), 214–20.

30 Fuhrmann, *Souvenir of the Diamond Jubilee*, 65, 86, 91; John F. Kempker, "Catholicity in Southeastern (Lee County) Iowa," in *Records of the American Catholic Historical Society of Philadelphia, Vol. II—1886–1888* (Philadelphia: American Catholic Historical Society, 1889), 139; "Father Emonds Says Farewell," *Catholic Messenger*, November 22, 1890, 8; "Impressive Services of Requiem Held in St. Mary's Church, Iowa City for the Late Father Emonds," *Catholic Messenger*, January 24, 1907, 1. As a young priest prior to arriving in Iowa City, Emonds had confronted ethnic politics in Keokuk, where he ran into trouble for building St. Peter the Apostle Church in 1856 without the full approbation of Bishop Loras, and then faced disappointed German Catholics who had thought the new parish would be exclusively for Germans, while Loras insisted it would serve a mixed congregation. In a trajectory similar to what occurred in Iowa City, German Catholics in Keokuk would form a national parish, St. Mary's, in 1867. Emonds left St. Mary's in 1890 and went to the Pacific Northwest, where he built and pastored St. Patrick's Church in Tacoma, Washington.

31 Fuhrmann, *Souvenir of the Diamond Jubilee*, 91; "Impressive Funeral Rites," *Iowa City Daily Press*, November 12, 1894, 4; "Imposing Rite First Communion," *Iowa City Daily Press*, April 15, 1912, 4; "Choir Feasts with Good Priest," *Iowa City Daily Press*, January 5, 1905, 1; "Beloved Priest Wins Appointment," *Iowa City Daily Press*, February 6, 1907, 5.

32 Ethno-cultural tensions between German Catholics, who led the Catholic hierarchy in Wisconsin, and non-German-speaking Catholics are explored at length in Avella, *In the Richness of the Earth*, esp. 177–87, 190–97. Shaw, "Cities and the Plains," 297–99; Kathleen Neils Conzen, *Germans in Minnesota* (St. Paul: Minnesota Historical Society, 2003); Steven J. Gross, "'Perils of Prussianism': Main Street German America, Local Autonomy, and the Great War," *Agricultural History* 78, no. 1 (Winter 2004): 91. For the German-Russians in the Dakotas, see Terence Kardong, *Beyond the Red River: The Diocese of Fargo, 1889–1989* (Fargo, ND: Diocese of Fargo, 1988), esp. 65–66; Robert F. Karolevitz, *With Faith, Hope, and Tenacity: The First One Hundred Years of the Catholic Diocese of Sioux Falls, 1889–1989* (Mission Hills, SD: Dakota Homestead, 1989), 29. For the contested memory of Métis Catholicism in North Dakota, see Ruth Swan and Edward A. Jerome, "The History of the Pembina Métis Cemetery: Inter-ethnic Perspectives on a Sacred Site," *Plains Anthropologist* 44, no. 170 (1999): 81–94. The Conzen quotation is in Kathleen Neils Conzen, "Making Their Own America: Assimilation Theory and the German Peasant Pioneer," German Historical Institute, Annual Lecture Series, no. 3 (Providence, RI: Berg, 1990), 2, and is also quoted in Dolan, "Catholics in the Midwest." For the debate pitting the Americanizing wing of the American Catholic Church led by Irish American archbishops James Gibbons and John Ireland versus German and other immigrant Catholics who sought parishes and possibly dioceses organized by ethnicity and language (the latter position famously advocated by German philanthropist Peter Paul Cahensly), see Rowland Berthoff, *An Unsettled People: Social Order and Disorder in American History* (New York: Harper & Row, 1971), 418–21.

33 For parish histories of St. John's Church, Waunakee, see *Souvenir of the Diamond Jubilee, St. John's Congregation, 1874–1949: And the Solemn Dedication of St. John's New School on Sunday, August 14, 1949, Waunakee, Wisconsin* (Waunakee, WI: St. John's Catholic Church, 1949). For the investigation of Fr. Hausner, see C. I. Rukes, "Re: Father Hausner," Madison, WI, February 13, 1919, Federal Bureau of Investigation Case Files, 1908–1922, Record Group 65, National Archives, Washington, DC. I am indebted to William H. Thomas for this source. For the World War I era Justice Department's efforts to investigate and prosecute German American clergy and other dissenters, see William H. Thomas, *Unsafe for Democracy: World War I and the U.S. Justice Department's Covert Campaign to Suppress Dissent* (Madison: University of Wisconsin Press, 2009), esp. 68–88. For Fr. Hausner's efforts to compel community observation of Good Friday in southern Wisconsin, see "Governor Asks Observance of Good Friday," *Waunakee (WI) Tribune*, April 1, 1916, 1; "Reverend Hausner Seeking Good Friday Closing,"

Madison Capital Times, March 20, 1931, 12; "Good Friday Plan Has Been Father Hausner's Chief Work," *Madison Capital Times*, March 26, 1931, 13; "Father Hausner Tells of Good Friday Custom," *Madison Wisconsin State Journal*, April 2, 1931, 4; "The Rambler," *Madison Wisconsin State Journal*, April 2, 1933, 6; "Rev. Hausner Issues Good Friday Plea," *Madison Wisconsin State Journal*, April 2, 1933, 8; "The Rambler," *Madison Wisconsin State Journal*, March 18, 1934, 4; "The Rambler," *Madison Wisconsin State Journal*, January 27, 1935, 4.

34 Fuhrmann, *Souvenir of the Diamond Jubilee*, 91; "Father Schulte Worthily Honored," *Iowa City Daily Press*, October 6, 1911, 7; Nancy Derr, "The Babel Proclamation," *Palimpsest* 60, no. 4 (July/August 1979): 100–101; Frederick C. Luebke, *Bonds of Loyalty: German-Americans and World War I* (DeKalb, IL: Northern University Press, 1974); "K.C.'s Start Drive for Million for Their Soldiers," *Iowa City Daily Citizen*, July 23, 1917, 1; "Dedication of St. Patrick's," *Iowa City Citizen*, January 31, 1916, 1; "Dean Schulte in Fine Talk to Kiwanians," *Iowa City Press Citizen*, October 9, 1923, 2. For German Catholics' antipathy to socialism and tendencies toward antistatism and communalism, see Conzen, "German Catholics in America," 580; Kathleen Neils Conzen, "Immigrant Religion and the Republic: German Catholics in Nineteenth-Century America," *German Historical Institute Bulletin* 35 (Fall 2004): 43–56; Conzen, "Immigrant Religion in the Public Sphere." For German American Catholics, social reform, and progressivism, with a particular focus on the Central-Verein, see Philip Gleason, "An Immigrant Group's Interest in Progressive Reform: The Case of the German-American Catholics," *American Historical Review* 73, no. 2 (December 1967): 367–379, and Philip Gleason, *The Conservative Reformers: German-American Catholics and the Social Order* (Notre Dame, IN: University of Notre Dame Press, 1968).

35 For this process of cultural change among Catholics of German descent, see Conzen, "German Catholics in America," 582. For shifts more generally in American Catholicism in the twentieth century, see Orsi, "Center Out There"; Dolan, *In Search of an American Catholicism*, 180–89; James T. Fisher, *Communion of Immigrants: A History of Catholics in America* (New York: Oxford University Press, 2008), 114–33; Timothy Matovina, *Latino Catholicism: Transformation in America's Largest Church* (Princeton, NJ: Princeton University Press, 2011); Kristy Nabhan-Warren, *The Virgin of El Barrio: Marian Apparitions, Catholic Evangelizing, and Mexican American Activism* (New York: New York University Press, 2005); Carl L. Bankston III, "Vietnamese-American Catholicism: Transplanted and Flourishing," *U.S. Catholic Historian* 18, no. 1 (Winter 2000): esp. 45–51. For the 1991 sesquicentennial ethnic dinners at St. Mary's, see Lalor, *Celebrating Thanks!*, 145–46.

3. WISCONSIN MARIANISM AND UPPER MIDWESTERN CATHOLIC CULTURE, 1858–2010

1 "Mary Appeared Thrice in Wisconsin, Bishop Says," *Christian Century*, January 11, 2011, 16; Sister M. Dominica, *The Chapel, Our Lady of Good Help: A Shrine of Mary on the Green Bay Peninsula* (Green Bay, WI: Sisters of St. Francis of Bay

Settlement, 1955); "Strange Story of a Chapel," *Milwaukee Sentinel*, September 4, 1891, 5. For an important interpretation stressing the role of gender, power relations, and clerical authority in the shaping of the narratives surrounding the apparitions to Adèle Brise, see Karen E. Park, "The Negotiation of Authority at a Frontier Marian Apparition Site: Adèle Brise and Our Lady of Good Help," *American Catholic Studies* 123, no. 3 (Fall 2012): 1–26.

2   "Crowds Jam Necedah for Miracle," *La Crosse Tribune*, August 14, 1950, 1; "Church Spokesman Discounts Report of Necedah Miracle," *Madison Capital Times*, August 16, 1950, 6. The "Russia is more powerful than America" quotation is from "Vision Appeared Again Today, Necedah Farm Woman Says," *Madison Capital Times*, August 15, 1950, 6. For the Cold War context and the fullest available analysis of the Necedah, Wisconsin, apparitions, see Thomas A. Kselman and Steven Avella, "Marian Piety and the Cold War in the United States," *Catholic Historical Review* 72, no. 3 (July 1986): 403–24. Another useful discussion of the Necedah apparitions can be found in Sandra L. Zimdars-Swartz, "Religious Experience and Public Cult: The Case of Mary Ann Van Hoof," *Journal of Religion and Health* 28, no. 1 (Spring 1989): 36–57.

3   Quotations are from Kselman and Avella, "Marian Piety and the Cold War," 417, and Steven M. Avella, *In the Richness of the Earth: A History of the Archdiocese of Milwaukee, 1843–1958* (Milwaukee: Marquette University Press, 2002), 724. "100,000 Cram Vision Site," *Madison Wisconsin State Journal*, August 16, 1950, 1, also describes the August 15, 1950, gathering at Van Hoof's Necedah farm as "the largest crowd in rural Wisconsin history."

4   Kselman and Avella, "Marian Piety and the Cold War"; Thomas A. Kselman and Steven Avella, 423–24, intriguingly write, "Our Lady of Guadalupe in Mexico is another example of a Marian shrine that has become a symbol of national independence in the modern world. Our Lady of Necedah represents a failed attempt to establish a similar shrine in the United States."

Mary Ann Van Hoof, *Revelations and Messages as Given through Mary Ann Van Hoof at Necedah, Wisconsin, 1950–1970* (Necedah, WI: For My God and Country, 1971); Leo A. Scheetz, *Necedah: Believe It . . . or Not!* (Necedah, WI: For My God and Country, 1982); "Necedah Shrine," http://en.wikipedia.org. I visited the Necedah shrine in September 2014, and that experience informs some of the characterization here. Detailed descriptions of the shrine can be found in pamphlets available in Queen of the Holy Rosary Mediatrix of Peace Shrine, Miscellaneous Publications, Pam 90–2790, Pamphlet Collection, Wisconsin Historical Society Libraries, Madison. "Religious Services," *Juneau County* (WI) *Star-Times*, December 20, 2018, A15. For the complicated history of the Guadalupe devotion in Mexico and its eventual evolution into an emblem of Mexican national identity, see Jeanette Favrot Peterson, "The Virgin of Guadalupe: Symbol of Conquest or Liberation?," *Art Journal* 51, no. 4 (Winter 1992): 39–47; Timothy Matovina, *Guadalupe and Her Faithful: Latino Catholics in San Antonio, from Colonial Origins to the Present* (Baltimore:

Johns Hopkins University Press, 2005); D. A. Brading, *Mexican Phoenix, Our Lady of Guadalupe: Image and Tradition across Five Centuries* (Cambridge: Cambridge University Press, 2001). For Marianism, gender, and the Mexican American community in recent years, see Kristy Nabhan-Warren, *The Virgin of El Barrio: Marian Apparitions, Catholic Evangelizing, and Mexican American Activism* (New York: New York University Press, 2005); Kristy Nabhan-Warren, "Little Slices of Heaven and Mary's Candy Kisses: Mexican American Women Redefining Feminism and Catholicism," in *The Religious History of American Women: Reimagining the Past*, ed. Catherine A. Brekus (Chapel Hill: University of North Carolina Press, 2007), 294–318. For the origins and belief structure of spiritualism, see Emily Suzanne Clark, *A Luminous Brotherhood: Afro-Creole Spiritualism in Nineteenth-Century New Orleans* (Chapel Hill: University of North Carolina Press, 2016), 6–13. My account and interpretation of the Wisconsin apparitions seeks to respect their "intersubjectivity," avoiding the pitfalls of a "historiography without gods" that Robert A. Orsi argues has imposed distorting and negating discursive and social constructionist models on Catholic and other religious experiences of "presence," that is, of an understanding of religious phenomena as active and real rather than as an "absence," experienced only as symbol, metaphor, discourse, or social relations. Robert A. Orsi, *History and Presence* (Cambridge, MA: Belknap, 2016), esp. 62–65. Important critiques of Orsi's interpretation can be found in Kristy Nabhan-Warren, Adam Park, and Michael Pasquier, review of Robert A. Orsi, *History and Presence* (H-AmRel, H-Net Reviews, November, 2016), www.networks.h-net.org.

5   For a rich analysis of the ways in which Jesuits in the nineteenth-century United States, and their counterparts elsewhere in the world, responded to the emergence of nationalism and the nation-state, see John T. McGreevy, *American Jesuits and the World: How an Embattled Religious Order Made Modern Catholicism Global* (Princeton, NJ: Princeton University Press, 2016). Kselman and Avella, "Marian Piety and the Cold War," 405–9, offer a helpful discussion of the Marian revival in modern Europe and elsewhere, noting the origins of the graces afforded by Marian shrines in premodern peasant cultures with arguably pre-Christian roots in some cases. For the Gallic context of the modern Marian revival, see Thomas A. Kselman, *Miracles and Prophecies in Nineteenth-Century France* (New Brunswick, NJ: Rutgers University Press, 1983); Richard D. E. Burton, *Holy Tears, Holy Blood: Women, Catholicism, and the Culture of Suffering in France, 1840–1970* (Ithaca, NY: Cornell University Press, 2004). For the transatlantic context of the Lourdes devotion in the United States, see John T. McGreevy, "Bronx Miracle," *American Quarterly* 52, no. 3 (September 2000): 413–21. An important overview of apparitions and Marianism in the modern era can be found in Sandra L. Zimdars-Swartz, *Encountering Mary: From La Salette to Medjugorje* (Princeton, NJ: Princeton University Press, 1991). For the transformation of the understanding of the apparitions at Fatima in the context of American Cold War Catholic culture, see Una M. Cadegan, "The Queen of Peace in the Shadow of War: Fatima and U.S. Catholic

Anticommunism," *U.S. Catholic Historian* 22, no. 4 (2004): 1–15. For a thought-ful, thick case study of apparitions in Germany's Saarland in the 1870s, see David Blackbourn, *Marpingen: Apparitions of the Virgin Mary in Bismarckian Germany* (New York: Knopf, 1994). Materialistic interpretations arguing the Marian cult's efficacy for the accumulation of clerical and political power or for assuaging culturally rooted psychological needs can be found in Nicholas Perry and Loreto Echeverria, *Under the Heel of Mary* (New York: Routledge, 1988), and Michael P. Carroll, *The Cult of the Virgin Mary: Psychological Origins* (Princeton, NJ: Princeton University Press, 1986). For an important foundational study of the history of the Marian image, see Marina Warner, *Alone of All Her Sex: The Myth and the Cult of the Virgin Mary* (New York: Knopf, 1976). The American context for the Marian revival, especially the response of U.S. Protestants to the Marian image, is explored in Elizabeth Hayes Alvarez, *The Valiant Woman: The Virgin Mary in 19th-Century American Culture* (Chapel Hill: University of North Carolina Press, 2016). For a Marian devotion with origins in the Gallic Catholic culture of French Ursulines in late eighteenth- and early nineteenth-century New Orleans, see Michael Pasquier, "Our Lady of Prompt Succor: The Search for an American Marian Cult in New Orleans," in *Saints and Their Cults in the Atlantic World*, ed. Margaret Cormack (Columbia: University of South Carolina Press, 2006), 128–49.

6   The history of Wisconsin's Catholicism is masterfully explored in Avella, *In the Richness of the Earth*. Marian cults in various American regions are analyzed in McGreevy, "Bronx Miracle"; Zimdars-Swartz, *Encountering Mary*; Pasquier, "Our Lady of Prompt Succor"; Nabhan-Warren, *Virgin of El Barrio*.

7   "Strange Story of a Chapel," *Weekly Sentinel and Wisconsin Farm Journal* (Milwaukee), September 10, 1891, 2 (reprinted story from *Green Bay Daily Gazette*); "Visions Lead to Pilgrimage," *Milwaukee Journal*, August 3, 1919, 1–2; "Robinsonville Ready to Receive Crowds on Assumption Day; Altar in Open Air," *Milwaukee Journal*, August 13, 1922, 1–3; Most Reverend David Laurin Ricken, D.D., J.C.L., "Decree on the Authenticity of the Apparitions of 1859 at the Shrine of Our Lady of Good Help Diocese of Green Bay" (December 8, 2010). Sister M. Dominica concedes the ambiguity of the exact year but interprets an 1889 letter from Adèle Brise stating, "It was thirty years the 9th of last October, when she appeared for the last time." The Franciscan sister interprets this to mean 1859, a correspondence she finds strengthened by the fact that October 9 occurred on a Sunday in 1859, as this third apparition occurred as Adèle was returning from Mass at Bay Settlement. While Sister M. Dominica's analysis is reasonable, Brise's letter may refer in fact to October of the previous year, making the actual date 1858, which would be consistent with how the date and the anniversary of the apparitions was locally understood and observed at least into the 1920s. Sister M. Dominica, OSF, *The Chapel*, 49. Xavier Martin, a Belgian contemporary of Adèle Brise writing in 1895, also held the year to be 1858, although he gave the date of the apparition as August 15, apparently conflating the date of the apparition with the Bon Secours cult's by then familiar custom of processions at the apparition site on the Feast of the As-

sumption. Xavier Martin, "Belgians of Northeastern Wisconsin," in *Collections of the State Historical Society of Wisconsin*, vol. 13 (Madison: State Historical Society of Wisconsin, 1895), 384–85.

8 Sister M. Dominica, OSF, *The Chapel*, 7–8, which cites "Pauline, Sister. Account of the apparitions as Pauline LaPlant often heard it from the lips of Sister Adèle." Also see the nearly identical account—differing only in stating that the apparitions occurred in 1858 rather than in 1859—reprinted from the *Green Bay Daily Gazette* in "Strange Story of a Chapel," *Milwaukee Sentinel*, September 4, 1891, 5.

9 Sister M. Dominica, OSF, *The Chapel*, 8.

10 Ibid., 8.

11 Ibid., 8–9.

12 Ibid., 9; Park, "Negotiation of Authority," 7.

13 For the history of the Belgian community in northeastern Wisconsin, see Martin, "Belgians of Northeastern Wisconsin," 375–96, quotation is from 378. For church-state relations and Belgian Catholic society in the early to mid-nineteenth century, see Thomas J. Shelley, "Mutual Independence: Church and State in Belgium: 1825–1846," *Journal of Church and State* 32, no. 1 (Winter 1990): 49–64.

14 Sister M. Dominica, OSF, *The Chapel*, 2–7; "Quaint Church in Belgian Colony Near Green Bay Goal of Many Pilgrimages," *Milwaukee Sentinel*, August 14, 1924, 2; Martin, "Belgians of Northeastern Wisconsin," 375–96; Hjalmar Rued Holand, *Wisconsin's Belgian Community* (Sturgeon Bay, WI: Door County Historical Society, 1933). The development of Catholicism in multiethnic antebellum Wisconsin is insightfully treated in Avella, *In the Richness of the Earth*, 8–131.

15 "Robinsonville Ready to Receive Crowds on Assumption Day; Altar in Open Air," *Milwaukee Journal*, August 13, 1922, 1–3. For analysis of the dissemination of an early modern Brabantian Marian cult, see Cordula Van Wyhe, "Reformulating the Cult of Our Lady of Scherpenheuvel: Marie de' Médicis and the Regina Pacis Statue in Cologne (1635–1645)," *Seventeenth Century* 22, no. 1 (Spring 2007): 42–75.

16 Sister M. Dominica, OSF, *The Chapel*, 17–20; "Robinsonville Ready to Receive Crowds on Assumption Day; Altar in Open Air," *Milwaukee Journal*, August 13, 1922, 1–3; Park, "Negotiation of Authority," 14; Martin, "Belgians of Northeastern Wisconsin," 385, 389–90.

17 Sister M. Dominica, OSF, *The Chapel*, 32–35; "Robinsonville Ready to Receive Crowds on Assumption Day; Altar in Open Air," *Milwaukee Journal*, August 13, 1922, 1–3. The late nineteenth-century development of the annual, heavily attended procession at the Bon Secours chapel would seem to reflect continental European models of public devotional practice rather than the private "household of faith" circumscribed by the United States' dominant public culture of Protestantism that is described by scholars Ann Taves, Joseph Chinnici, and Paula Kane in their work on U.S. Catholic devotions. The Upper Midwest, with its heavy concentrations of diverse European Catholic immigrants living in both rural and urban areas, may have displayed devotional patterns that diverged from those in the Northeast, where Irish Catholics lived predominantly in cities. For Kane's im-

portant synthesis that draws on Taves and Chinnici, see Paula M. Kane, "Marian Devotion since 1940: Continuity or Casualty?," in *Habits of Devotion: Catholic Religious Practice in Twentieth-Century America*, ed. James M. O'Toole (Ithaca, NY: Cornell University Press, 2004), 89–129, esp. 92–93; Ann Taves, *The Household of Faith: Roman Catholic Devotions in Mid-Nineteenth-Century America* (Notre Dame, IN: University of Notre Dame Press, 1986); Joseph Chinnici, "Deciphering Religious Practice: Material Culture as Social Code in the Nineteenth Century," *U.S. Catholic Historian* 19, no. 3 (Summer 2001): 1–19.

18 Sister M. Dominica, OSF, *The Chapel*, 23 (quotation). For anti-conscription sentiment and protest among Belgian farmers in Brown County during the Civil War, see Avella, *In the Richness of the Earth*, 120.

19 Sister M. Dominica, OSF, *The Chapel*, 24–26.

20 Kselman and Avella, "Marian Piety and the Cold War," 424.

21 Quotations are from Blackbourn, *Marpingen*, 3–22. See also Kselman, *Miracles and Prophecies*; Orsi, *History and Presence*, 30–31.

22 Sister M. Dominica, OSF, *The Chapel*, 6–7, 9.

23 Ibid., 10 (quotations); Park, "Negotiation of Authority," 3.

24 Sister M. Dominica, OSF, *The Chapel*, 11 (quotations).

25 "Robinsonville Ready to Receive Crowds on Assumption Day; Altar in Open Air," *Milwaukee Journal*, August 13, 1922, 1–3.

26 Martin, "Belgians of Northeastern Wisconsin," 384–85.

27 Sister M. Dominica, OSF, *The Chapel*, 21–22 (quotations from 22); "Quaint Church in Belgian Colony Near Green Bay Goal of Many Pilgrimages," *Milwaukee Sentinel*, August 14, 1924, 1–2.

28 Sister M. Dominica, OSF, *The Chapel*, 23–24.

29 Park, "Negotiation of Authority," 10–11.

30 Ibid., 11.

31 Ibid., 11–15. Important treatments of the La Salette apparition can also be found in Zimdars-Swartz, *Encountering Mary*, 27–43, and Kselman, *Miracles and Prophecies*, esp. 62–68, 174–79.

32 Ibid., 10. Bishop Ricken's official pronouncement of the date of the Robinsonville/Champion apparitions as October 1859, despite the ambiguity of the historical record, also could be construed as part of an effort to construct a connection to the apparitions to Bernadette Soubirous at Lourdes between February and July 1858. If Adèle Brise saw Mary in October 1858, as the nineteenth-century local tradition suggested, it is unlikely that she would have been aware of the Lourdes apparitions, news of which first appeared in the American press only that month, although there remains the possibility that news of Lourdes may have circulated by that time among transatlantic French speakers. Ricken, "Decree on the Authenticity of the Apparitions of 1859"; McGreevy, "Bronx Miracle," 413–21.

33 Martin, "Belgians of Northeastern Wisconsin," 386; Sister M. Dominica, OSF, *The Chapel*, 23–42; "Shrine of Our Lady of Good Help: A Brief Historical Account; Historical Chronology" (Champion, WI: Shrine of Our Lady of Good Help, 2010).

34 "Robinsonville Ready to Receive Crowds on Assumption Day; Altar in Open Air,"
    Milwaukee Journal, August 13, 1922, 1 (quotation).

35 Kselman and Avella, "Marian Piety and the Cold War," 407–11; Kselman, *Miracles
    and Prophecies*; McGreevy, "Bronx Miracle," 413–21; Zimdars-Swartz, *Encounter-
    ing Mary*.

36 Ricken, "Decree on the Authenticity of the Apparitions of 1859."

37 Martin, "Belgians of Northeastern Wisconsin," 385; also quoted in Park, "Negotia-
    tion of Authority," 19.

38 Park, "Negotiation of Authority," 18–19.

39 I am grateful to Steven Avella of Marquette University for this point regarding the
    potential factor of the rural nature of the Green Bay diocese. The Green Bay par-
    ish closures are discussed in "Church Closings in New Orleans Reflect a National
    Trend," *National Catholic Reporter*, April 29, 2008.

40 For an overview of global and American Marianism since World War II, see
    Zimdars-Swartz, *Encountering Mary*, esp. 121 (quotation); Kane, "Marian Devo-
    tion since 1940," 119–26; and, more experientially, Mark Garvey, *Searching for
    Mary: An Exploration of Marian Apparitions across the U.S.* (New York: Penguin,
    1998). I visited the Our Lady of Good Help shrine in September 2014, and that
    visit informs some of the analysis here.

41 Zimdars-Swartz, "Religious Experience and Public Cult," 36–38.

42 Ibid., 40–41; "Necedah," *La Crosse Tribune*, August 15, 1950, 3.

43 Zimdars-Swartz, "Religious Experience and Public Cult," esp. 53 and 57n107.

44 Van Hoof herself had been born to German-speaking parents (her mother had im-
    migrated from Hungary) in Philadelphia in 1909. Her father suffered an accident at
    work in which he severely injured his hand; compensation by his employer enabled
    a brief return to Hungary before the family returned to the United States and moved
    to Kenosha when she was a young child. Van Hoof had apparently married in 1934
    but left the first husband when she learned of his previous marriage and married
    Godfred Van Hoof in 1935. Zimdars-Swartz, "Religious Experience and Public
    Cult," esp. 40; Kselman and Avella, "Marian Piety and the Cold War"; "Necedah,"
    La Crosse Tribune, August 15, 1950, 3; "Reaction on Necedah," *Milwaukee Sentinel*,
    August 17, 1950; *Testimonials of Pilgrims, Queen of the Holy Rosary Mediatrix of
    Peace Shrine, Necedah, Wisconsin, 1950–1966* (Necedah, WI: For My God and Coun-
    try, n.d.); "As Woman Told 100,000 of Her Vision," *Madison Capital Times, Times*,
    August 16, 1950, 6; George A. Hammes, Chancellor of La Crosse Diocese, letter,
    October 26, 1950. For periodic conflict between Poles and non-Polish archdiocesan
    leadership in Milwaukee, see Avella, *In the Richness of the Earth*, 316–42, 441. While
    the La Crosse chancery's concern for the canonical validity of Van Hoof's claims is
    understandable, it was expressed in an idiom highly skeptical of lay and feminine
    experiences of divine presence unmediated by clerical authority.

45 Zimdars-Swartz, "Religious Experience and Public Cult"; Kselman and Avella,
    "Marian Piety and the Cold War." Garvey, *Searching for Mary*, 201–30, has a use-
    ful discussion of the Necedah cult's history, including the period after 1970. For

post–Vatican II "extremist Marian movements," see Kane, "Marian Devotion since 1940," esp. 121–22. For an important discussion of a post–Vatican II local Marian cult in the American South, see Michael Pasquier, "Medugorje in the American South: Our Lady of Tickfaw and the Politics of Devotion," *U.S. Catholic Historian* 24, no. 4 (Fall 2006): 125–48. For a recent journalistic treatment of Necedah and the traditionalistic Catholic fringe in Wisconsin, see "The Devil You Know," *Milwaukee Journal Sentinel*, January 27–March 23, 2019, https://projects.jsonline.com.

4. LA PLACITA AND THE EVOLUTION OF CATHOLIC RELIGIOSITY IN LOS ANGELES

1   "Reina," that is "Queen," was added to the church's title in 1861. Rev. Francis J. Weber, ed., *The Old Plaza Church: A Documentary History* (Los Angeles: Libra Press, 1980), "Owen's Historical Account (1784–1960)," 54. For overviews of Mexican American Catholicism, see Jeffrey M. Burns, *Building the Best: A History of Catholic Parish Life in the Pacific States*, chap. 7, "The Mexican-American Catholic Community," in Jay P. Dolan, ed., *The American Catholic Parish: A History from 1850 to the Present*, vol. 2 (Mahwah, NJ: Paulist Press, 1987), 79–95; Jay P. Dolan and Gilberto M. Hinojosa, eds., *Mexican Americans and the Catholic Church, 1900–1965* (Notre Dame, IN: University of Notre Dame Press, 1994); Timothy Matovina, *Horizons of the Sacred: Mexican Traditions in U.S. Catholicism* (Ithaca, NY: Cornell University Press, 2002); Eduardo C. Fernández, *Mexican-American Catholics* (Mahwah, NJ: Paulist Press, 2007); Mario T. García, *Católicos. Resistance and Affirmation in Chicano Catholic History* (Austin: University of Texas Press, 2008). For key analyses of Mexican American Catholicism, see Timothy Matovina and Gary Riebe Estrella, SVD, eds., *Horizons of the Sacred: Mexican Traditions in U.S. Catholicism* (Ithaca, NY: Cornell University Press, 2002); Luis D. León, *La Llorona's Children: Religion, Life, and Death in the U.S.-Mexican Borderlands* (Berkeley: University of California Press, 2004); Timothy Matovina, *Guadalupe and Her Faithful: Latino Catholics in San Antonio, from Colonial Origins to the Present* (Baltimore: Johns Hopkins University Press, 2005); Kristy Nabhan-Warren, *The Virgin of El Barrio: Marian Apparitions, Catholic Evangelizing, and Mexican American Activism* (New York: New York University Press, 2005); Kristy Nabhan-Warren, "Little Slices of Heaven and Mary's Candy Kisses: Mexican American Women Redefining Feminism and Catholicism," in *The Religious History of American Women: Reimagining the Past*, ed. Catherine A. Brekus (Chapel Hill: University of North Carolina Press, 2007), 294–318. For the larger context of Latino Catholicism, including Mexican American Catholicism, see Jay P. Dolan and Allan Figueroa Deck, eds., *Hispanic Catholic Culture in the U.S.: Issues and Concerns* (Notre Dame, IN: University of Notre Dame Press, 1994); Timothy Matovina, *Latino Catholicism: Transformations in America's Largest Church* (Princeton, NJ: Princeton University Press, 2011).

2   Steven M. Avella, "Region and Religion in California," *U.S. Catholic Historian* 18, no. 3 (Summer 2000): 28–53. San Antonio's San Fernando Cathedral parallels

La Placita in some respects in terms of a lengthy history of Mexican American Catholicism spanning Spanish colonialism, Mexican independence, American annexation, and later waves of Mexican immigration. For the development of Mexican American devotions at San Fernando in the early twentieth century, see Timothy Matovina, "Guadalupan Devotion at San Fernando Cathedral, San Antonio, Texas, 1900–1940," in Matovina and Estrella, *Horizons of the Sacred*, 17–40.

3 Avella, "Region and Religion in California"; Wade Clark Roof, "Religion in the Pacific Region: Demographic Patterns," in *Religion and Public Life in the Pacific Region: Fluid Identities*, ed. Wade Clark Roof and Mark Silk (Walnut Creek, CA: AltaMira Press, 2005), 25–56. Roof finds that Catholics composed 28.7 percent of the Pacific region's (California, Nevada, and Hawaii) population in 2000, the third largest concentration of Catholics in the United States after New England and the Mid-Atlantic, yet within a regional Pacific pattern of "'weak' religious identity" and "low-commitment" to religious congregations. The essential survey of Latino Catholic history is Matovina, *Latino Catholicism*, see esp. viii, 3–6. Matovina, 46, convincingly argues the inadequacy of the Americanization assimilation model based on the experience of European Catholic immigration for understanding the historical and contemporary experience of Latino Catholics, whose encounter with American Catholicism is more accurately characterized as a complex acculturation. The Americanization model also fails to accurately represent the historical experience of European Catholic immigrants such as Italians. For a prominent and influential example of the pronounced neglect of Latino Catholics in American Catholic studies, see John Tracy Ellis's pivotal foundational survey of American Catholic history. Ellis briefly noted the significance of Mexican American Catholics in California and Arizona dioceses, but, essaying mid-twentieth-century demographic shifts, problematically argued that "the entrance of thousands of Puerto Ricans and Mexicans has presented an added anxiety rather than a solution to the Church's problems." John Tracy Ellis, *American Catholicism*, 2nd ed. (Chicago: University of Chicago Press, 1969), 127–28, 165 (quotation).

4 Weber, *Old Plaza Church*, "Preface," ix–viii, "Juan Crespi Bestows Name (1769)," 1–6, "The Pobladores (1781)," 6–9, "Owen's Historical Account (1784–1960)," 22–23, includes quotation.

5 Weber, *Old Plaza Church*, "Preface," vii; "Juan Crespi Bestows Name (1769)," 1–6; "The Pobladores (1781)," 7–9; "Owen's Historical Account (1784–1960)," 23–24, includes quotation. Essential context for race and gender in early Los Angeles can be found in David Samuel Torres-Rouff, *Before L.A.: Race, Space, and Municipal Power in Los Angeles, 1781–1894* (New Haven, CT: Yale University Press, 2013), 18–19, 24–25, and William David Estrada, *The Los Angeles Plaza: Sacred and Contested Space* (Austin: University of Texas Press, 2008), 15–41.

6 Weber, *Old Plaza Church*, "Preface," vii; "Monument to the Missions (1784)," 18–19; "Architectural Observations (1822)," 68–69; "Owen's Historical Account (1784–1960)," 24–29. For information on Joseph Chapman, see "Strange Story of a Church," in ibid., 75–78; Estrada, *Los Angeles Plaza*, 47. For U.S. immigrant

men and their integration into power networks in early nineteenth-century Los Angeles, see Torres-Rouff, *Before L.A.*, 55–65.

7 I am indebted to J. Thomas Owen's 1960 analysis in the *Historical Society of Southern California Quarterly* reprinted in Weber, *Old Plaza Church*, 29–31, for this physical description of the church including the quotations.

8 For a rich discussion of the European, pre-Columbian, and colonial Spanish antecedents and origins of the Los Angeles Plaza, see Estrada, *Los Angeles Plaza*, 41.

9 For overviews of Spanish colonialism and Catholicism in what would become the United States, see James Hennessey, *American Catholics: A History of the Roman Catholic Community in the United States* (New York: Oxford University Press, 1983), 9–22; James T. Fisher, *Communion of Immigrants: A History of Catholics in America* (New York: Oxford University Press, 2008), 1–10. For Spanish colonialism and Catholicism in Florida, see Robert L. Kapitzke, *Religion, Power, and Politics in Colonial St. Augustine* (Gainesville: University Press of Florida, 2001). For colonial New Mexico, see Ramón Arturo Gutiérrez, *When Jesus Came the Corn Mothers Went Away: Marriage, Sexuality, and Power in New Mexico, 1500–1846* (Stanford, CA: Stanford University Press, 1991). For Catholicism in Texas after Texan independence and American annexation, see James Talmadge Moore, *Through Fire and Flood: The Catholic Church in Frontier Texas, 1836–1900* (College Station: Texas A&M University Press, 1993).

10 Hennessey, *American Catholics*, 9–22; Fisher, *Communion of Immigrants*, 1–10. Timothy Matovina persuasively argues that Catholic decline in the Southwest during the Mexican period has been exaggerated by historians asserting a racialist trope of Mexican "decadence." Matovina, *Latino Catholicism*, 19–20.

11 For the debate over the canonization of the spiritual leader of the missions, Fr. Junípero Serra, see James A. Sandos, "Junípero Serra's Canonization and the Historical Record," *American Historical Review* 93, no. 5 (December 1988): 1253–69. For a biography of Serra in full historical context, see Steven W. Hackel, *Junípero Serra: California's Founding Father* (New York: Hill & Wang, 2013); Hackel's assessment of Serra as a complex figure is succinctly expressed in 237–43. For Serra across a range of historical milieus, see Steven W. Hackel, ed., *The Worlds of Junípero Serra: Historical Contexts and Cultural Representations* (Berkeley: University of California Press, 2018). For the larger issue of the nature of indigenous conversions to Catholicism under Spanish colonization in Latin America, see R. Po-Chi Hsia, *The World of Catholic Renewal, 1540–1770*, 2nd. ed. (New York: Cambridge University Press, 2005), chap. 12, "The Iberian Church and Empires," 187–98.

12 For Native peoples and the Spanish mission system in colonial California, see Steven W. Hackel, *Children of Coyote, Missionaries of Saint Francis: Indian-Spanish Relations in Colonial California, 1769–1850* (Chapel Hill: University of North Carolina Press, 2005), 2–3, 236–37, 280–81, 308–34. For the Gabrielino-Tongva indigenous people before and after the founding of the Los Angeles pueblo, see Estrada, *Los Angeles Plaza*, 9, 15–41. For tensions between the Franciscans and Spanish civil authorities in early Los Angeles, see Torres-Rouff, *Before L.A.*, 34.

13 Estrada, *Los Angeles Plaza*, 39–50. For additional key treatments of Los Angeles and California in the Spanish, Mexican, and early American periods, see Miroslava Chávez-García, *Negotiating Conquest: Gender and Power in California, 1770s to 1880s* (Tucson: University of Arizona Press, 2004); Michael J. González, *Exploring the Origins of Mexican Culture in Los Angeles, 1821–1946* (Albuquerque: University of New Mexico Press, 2005); Richard Griswold del Castillo, *The Los Angeles Barrio, 1850–1890: A Social History* (Berkeley: University of California Press, 1979), 1–102; Albert Camarillo, *Chicanos in a Changing Society: From Mexican Pueblos to American Barrios in Santa Barbara and Southern California, 1848–1930* (Cambridge, MA: Harvard University Press, 1979); Douglas Monroy, *Thrown among Strangers: The Making of Mexican Culture in Frontier California* (Berkeley: University of California Press, 1990); Ricardo Romo, *East Los Angeles: History of a Barrio* (Austin: University of Texas Press, 1983). The classic treatment of Los Angeles's and California's evolution after the American conquest is Leonard Pitt, *Decline of the Californios: A Social History of the Spanish-Speaking Californians, 1846–1890* (Berkeley: University of California Press, 1966; repr., 1994).

14 Torres-Rouff, *Before L.A.*, 36–54 (quotation is from 51); Chávez-García, *Negotiating Conquest*, 26–51, esp. 33, and 163–64.

15 Michael E. Engh, SJ, *Frontier Faiths: Church, Temple, and Synagogue in Los Angeles, 1846–1888* (Albuquerque: University of New Mexico Press, 199), 175; Michael J. González, *This Small City Will Be a Mexican Paradise: Exploring the Origins of Mexican Culture in Los Angeles, 1821–1846* (Albuquerque: University of New Mexico Press, 2005), 80–87 (quotation is from 81). For Pío Pico and the Plaza Church, see Estrada, *Los Angeles Plaza*, 45, 49. For the forces shaping institutional Catholicism in the Mexican borderlands including Alta California, which lay within the jurisdiction of the bishop of Sonora until 1840, and the creation of the Diocese of the Californias, which would be seated in 1841 at Santa Barbara, see David J. Weber, "Failure of a Frontier Institution: The Secular Church in the Borderlands under Independent Mexico, 1821–1846," *Western Historical Quarterly* 12, no. 2 (1981): 125–43; Harlan Edward Hogue, "A History of Religion in Southern California: 1846–1880" (Ph.D. diss., Columbia University, 1958), 12–19.

16 Torres-Rouff, *Before L.A.*, 55–132; Estrada, *Los Angeles Plaza*, 52–54. See also Pitt, *Decline of the Californios*, 89–124, and Chávez-García, *Negotiating Conquest*, 3–122. Henry Standage's description of the 1847 Corpus Christi procession around the plaza is quoted in Engh, *Frontier Faiths*, 9–10.

17 *Pioneer Notes from the Diaries of Judge Benjamin Hayes, 1849–1875* (1929; repr., New York: Arno Press, 1976), 71–72. For the "matriarchal core of Latino Catholicism," see Ana María Díaz-Stevens, "The Saving Grace: The Matriarchal Core of Latino Catholicism," *Latino Studies Journal* 4 (September 1993): 60–78, and Matovina, *Latino Catholicism*, 24.

18 For information on the *Los Angeles Star/La Estrella de Los Angeles*, see Estrada, *Los Angeles Plaza*, 64. The August 22, 1857, *Los Angeles Star/La Estrella de Los An-*

geles account of the Assumption fiesta is reprinted in Hogue, "History of Religion in Southern California," 174–75, and Weber, *Old Plaza Church*, "Fiesta Day at Los Angeles" (1857), 101.

19 Torres-Rouff, *Before L.A.*, 103–203. Pitt, *Decline of the Californios*, 185, 218–19, describes the central role of the Plaza Church and analyzes the varying reactions of Newmark and Ramirez to Los Pastores; the quotations from Francisco Ramirez are on 219. For the Harris Newmark quotation on the Plaza Church's bells, see Maurice H. Newmark and Marco R. Newmark, eds., *Sixty Years in Southern California, 1853–1913, Containing the Reminiscences of Harris Newmark* (New York: Knickerbocker Press, 1926), chap. 7.

20 Newmark and Newmark, *Sixty Years in Southern California*, chap. 7.

21 Torres-Rouff, *Before L.A.*, 103–203; quotation is from 108. For the French colony near the Plaza in the nineteenth century, see Estrada, *Los Angeles Plaza*, 61, 95. For the anti-Chinese Massacre of 1871, also see Scott Zesch, *The Chinatown War: Chinese Los Angeles and the Massacre of 1871* (New York: Oxford University Press, 2012); Paul R. Spittzeri, "The Retirement of Judge Lynch: Justice in 1870s Los Angeles" (Ph.D. diss., California State University, Fullerton, 1999), 46–204; Isabella Seong-Leong Quintana, "National Borders, Neighborhood Boundaries: Gender, Space, and Border Formation in Chinese and Mexican Los Angeles, 1871–1938" (Ph.D. diss., University of Michigan, 2010), 32–52; Lawrence E. Guillow, "The Origins of Race Relations in Los Angeles, 1850–1900: A Multiethnic Study" (Ph.D. diss., Arizona State University, 1996), 215–52. The death toll of the anti-Chinese massacre is unclear; I have used the total included in David Samuel Torres-Rouff's thorough account. For religiosity in Los Angeles's nineteenth-century Chinese community, including Taoism, Confucianism, and Protestant missions, see the thoughtful discussion in Engh, *Frontier Faiths*, xii, 122–37.

22 My discussion closely follows Griswold del Castillo's valuable analysis of Mexican American religiosity in *Los Angeles Barrio*, 161–70, and the thoughtful interpretation in Chávez-García, *Negotiating Conquest*, 165–69, as well as the perceptive analysis in Engh, *Frontier Faiths*, 57, 68, 93–94. Fr. Lestrade's first name is given variously depending on the source. For the robbery of Fr. Lestrade's rectory, see Hogue, "History of Religion in Southern California," 169; "Plaza Was Scene of Church Festivals, Bull Fights, and Clashes of Old Armies," *Los Angeles Times*, October 11, 1925, 21; Pitt, *Decline of the Californios*, 220, 227; "Father Peter's Farewell," *Los Angeles Times*, August 24, 1898, 8. For the remodeling of the Plaza Church under Bishop Amat, see Weber, *Old Plaza Church*, "Owen's Historical Account (1784–1960)," 38–48; "'Old Cathedral' of Los Angeles (1859)," 104–5; "Religion in Los Angeles (1946)," 181; "What Happened to the *Plaza* Church?" (1965), 187.

23 Griswold del Castillo, *Los Angeles Barrio*, 161–70; Chávez-García, *Negotiating Conquest*, 165–69; Engh, *Frontier Faiths*, 57, 68, 93–94; Pitt, *Decline of the Californios*, 220, 227. The *Pacific* is quoted on the procession in Hogue, "History of Religion in Southern California," 67. For background on the publication of the *Pacific*, see ibid., 56–59.

24 Griswold del Castillo, *Los Angeles Barrio*, 161–70; Chávez-García, *Negotiating Conquest*, 165–69, including Indian baptism statistics; Rev. Francis J. Weber, *Catholic Footprints in California* (Newhall, CA: Hogarth Press, 1970), 28–32; Rev. Francis J. Weber, *A History of the Archdiocese of Los Angeles and Its Precursor Jurisdictions in Southern California, 1840–2007* (Los Angeles: Archdiocese of Los Angeles, 2006), 60; Weber, *Old Plaza Church*, "Owen's Historical Account (1784–1960)," 49–53; "What Happened to the *Plaza* Church?" (1965), 188–89. Engh, *Frontier Faiths*, 109–10, 161, 174–83; Estrada, *Los Angeles Plaza*, 83–108. Amat later would recruit Irish clergy to Southern California, although this had less implication for the Plaza Church where the clerical profile tended to involve continental Europeans that could speak Spanish in ministry to Mexican Americans. Engh notes that the Daughters of Charity, who were significantly involved in ministry in the diocese, including an orphanage that they had established just off the Plaza in 1856, were more respectful of local Hispanic Catholic traditions and more successful in recruiting Californios into their religious order, albeit in small numbers. In another example of how Amat sought to "Romanize" Southern California's Hispanic-rooted Catholicism, the Catalan bishop also replaced the Mexican madonna patroness of the diocese, Nuestra Señora del Refugio (Our Lady of Refuge), with a third-century martyr, St. Vibiana, whose relics Pope Pius IX had given him with the proviso that a cathedral be built in her honor.

25 Torres-Rouff, *Before L.A.*, 202–68. For gender in the Americanization of Los Angeles, see Chávez-García, *Negotiating Conquest*, 89–173. The mid- to late nineteenth-century emergence of a segregated Mexican American barrio is charted in Griswold del Castillo, *Los Angeles Barrio*, 139–70. For the argument that "no section of the continent was less hospitable to the establishment and maintenance of institutional religion than was southern California" from 1846 until 1880, see Hogue, "History of Religion in Southern California," 1, 204–5, 357. The classic interpretation of the rise of Los Angeles as a major American metropolis in the late nineteenth century and early twentieth, defined by its "ambivalent attitude toward urbanization," is Robert M. Fogelson, *The Fragmented Metropolis: Los Angeles, 1850–1930* (Cambridge, MA: Harvard University Press, 1967). For the "Protestantization" of Los Angeles by the 1870s and 1880s, see Engh, *Frontier Faiths*, xvii, 186–221; Gregory H. Singleton, "Religion in the City of the Angels: American Protestant Culture and Urbanization Los Angeles 1850–1930" (Ph.D. diss., University of California, Los Angeles, 1976). For Protestant Americans' development of a romantic view of Southern California's Catholic Spanish and Mexican past that became an important trope in Los Angeles boosterism and in Angelenos' efforts to create a usable past, see Roberto Ramón Lint Sagarena, *Aztlán and Arcadia: Religion, Ethnicity and the Creation of Place* (New York: New York University Press, 2014), 1–128. For an influential mid-twentieth-century argument that Los Angeles's romanticization of its Spanish mission past belied the city's "non-Catholic" character, see Carey McWilliams, *Southern California Country: An Island on the Land* (New

York: Duell, Sloan & Pearce, 1946), 80–81. For the early twentieth-century Great Migration of Mexicans to Los Angeles, see Douglas Monroy, *Rebirth: Mexican Los Angeles from the Great Migration to the Great Depression* (Berkeley: University of California Press, 1999).

26   Begue de Packman's letter is quoted verbatim in Weber, *Old Plaza Church*, "Ana Begue de Packman Remembers (Early 1890s)," 112–13.

27   Estrada, *Los Angeles Plaza*, 109–32; Fogelson, *Fragmented Metropolis*. For the late nineteenth-century origins of a "Spanish myth" that separated Mexicans, including recent immigrants, from "Spanish" settlers of Los Angeles (who were in fact mixed-race Mexicans), see McWilliams, *Southern California Country*, 278; Estrada, *Los Angeles Plaza*, 98. For the efforts of Ana Begue de Packman and other mid-twentieth-century Los Angeles preservationists to promote an "Anglo birth legend" that whitewashed Los Angeles's multiracial roots, see Estrada, *Los Angeles Plaza*, 247–50. For an extended discussion of *México de afuera* in the Mexican Great Migration, see Monroy, *Rebirth*, esp. 4, 106, and of Mexican Catholic religiosity in early twentieth-century Los Angeles, Monroy, *Rebirth*, esp. 49–56. The lengthy and complex history of the Guadalupe devotion in Mexico is explored in D. A. Brading, *Mexican Phoenix, Our Lady of Guadalupe: Image and Tradition across Five Centuries* (Cambridge: Cambridge University Press, 2001).

28   Estrada, *Los Angeles Plaza*, 109–32.

29   The quotation is from Monroy, *Rebirth*, 54.

30   "Latin Races' Reception," *Los Angeles Times*, May 6, 1903, A6; "Plaza Church to Greet and Speed," *Los Angeles Times*, July 6, 1903, A1.

31   Eileen Wallis, *Earning Power: Women and Work in Los Angeles, 1880–1930* (Reno: University of Nevada Press, 2000), 136–37; "Church Outing, *Los Angeles Times*, August 9, 1908, II1"; "Charity Entertainment: Hundred Children of Industrial Classes to Appear Tonight at the Old Plaza Church," *Los Angeles Times*, November 26, 1908, II6.

32   "Mexican Feast of Guadalupe Celebrated at Plaza Church," *Los Angeles Times*, December 13, 1901, 9; "Touch of Old Days," *Los Angeles Times*, May 15, 1906, II2; "Mexican Independence," *Los Angeles Times*, September 15, 1907, V12.

33   "Camino Real Is Road Again," *Los Angeles Times*, August 6, 1906, II3; *Hoffman's Catholic Directory, Almanac, and Clergy List*, vol. 12, no. 1 (Milwaukee: M. H. Wiltzius, 1897), 343. For El Camino Real and "mission nostalgia" in the nineteenth and early twentieth centuries, see Phoebe S. Kropp, *California Vieja: Culture and Memory in a Modern American Place* (Berkeley: University of California Press, 2006), 47–102.

34   "Restoring Old Plaza Church on Simple Lines of Long Ago," *Los Angeles Times*, May 25, 1907, II2.

35   "A Walk along L.A.'s Claretian Way," *National Catholic Reporter*, February 28, 2003, 14. For the Spanish Claretians' Hispanophilism, see Mario T. García, *Father Luis Olivares, a Biography: Faith Politics and the Origins of the Sanctuary Movement in Los Angeles* (Chapel Hill: University of North Carolina Press, 2018), 79.

36 Estrada, *Los Angeles Plaza*, 126–27, 133–68; "Big Church on Historic Site," *Los Angeles Times*, September 16, 1916, II1.

37 "Fiesta at Old Plaza Church: Ancient Mission Gay with Spain's Colors," *Los Angeles Times*, June 16, 1913, II2; Weber, *Old Plaza Church*, "What Happened to the *Plaza* Church?" (1965), 189.

38 "Plaza Church Members Plan Festival Concert," *Los Angeles Times*, July 9, 1917, II2.

39 "Santa's Belated, Welcomed, Arrival at Old Plaza Church," *Los Angeles Times*, January 1, 1917, II8; "Santa at Plaza Church," *Los Angeles Times*, January 3, 1914, I8; "To Celebrate Novena in Ancient Church Court," *Los Angeles Times*, August 27, 1916, I10. For the Claretian nexus of Spanish-born and -ordained priests serving in Mexico and the American Southwest including Los Angeles, see "Priest Will Celebrate 50th Anniversary of Ordination," *Los Angeles Times*, September 21, 1941, A2.

40 "Plaza Church to Shine Again in Olden Glory," *Los Angeles Times*, June 19, 1921, II1; "Church to Celebrate Dedication," *Los Angeles Times*, December 7, 1922, II1.

41 Estrada, *Los Angeles Plaza*, 169–29; quotation is on 181.

42 Ibid., 169–29; quotation is on 201. Kropp, *California Vieja*, 207–60, quotation is on 252. See also César López, "*El Descanso*: A Comparative History of the Los Angeles Plaza Area and the Shared Racialized Space of the Mexican and Chinese Communities, 1853–1933" (Ph.D. diss., University of California, Berkeley, 2002), 157–61; "Suited to Civic Center: State Engineers Show Plaza Terminal Fits In," *Los Angeles Times*, October 12, 1920, II1.

43 Estrada, *Los Angeles Plaza*, 203–29. For the deportations/repatriations of 1931 and their impact on Los Angeles's Mexican community, see Monroy, *Rebirth*, 147–51, and "Ghosts of a 1931 Raid," *Los Angeles Times*, February 25, 2001.

44 Estrada, *Los Angeles Plaza*, 204–7. For the Plaza Church's role in the 1933 Fiesta, see "Fiesta Marks City Birthday: Plaza Church Scene of Colorful Event," *Los Angeles Times*, September 4, 1933, A1.

45 Marion Parks, *Doors to Yesterday—A Guide to Old Los Angeles* (Los Angeles: Los Fiesteros De La Calle Olvera, 1932), 1.

46 Weber, *Old Plaza Church*, "What Happened to the *Plaza* Church?" (1965), 189.

47 "Plaza Church Doors' Restoration Planned," *Los Angeles Times*, A22, December 29, 1935; "Native Daughters of Southern California to Place Plaque," *Los Angeles Times*, January 26, 1936, D8.

48 "Plaza's Welter of Nations Greet New Year Quietly," *Los Angeles Times*, January 4, 1937, A2.

49 "Thousands Flock to Old Plaza Church for Annual Feast of Corpus Christi," *Los Angeles Times*, June 12, 1939, B.

50 Estrada, *Los Angeles Plaza*, 230–58. A signal treatment of the Zoot Suit Riots remains Mauricio Mazón, *The Zoot-Suit Riots: The Psychology of Symbolic Annihilation* (Austin: University of Texas Press, 1984). For the Sleepy Lagoon case and the Zoot Suit Riots, see also Monroy, *Rebirth*, 262–65, Eduardo Obregón Pagán, *Murder at the Sleepy Lagoon: Zoot Suits, Race, and Riot in Wartime L.A.* (Chapel

Hill: University of North Carolina Press, 2003); Richard Griswold del Castillo, "The Los Angeles 'Zoot Suit Riots' Revisited: Mexican and Latin American Perspectives," *Mexican Studies/Estudios Mexicanos* 16, no. 2 (Summer 2000): 367–91; Elizabeth R. Escobedo, "The Pachuca Panic: Sexual and Cultural Battlegrounds in World War II Los Angeles," *Western Historical Quarterly* 38, no. 2 (Summer 2007): 133–56.

51 See, for example, "Peace Theme of Holy Hour: Archbishop Cantwell Presides at Services Climaxing Church Watch," *Los Angeles Times*, October 28, 1940, 2. For the expansion of predominantly Mexican parishes in the Los Angeles Archdiocese in the first half of the twentieth century and for Latinos and "public Catholicism," see Matovina, *Latino Catholicism*, 32, 190–218.

52 "Catholics to Conduct Solemn Ceremony at Plaza Church," *Los Angeles Times*, June 23, 1943, A2. For the Sacred Heart procession at the Plaza Church in wartime Los Angeles, see also "Catholics to Join a Sacred Event," *Los Angeles Times*, June 21, 1941, A16, and "Colorful Procession Climaxes Ceremony at Plaza Church," *Los Angeles Times*, June 23, 1941, 10, which notes the participation of "Catholic veterans of the American Legion" and "Mexican religious groups and various Holy Name societies."

53 "Pets of Olvera St. Receive Spring Blessing and Food in Colorful Parade and Ceremony at Plaza Church Patio," *Los Angeles Times*, February 25, 1940, A1. See also "Animals to Receive Annual Blessing in the Plaza Tomorrow," *Los Angeles Times*, February 23, 1940, 20; "Animals Get Blessing at Plaza Church Rites," *Los Angeles Times*, April 21, 1946, 14; "Plaza Pastor Gets High Post," *Los Angeles Times*, September 7, 1941, A2. For the Blessing of the Animals at the Plaza Church in the 1950s, when the rite saw similar popularity and cultural reception, see "Animals Receive Easter Blessing at Plaza Church," *Los Angeles Times*, April 13, 1952, A8; "Blessing of Animals at Old Plaza Church," *Los Angeles Times*, April 10, 1955, B. Christine Sterling's role in facilitating the rite of Mexican popular Catholicism for Anglo consumption was particularly evident in 1958, when actor Leo Carrillo jointly presided with Fr. Victor Marin, Olvera Street's well-known burro was blessed, and a *Los Angeles Times* reporter noted that Sterling, executive director of the Pueblo de Los Angeles park, had arranged the "ceremony . . . to help keep California colorful." "Pets by Hundreds Get Blessings at Church," *Los Angeles Times*, April 6, 1958, 23.

54 "Annual Animal Blessing Conducted at Plaza," *Los Angeles Times*, April 6, 1947, 1; "Bendicion de Los Animales Old as Los Angeles," *Los Angeles Times*, March 28, 1948, A1; "Plaza to Hold Annual Blessing Rites," Los Angeles Times, April 13, 1949, A1; "Los Animales Get Padre's Blessing," *Los Angeles Times*, April 17, 1949, A1.

55 "Pageant Staged at Plaza Church," *Los Angeles Times*, April 24, 1943, A1. For interpretation of the Way of the Cross (Via Crucis) in Mexican American and Latino traditions, see Matovina, *Latino Catholicism*, 171–72; Karen Mary Davalos, "'The Real Way of Praying': The Via Crucis, Mexicano Sacred Space, and the Architecture of Domination," in Matovina and Estrella, *Horizons of the Sacred*, 41–68.

56 Estrada, *Los Angeles Plaza*, 230–58; Sterling's quotation is on 245. "Church Service to Celebrate New Plaza Park," *Los Angeles Times*, March 26, 1953, 19; "175th Birthday Celebration of City Planned," *Los Angeles Times*, July 31, 1956, B2; "Old Plaza Church Rites to Open City Birthday," *Los Angeles Times*, August 26, 1956, B15. For urban renewal, freeway construction, and the state park designation for the Plaza in the 1950s, see "Detailed Plan for Preserving of City Plaza Area Presented," *Los Angeles Times*, September 26, 1950, A1; "Progress Is Laying the Plaza Low," *Los Angeles Times*, February 14, 1951, A5; "Plaza State Park Receives Final OK," *Los Angeles Times*, March 25, 1953, A1; "Fiesta Opens First Unit of Plaza Restoration," *Los Angeles Times*, May 14, 1959, B3; "Old Plaza Area Awakes from Prolonged Siesta," *Los Angeles Times*, November 8, 1959. For an overview of Plaza redevelopment schemes from the 1920s through the 1960s, see "Compromise Could Blend Best Points of Two Plaza Plans," *Los Angeles Times*, August 16, 1970, I1.

57 "Miracle of Roses Celebrated: Archbishop Officiates at Old Plaza," *Los Angeles Times*, December 13, 1949, A2.

58 Estrada, *Los Angeles Plaza*, 247–53; for Operation Wetback, see Monroy, *Rebirth*, 265. "Fiesta Opens First Unit of Plaza Restoration," *Los Angeles Times*, May 14, 1959, B3 (includes quotations); "Mrs. Sterling, Plaza Restorer, Dies at 82," *Los Angeles Times*, June 22, 1963, B5.

59 Estrada, *Los Angeles Plaza*, 254–58. For Mexican American Catholics' identification with Kennedy, see García, *Father Luis Olivares*, 124. For Kennedy's visit to Los Angeles on November 1, 1960, see "Kennedy Here Today for Talk, Rallies," *Los Angeles Times*, November 1, 1960, 1; "200,000 Hail Kennedy on Downtown Route," *Los Angeles Times*, November 2, 1960, 1.

60 "Los Angeles Celebrates Name Day at Old Plaza," *Los Angeles Times*, August 3, 1960, B1.

61 Weber, *Old Plaza Church*, "Plaza Church Renovation (1965)," 194.

62 "Catholic Laymen Accept Challenge of Christ," *Los Angeles Times*, March 11, 1962, N4.

63 Weber, *Old Plaza Church*, "Plaza Church Renovation (1965)," 191–94; "Comments about the Restoration (1966)," 195–200, quotation from Robert Bobrow is on 198.

64 "Church 'Restoration' Assailed as Tasteless," *Los Angeles Times*, July 24, 1971, 25.

65 Estrada, *Los Angeles Plaza*, 255–57, 265–66; "17 Miles of Boulevard to the Sunset," *Los Angeles Times*, March 27, 1977, F1.

66 García, *Father Luis Olivares*, 248.

67 "What Began as a Sprinkle Has Turned into a Flood," *Los Angeles Times*, June 11, 1984, D3; García, *Father Luis Olivares*, 391–98. For an ethnographic discussion of the performance of Las Posadas in Los Angeles, including Olvera Street / La Placita, in the 1970s, see Mary MacGregor-Villareal, "Celebrating Las Posadas in Los Angeles," *Western Folklore* 39, no. 2 (April 1980): 71–105.

68 García, *Father Luis Olivares*, 11–14, 37, 47, 57–85, 118–23, 131, 136–42, 146, 152–55.

69 Ibid., 158–79, 182–233

70 Ibid., 234–46.

71 "Ruins of 160-Year-Old Rectory Unearthed," *Los Angeles Times*, July 15, 1981, D1; "Probing Ruins Near Plaza Church," *Los Angeles Times*, July 16, 1981, C2; "Plaza Church Construction Given Approval by Cultural Board," *Los Angeles Times*, July 30, 1981, B15. Quotations are from "Rectory Ruins at L.A. Plaza: Archeology Find Holds Up Project," *Los Angeles Times*, July 16, 1981.

72 García, *Father Luis Olivares*, 394–96.

73 Ibid., 400–409.

74 Ibid., 256–305; "Salvadorans Pray, Fast, Demonstrate at L.A. Church," *Los Angeles Times*, March 7, 1983, I2; "Salvadoran Archbishop on Hand as Church Marks a Year as Sanctuary," *Los Angeles Times*, December 13, 1986, A1.

75 García, *Father Luis Olivares*, 256–305. For Latino sacramentalism and the hemispheric perspective of U.S. Latino Catholics linking the United States with Latin America and La Placita as an example of a "national parish" model of Hispanic ministry in the United States in the post–Vatican II era, see Matovina, *Latino Catholicism*, 31, 38, 40, 51. For the communitarian emphasis of Latino Catholicism, see ibid., 184–86; Roberto S. Goizeta, "The Symbolic World of Mexican American Religion," in Matovina and Estrella, *Horizons of the Sacred*, 120–21. For the dynamic of the "Hispanic poor in a middle class" American Church and the complex relations of Latino immigrants and Euro-Americans in predominantly English-language parishes, see Matovina, *Latino Catholicism*, 58, 246. This passage is influenced by my observation of and participation as worshipper in around a dozen Masses at La Placita from 2000 to 2019.

76 García, *Father Luis Olivares*, 307–29, 373, 381; "Sanctuary Designation to Include Archbishop?," *Los Angeles Times*, November 15, 1985, G1; "Old Plaza Church to Become a Sanctuary," *Los Angeles Times*, December 6, 1985, B1; "Church to Be Sanctuary for Political Refugees," *Los Angeles Times*, December 6, 1985, A6.

77 García, *Father Luis Olivares*, 14–22, 337–58, 432–43; Estrada, *Los Angeles Plaza*, 255–57, 265–66; "Plaza Church Serves as Haven for Illegals Trapped by Amnesty Law," *Los Angeles Times*, June 15, 1988, C1; "Priests Accuse FBI of Plan to Spy on Church," *Los Angeles Times*, April 11, 1990, VCB5; "Pastor Celebrates Controversial Past," *Los Angeles Times*, August 16, 1989, B3; "Church Leaders Ask More Pastors to House Illegals," *Los Angeles Times*, August 24, 1989, A3; "Fund Drive to Keep Alive Priest's Legacy," *Los Angeles Times*, March 22, 1994, B3. For a succinct discussion of Olivares and the Sanctuary Movement, see Rodolfo Acuña, *Anything But Mexican: Chicanos in Contemporary Los Angeles* (London: Verso, 1996), 120. For an analysis of the larger Sanctuary Movement in 1980s Los Angeles, see Norma Stoltz Chinchilla, Nora Hamilton, and James Loucky, "The Sanctuary Movement and Central American Activism in Los Angeles," *Latin American Perspectives*, Issue 169, 36, no. 6 (November 2009): 101–26.

78 "New Pastor Faces Conflicts at Activist Queen of Angels," *Los Angeles Times*, October 16, 1990, A1 (quotations); "Salvadorans' Eviction from Church Stirs Debate," *Los Angeles Times*, December 5, 1990, B3; "Church to Stop Giving Shelter to Homeless," *Los Angeles Times*, January 14, 1991, VYB1.

79 Estrada, *Los Angeles Plaza*, 255–57, 265–66, 443, 450–500; Matovina, *Latino Catholicism*, 71–91.

80 Estrada, *Los Angeles Plaza*, 260–70.

81 "A Walk along L.A.'s Claretian Way," "Parish of La Placita is a 'Pentecost' Community," *National Catholic Reporter*, February 28, 2003, 15 (Gallo quotation); "L.A. Church in Forefront of Sanctuary Movement," *Los Angeles Times*, March 23, 2007; "Gimme Shelter: Immigrants Facing Deportation Find Shelter with the New Sanctuary Movement," *Nation*, February 7, 2008; "Latinos and Religion: Separated Brothers," *Economist*, July 16, 2009; "Evicted but Defiant, Occupy LA Faces Crisis Moment," *Christian Science Monitor*, November 30, 2011, www.csmonitor.com; "When His Religion No Longer Matched His Moral Beliefs," *Los Angeles Times*, January 30, 2015; "The Long Road to Los Angeles," *Occidental Weekly*, January 1, 2016, www.theoccidentalweekly.com; Jenna M. Lloyd and Andrew Burridge, "La Gran Marcha: Anti-racism and Immigrants' Rights in Southern California," *ACME: An International E-Journal for Critical Geographies* 6, no. 1 (2007): 1–35.

82 Adolfo Guzman-Lopez, "News and Analysis, Preach," KCET, May 20, 2010, www.kcet.org; "LA Names Street after Priest Olivares," *Daily Breeze*, May 20, 2010, www.dailybreeze.com.

83 "A Century of Serving the Disenfranchised," *Los Angeles Times*, May 30, 2010.

84 "The Claretians USA Return La Placita," Radio Claret America, August 6, 2015, http://radioclaretamerica.com.

5. HOLY CROSS ON WEST FORTY-SECOND AND THE TRANSFORMATION OF NEW YORK CITY'S IRISH AMERICAN CATHOLICISM

1 Emmett Larkin, "The Devotional Revolution in Ireland, 1850–1875," *American Historical Review* 77, no. 3 (June 1972): 625–52.

2 Andrew Walsh and Mark Silk, eds., *Religion and Public Life in New England: Steady Habits, Changing Slowly* (Walnut Creek, CA: AltaMira Press, 2004); James T. Fisher, "Catholicism in the Middle Atlantic," in *Religion and Public Life in the Middle Atlantic Region: The Fount of Diversity*, ed. Randall Balmer and Mark Silk (Walnut Creek, CA: AltaMira Press, 2006), 71–93.

3 James T. Fisher, *Communion of Immigrants: A History of Catholics in America* (New York: Oxford University Press, 2008), 14–15; Thomas J. Shelley, *The Archdiocese of New York: The Bicentennial History, 1808–2008* (Strasbourg: Editions du Signe, 2007), 23, 25. The best treatment of Catholicism and anti-Catholicism in early New York is Jason K. Duncan, *Citizens or Papists? The Politics of Anti-Catholicism in New York, 1685–1821* (New York: Fordham University Press, 2005).

4 Fisher, *Communion of Immigrants*, 15–24; John Tracy Ellis, *American Catholicism*, 2nd ed. (Chicago: University of Chicago Press, 1969), 21–28; *Catholic Colonial Maryland: A Sketch* (Milwaukee: Bruce, 1931); Thomas W. Spalding, *The Premier See: A History of the Archdiocese of Baltimore, 1789–1989* (Baltimore: Johns Hopkins University Press, 1989); Antoinette Patricia Sutto, *Loyal Protestants and Dangerous Papists: Maryland and the Politics of Religion in the English Atlantic,*

1630-1690 (Charlottesville: University of Virginia Press, 2015); Thomas Murphy, *Jesuit Slaveholding in Maryland, 1717-1838* (New York: Routledge, 2001); Thomas R. Ulshafer, PSS, "Slavery and the Early Sulpician Community in Maryland," *U.S. Catholic Historian* 37, no. 2 (Spring 2019), 1–21.

5 Shelley, *Archdiocese of New York*, 25–30; James Hennessey, *American Catholics: A History of the Roman Catholic Community in the United States* (New York: Oxford University Press, 1983), 52–54; James M. O'Toole, *The Faithful* (Cambridge, MA: Harvard University Press, 2008), 11–49; Duncan, *Citizens or Papists?*, 30–80, 119–32.

6 Shelley, *Archdiocese of New York*, 38–43, 70–72; Duncan, *Citizens or Papists?*, 167–72; Anne Hartfield, "Profile of a Pluralistic Parish: St. Peter's Roman Catholic Church, New York City, 1785–1815," *Journal of American Ethnic History* 12, no. 3 (Spring 1993): 30–59; "Canonizing a Slave: Saint or Uncle Tom?," *New York Times*, February 23, 1992 (includes quotation). For a sympathetic recent biography of Pierre Toussaint, see Arthur Jones, *Pierre Toussaint: A Biography* (New York: Doubleday, 2003).

7 Shelley, *Archdiocese of New York*, 44–55; Hennessey, *American Catholics*, 90–91; Maxwell Bloomfield, "William Sampson and the Codifiers: The Roots of American Legal Reform, 1820–1830," *American Journal of Legal History* 11, no. 3 (1967): 234–52.

8 Shelley, *Archdiocese of New York*, 56–98; Jay P. Dolan, *The Immigrant Church: New York's Irish and German Catholics, 1815–1865* (1975; repr., Notre Dame, IN: University of Notre Dame Press, 1983), 11–86, 136.

9 Shelley, *Archdiocese of New York*, 72; Judith Metz, "The Founding Circle of Elizabeth Seton's Sisters of Charity," *U.S. Catholic Historian* 14, no. 1 (Winter 1996): 19–33; Margaret M. McGuinness, *Called to Serve: A History of Nuns in America* (New York: New York University Press, 2013), 29–31 (quotations).

10 Shelley, *Archdiocese of New York*, 108–12; O'Toole, *Faithful*, 53–64; John Loughery, *Dagger John: Archbishop John Hughes and the Making of Irish America* (Ithaca, NY: Three Hills, Cornell University Press, 2018), 22–91, 103–6, 118, 144–45, 261; quotation, 24. The U.S. bishops' meeting in Baltimore in October 1829 had previously urged the end of lay trustee control of property and recruitment of priests, asserting that such arrangements undermined church authority.

11 Shelley, *Archdiocese of New York*, 112–30; Loughery, *Dagger John*, 121–38, 156–60, 164–65, 212–13, 217–19, 347.

12 Shelley, *Archdiocese of New York*, 64, 137, 139; Loughery, *Dagger John*, 184–89. For tensions between Irish and Germans at St. Alphonsus Parish in antebellum New York City and the creation of national parishes as a solution, see Jay P. Dolan, "Immigrants in the City: New York's Irish and German Catholics," *Church History* 41, no. 3 (September 1972): 354–68, esp. 360, 362.

13 Annabel Jane Wharton, "The Baptistery of the Holy Sepulchre in Jerusalem and the Politics of Sacred Landscape," *Dumbarton Oaks Papers* 46 (1992): 323–24.

14 *1852-1927 Diamond Jubilee of Holy Cross Church* (New York, 1927), 3; Rev. Michael Corrigan, "Register of the Clergy Laboring in the Archdiocese of New York from

Early Missionary Times to 1885," in United States Catholic Historical Society, *Historical Records and Studies* 4, nos. 1–2 (October 1906): 96–97; "Benevolent Lares' Fare," *Irish American Weekly*, December 24, 1853, 3; "The Church of the Holy Cross," *Irish American Weekly*, December 16, 1854, 4; John Gilmary Shea, *The Catholic Churches of New York City with Sketches of Their History and Lives of Their Present Pastors* (New York: L.G. Goulding, 1878), 327–28.

15 Rev. John T. Conway, *Holy Cross Church on West Forty-Second Street 1852–1952* (New York, 1952), 42. I am grateful to Thomas J. Shelley for his thoughts on the context of the appointment of Fr. Lutz. Email conversation with the author, November 21, 2013.

16 For the predominance of a transient, transnational clergy that moved frequently among dioceses in the nineteenth-century American Church, including in New York, see Shelley, *Archdiocese of New York*, 74–77.

17 Corrigan, "Register of the Clergy," 96–97; Rev. F. G. Holweck, "The Language Question in the Old Cathedral of St. Louis," *St. Louis Catholic Historical Review* 2, no. 1 (January 1920): 6–17; John F. Kempker, "Catholic Missionaries in the Early and in the Territorial Days of Iowa," *Annals of Iowa* 10, no. 1 (April 1911): 54–62. Lutz's final assignment was also in a non-German parish. In 1855, Lutz was transferred from Holy Cross to Immaculate Conception on East Fourteenth Street, where he served as assistant until his death in 1861.

18 Shea, *Catholic Churches of New York*, 328–29; "The Church of the Holy Cross," *Irish American Weekly*, December 16, 1854, 4; Joseph George Jr., "Very Rev. Dr. Patrick E. Moriarty, O.S.A., Philadelphia's Fenian Spokesman," *Pennsylvania History* 48, no. 3 (July 1981):2–15. For Archbishop John Hughes's differences with Bishop James Wood over the Fenians (and Hughes's own shifting views), see Loughery, *Dagger John*, 305–7.

19 Shea, *Catholic Churches of New York*, 329.

20 *1852–1927 Diamond Jubilee of Holy Cross Church*, 13.

21 Shea, *Catholic Churches of New York*, 328–29.

22 "Roman Catholic Schools in New York: Their Origin and Importance," *Irish American Weekly*, January 30, 1857, 1.

23 Jay P. Dolan, *The Irish Americans: A History* (New York: Bloomsburg, 2010), 108–11. For overviews of the history of Irish Catholicism, see Daniel Rops, *The Miracle of Ireland*, trans. Earl of Wicklow (Baltimore: Helicon Press, 1959); Patrick J. Corish, *The Irish Catholic Experience: A Historical Survey* (Wilmington, DE: Michael Glazier, 1985); Lawrence J. Glazier, *Occasions of Faith: An Anthropology of Irish Catholics* (Philadelphia: University of Pennsylvania Press, 1995). For Catholicism in early modern Ireland, see Patrick J. Corish, *The Catholic Community in the Seventeenth and Eighteenth Centuries* (Dublin: Helicon Limited, 1981); Oliver P. Lafferty, *Catholicism in Ulster, 1603–1983: An Interpretative History* (Columbia: University of South Carolina Press, 1994). For Catholicism in nineteenth-century Ireland in the pre-famine and post-famine eras, see James A. Reynolds, *The Catholic Emancipation Crisis in Ireland, 1823–1829*

(New Haven, CT: Yale University Press, 1954); S. J. Connolly, *Priests and People in Pre-Famine Ireland, 1780–1845* (Dublin: Gill and Macmillan, 1982); Desmond Keenan, *The Catholic Church in Nineteenth-Century Ireland: A Sociological Study* (Dublin: Gill and Macmillan, 1983); Larkin, "Devotional Revolution in Ireland"; Emmett Larkin, *The Making of the Roman Catholic Church in Ireland, 1850–1860* (Chapel Hill: University of North Carolina Press, 1980); Emmett Larkin, *The Historical Dimensions of Irish Catholicism* (Washington, DC: Catholic University of America Press, 1984); Emmett Larkin, *The Consolidation of the Roman Catholic Church in Ireland, 1860–1870* (Chapel Hill: University of North Carolina Press, 1987).

24 Dolan, *Irish Americans*, 108; Dolan, *Immigrant Church*, 45–67; "Rules and Regulations of the Church of Holy Cross," 11, in Holy Cross Parish File, Pastor Charles McCready, AANY; "Regulations for Lent: Diocese of New York," *Irish American Weekly*, February 28, 1857, 4. For the Feast of the Immaculate Conception at Holy Cross, see "Religious Services," *New York Herald*, December 10, 1866, 8. For listings of funeral Masses for Irish-surnamed parishioners at Holy Cross in the late 1860s, see, for example, "Murray," *New York Times*, January 30, 1867, 5; "Coulter," *New York Times*, October 5, 1867, 5. Baptismal Register, 1852–58, Holy Cross Church Rectory, New York; O'Toole, *Faithful*, 82–83.

25 Henry J. Browne, *The Parish of St. Michael 1857–1957: A Century of Grace on the West Side* (New York: Church of St. Michael, 1957), 7; I am grateful to Thomas J. Shelley for this source. Loughery, *Dagger John*, 327.

26 Herbert Asbury, *The Gangs of New York: An Informal History of the Underworld* (1927; repr., New York: Thunder's Mouth Press, 2001), 137; Albon P. Man Jr., "The Church and the New York Draft Riots of 1863," *Records of the American Catholic Historical Society of Philadelphia* 62, no. 1 (March 1951): 46; Loughery, *Dagger John*, 1–21, 31, 123–26, 138, 162–63, 290–91, 295–337, 343. Although he was a Protestant Whig (and eventually Republican), two decades before Seward had supported public funding for parochial schools in New York and forged a working relationship with Hughes, whom Seward had convinced Lincoln to designate as an emissary to France and the Vatican (successfully averting their recognition of the Confederacy) earlier in the war. For the larger context of the Draft Riots, Irish Catholic racism, and Irish Catholic racial violence, see Iver Bernstein, *The New York City Draft Riots: Their Significance for American Society and Politics in the Age of the Civil War* (New York: Oxford University Press, 1990); David R. Roediger, *The Wages of Whiteness: The Making of the American Working Class*, 2nd ed. (New York: Verso, 1997), esp. 133–63; Michael J. Pfeifer, "The Northern United States and the Genesis of Racial Lynching: The Lynching of African-Americans in the Civil War Era," *Journal of American History* 97, no. 3 (December 2010): 621–35. For a useful overview of Catholic opposition to Lincoln during the war, see Frank L. Clement, "Catholics as Copperheads during the Civil War," *Catholic Historical Review* 80, no. 1 (January 1994): 36–57.

27 For a summary of Catholic sermons in New York on the Draft Riots, see Man, "Church and the New York Draft Riots," 48–49. Also see *New York Herald*, July 20, 27, 1863; *New York Tribune*, July 20, 1863.

28 For Donnelly's sermon, see "St. Michael's Catholic Church," *New York Tribune*, July 20, 1863, 1.

29 Edwin G. Burrows and Mike Wallace, *Gotham: A History of New York City to 1898* (New York: Oxford University Press, 1998), 1004–6.

30 "Effects of the Storm," *New York Times*, June 19, 1867, 8.

31 "Church of the Holy Cross," *Irish American Weekly*, April 6, 1872, 5; Shea, *Catholic Churches of New York*, 334. For a detailed description of the functioning of the "Church Debt Paying Association" at Sacred Heart Parish on West Fifty-First Street, an Irish parish that was organized in 1876, carving away northern blocks of what had been Holy Cross territory, with Irish-born Martin J. Brophy, formerly an assistant priest at Holy Cross as rector, see Henry J. Browne, *One Stop above Hell's Kitchen: Sacred Heart Parish in Clinton* (South Hackensack, NJ: Custom Book, 1977), 15. I am grateful to Thomas J. Shelley for this reference. The classic work on the milieu of the Irish immigrant in the nineteenth-century United States is Kerby A. Miller, *Emigrants and Exiles: Ireland and the Irish Exodus to North America* (New York: Oxford University Press, 1985).

32 Shea, *Catholic Churches of New York*, 330.

33 S. J. Donleavy, "Right Reverend Monsignor Charles McCready," *Journal of the American Irish Historical Society* 14 (1915): 340–42; "Monsignor Charles McCready Biographical File," AANY.

34 "For the Home Rule Cause," *New York Times*, November 11, 1890, 5. For the nineteenth-century transformation of St. Patrick's Day celebrations and the creation of an Irish American national consciousness, see Kenneth Moss, "St. Patrick's Day Celebrations and the Formation of Irish-American Identity, 1845–1875," *Journal of Social History* 29, no. 1 (1995): 125–48.

35 "Justice O'Gorman Honored," *New York Times*, February 4, 1903, 9; "Emmett's Memory Honored," *New York Times*, September 21, 1903, 7.

36 "Rioting in Armagh," *New York Times*, July 25, 1904, 7; "200,000 Children in Church Jubilee," *New York Times*, April 28, 1908, 3.

37 Robert Emmett Curran, "The McGlynn Affair and the Shaping of the New Conservatism in American Catholicism, 1866–1894," *Catholic Historical Review* 66, no. 2 (April 1980): 184–204; *The Catholic Church in the United States of America: Undertaken to Celebrate the Jubilee of His Holiness, Pope Pius X* (New York: Catholic Editing, 1914), 329–30; Sylvester L. Malone, *Dr. Edward McGlynn* (New York: Dr. McGlynn Monument Association, 1918), 1; *Golden Jubilee of Holy Cross Church* (New York, 1902), 18–20, 22; "He Will Not Go to Rome," *New York Times*, January 9, 1887, 1; "No Notice of M'Glynn," *New York Times*, July 17, 1887; "Mgr. M'Cready Dead, Mgr. McMahon Dying," *New York Times*, April 10, 1915.

38 Curran, "McGlynn Affair"; Anthony D. Andreassi, "'The Cunning Leader of a Dangerous Clique?' The Burtsell Affair and Archbishop Michael Augustine Cor-

rigan," *Catholic Historical Review* 86, no. 4 (2000): 620–39. For the larger struggle between the conservative and the Americanist blocs in the late nineteenth century, see Joseph P. Chinnici, *Living Stones: The History and Structure of Catholic Spiritual Life in the United States* (New York: Macmillan, 1989), 119–33; Patrick W. Carey, *Catholics in America: A History* (Westport, CT: Praeger, 2004), 119–33; James R. Barrett and David R. Roediger, "The Irish and the 'Americanization' of the 'New Immigrants' in the Streets and in the Churches of the Urban United States, 1900–1930," *Journal of American Ethnic History* 24, no. 4 (2005): 3–33.

39 Curran, "McGlynn Affair," including quotations, 190; Andreassi, "'Cunning Leader'"; *Golden Jubilee of Holy Cross Church* (New York, 1902), 26–27; "He Will Not Go to Rome," *New York Times*, January 9, 1887, 1; "No Notice of M'Glynn," *New York Times*, July 17, 1887. For McGlynn's social views in theological context, see Patrick W. Carey, ed., *American Catholic Religious Thought: The Shaping of a Theological and Social Tradition* (New York: Paulist Press, 1987), 220–41.

40 Curran, "McGlynn Affair"; "Dr. M'Glynn to Say Mass in New York," *New York Times*, December 23, 1894, 1; "Dr. M'Glynn's Christmas: His First Mass in Seven Years in New-York Archdiocese," *New York Times*, December 26, 1894, 1; "Dr. M'Glynn's Letters: He Gives the Correspondence That Led to His Restoration," *New York Times*, September 28, 1895, 2; "Father M'Glynn Is Dead," *New York Times*, January 8, 1900.

41 Curran, "McGlynn Affair." For the growing influence of the papacy over American Catholic culture in the "immigrant church" of the late nineteenth century and a discussion of *Rerum Novarum*, see O'Toole, *Faithful*, 131–37, 143.

42 O'Toole, *Faithful*, 102–3; Browne, *Parish of St. Michael*, 1–8.

43 *Golden Jubilee of Holy Cross Church*, 26; Rev. Charles McCready to Archbishop Michael Corrigan, November 1, 1893, AANY; Rev. Charles McCready to Archbishop Michael Corrigan, April 5, 1894, AANY; Rev. Charles McCready to Rev. Malick A. Cunnion, November 1, 1900, AANY.

44 Browne, *One Stop above Hell's Kitchen*, 5–6, 31–33; "Aiding St. Benedict's Church: The Success of the Fair for the New Colored Congregation," *New York Times*, February 27, 1884, 2; Manhattan Community Board Four, "Re: 342 West 53rd Street St. Benedict the Moor Church" (June 11, 2019), www1.nyc.gov. For the nexus of parish, neighborhood, ethnicity, and race in the "immigrant church," see John T. McGreevy, *Parish Boundaries: The Catholic Encounter with Race in the Twentieth-Century Urban North* (Chicago: University of Chicago Press, 1996), 7–53. For the interaction of the Irish, the "new immigrants," and African Americans in the late nineteenth- and early twentieth-century urban United States, see Barrett and Roediger, "Irish and the 'Americanization' of the 'New Immigrants.'"

45 "Francis Patrick Duffy," in *New Catholic Encyclopedia*, 1093, Fr. Francis Duffy File, AANY; Miller, *Emigrants and Exiles*, 542–43; "Calls Father Duffy Ideal Parish Priest," *New York Times*, November 17, 1927, 4. Duffy's career as a theology professor at Dunwoodie Seminary and his role as an editor of the *New York Review* are considered in Thomas J. Shelley, "Never a Monsignor: Father Francis Patrick

Duffy" (address, Alumni Association of St. Joseph's Seminary, November 11, 2004), 5 for Duffy and Farley quotations, Fr. Francis Duffy File, AANY; Thomas J. Shelley, "'What the Hell Is an Encyclical?' Governor Alfred E. Smith, Charles C. Marshall, Esq., and Father Francis P. Duffy," *U.S. Catholic Historian* 15, no. 2 (1997): 92–94, 105; Rev. James Gilhooley, "Father Duffy: Priest with a Tin Hat," *America*, March 24, 1984, 204–7. Duffy destroyed his papers before he died in 1932, making it difficult to reconstruct aspects of his life and career. For an admiring biography that draws on firsthand accounts but ignores Duffy's work with the *New York Review*, see Ella M. Flick, *Chaplain Duffy of the Sixty-Ninth Regiment, New York* (Philadelphia: Dolphin Press, 1935). For the key role of Irish nationalism in the 69th Regiment's contribution to the Union Army in the Civil War, see Susannah Ural Bruce, "'Remember Your Country and Keep up Its Credit': Irish Volunteers and the Union Army, 1861–1865," *Journal of Military History* 69, no. 2 (2005): 331–59.

46 "Laud Father Duffy, 25 Years a Priest: Prominent Men of All Creeds Join in Great Celebration," *New York Times*, December 5, 1921, 11. For Alexander Wolcott's quotation on Father Duffy, see Flick, *Chaplain Duffy*, 173–74. For the late nineteenth-century rise in the understanding of American Catholic priests as social workers, see O'Toole, *Faithful*, 128.

47 Conway, *Holy Cross Church*, 24–25. The fullest treatment of New York's Irish waterfront, of which Hell's Kitchen formed the northern end, is James T. Fisher, *On the Irish Waterfront: The Crusader, the Movie, and the Soul of the Port of New York* (Ithaca, NY: Cornell University Press, 2009).

48 For the crucial trajectory of American anti-Catholicism in the antebellum era, see Jenny Franchot, *Roads to Rome: The Antebellum Protestant Encounter with Catholicism* (Berkeley: University of California Press, 1992). For analysis of the pivotal "conversation" between Protestant and Catholic America in the nineteenth century, see Jon Gjerde, *Catholicism and the Shaping of Nineteenth-Century America*, ed. S. Deborah Kang (New York: Cambridge University Press, 2012), quotation is from 7.

49 For analyses of Al Smith's political career, including the issue of his Catholicism in the 1928 presidential campaign, see Donn C. Neal, *The World beyond the Hudson: Alfred E. Smith and National Politics, 1918–1928* (New York: Garland, 1983); Robert A. Slayton, *Empire Statesman: The Rise and Redemption of Al Smith* (New York: Simon & Schuster, 2001); Christopher M. Finan, *Alfred E. Smith: The Happy Warrior* (New York: Hill & Wang, 2002). Al Smith kept what amounted to a voluminous file of anti-Catholic materials that were sent to him throughout his political career, often by political supporters seeking to alert him to anti-Catholic publications and activity in their locales. The extensive collection of anti-Catholic materials in his papers illustrates the strength of anti-Catholicism in the United States in 1920s and 1930s. Governor Alfred E. Smith Public and Private Papers, New York State Library, Albany, NY.

50 Charles C. Marshall, "An Open Letter to the Honorable Alfred E. Smith," *Atlantic Monthly* 139 (April 1927): 540–49.

51 Shelley, "'What the Hell Is an Encyclical?'"; "Catholic and Patriot: Governor Smith Replies," *Atlantic Monthly* 139 (May 1927): 721–28.

52 Shelley, "'What the Hell Is an Encyclical?,'" quotations from 104, 107.

53 Finan, *Alfred E. Smith*, 229–30; Slayton, *Empire Statesman*, 322–26.

54 "The Current Week: Dinner in Honor of the Rev. Father Joseph C. McCaffrey," *New York Times*, January 31, 1926; "Msgr. Joseph McCaffrey Dies: Warred on Smut Peddlers Here," *New York Times*, August 23, 1970; Conway, *Holy Cross Church*, 27–29; James P. Morrison, "The Bishop of Times Square," *Holy Name Journal*, January 1942, 8–9, Msgr. Joseph McCaffrey File, AANY. Jesuit waterfront labor priest Pete Corridan, brilliantly analyzed by James T. Fisher in *On the Irish Waterfront*, is in some ways an interesting counterpoint to McCaffrey, indicating that Irish American clergy seeking to inspire "Catholic Action" could take on both right-wing and left-wing inflections in New York City in the middle decades of the twentieth century.

55 Jay P. Dolan, *The American Catholic Experience: A History from Colonial Times to the Present* (Garden City, NY: Doubleday, 1985), 358, 384; Robert Orsi, "The Center Out There, in Here, and Everywhere Else: The Nature of Pilgrimage to the Shrine of Saint Jude, 1929–1965," *Journal of Social History* 25, no. 2 (1991): 217–25. For Father Coughlin, see Alan Brinkley, *Voices of Protest: Huey Long, Father Coughlin, and the Great Depression* (New York: Knopf, 1982); David H. Bennett, *The Party of Fear: From Nativist Movements to the New Right in American History* (New York: Vintage, 1988), 254–66; "U.S. Entry in War Is Laid to Money," *New York Times*, February 23, 1936 (McCaffrey quotations); Patrick J. Kelley, Secretary, American Citizens Committee, Brooklyn, to Rev. Joseph McCaffrey, March 22, 1939, in Msgr. Joseph McCaffrey File, AANY (quotations).

56 Morrison, "Bishop of Times Square," 8–9; interview with Ed Reigadas, Holy Cross Rectory, Manhattan, November 2, 2019. For views of the suffering of the ill and disabled in twentieth-century American Catholicism, see Robert Orsi, *Between Heaven and Hell: The Religious Worlds People Make and the Scholars Who Study Them* (Princeton, NJ: Princeton University Press, 2005), 18–47.

57 American Catholic anticommunism is considered in M. J. Heale, *American Anticommunism: Combating the Enemy Within, 1830–1970* (Baltimore: Johns Hopkins University Press, 1990), 172–73.

58 "Radical Students Scored: Their Behavior at City College Is Termed Insult to Taxpayers," *New York Times*, June 14, 1937, 13.

59 "Catholic Schools Held Curbs on Reds," *New York Times*, September 14, 1936, 15 (quotations).

60 Heale, *American Anticommunism*, 172–73. "Monsignor McCaffrey Retires after Thirty Years," *New York Police Magazine*, May 1954; Murray Kempton, "He Wept," *New York Post*, October 1953, Msgr. Joseph McCaffrey File, AANY (quotations).

McCaffrey had been made a monsignor in 1941. "Clergymen Here Honored by Pope," *New York Times*, October 25, 1941, 15.

61 John D'Emilio and Estelle B. Freedman, *Intimate Matters: A History of Sexuality in America*, 2nd ed. (Chicago: University of Chicago Press, 1999), 275–300; "The Bishop of Times Square," *Sunday Mirror Magazine*, October 15, 1939, in Msgr. Joseph McCaffrey File, AANY; "Burlesque Scored in New Affidavits," *New York Times*, March 22, 1942; "Lewd Book Sales Scored by Priest," *New York Times*, January 6, 1957, 6 (quotation); "Priest Denounces Smut in Times Square: McCaffrey Lays It to 'Broad-Minded Judges,'" *New York Times*, May 6, 1963, 32 (quotation).

62 Morrison, "Bishop of Times Square," 9, Msgr. Joseph McCaffrey File, AANY.

63 For the significant postwar Puerto Rican migration to New York City and an argument that the New York Archdiocese made limited efforts to accommodate Puerto Rican Catholics, see Jaime R. Vidal, "The American Church and the Puerto Rican People," *U.S. Catholic Historian* 9 (Winter–Spring 1990): 119–35. For a polemical overview of the rise of violent crime after 1965, including in New York City, see Barry Latzer, *The Rise and Fall of Violent Crime in America* (New York: Encounter Books, 2016).

64 "Priest Hits 'Coddling' at Youth's Funeral," Religious New Service, September 3, 1959; "Gang Violence Is Deplored by Msgr. Jos. A. McCaffrey," September 5, 1959, Msgr. Joseph McCaffrey File, AANY; "Wagner Will Add 1,080 Policemen to Fill Out Force," *New York Times*, September 3, 1959, 1.

65 "Msgr. McCaffrey, 'Bishop of Times Square,' Is Retiring," *New York Times*, June 29, 1968, 17.

66 "Civilian Review Foes Back Buckley's Bid," *New York Post*, October 28, 1965, 22; Thomas F. Heneghan, Vice Chancellor, to Right Reverend Monsignor Joseph A. McCaffrey, December 15, 1965; Rev. Joseph A. McCaffrey to Rt. Rev. Thomas F. Henegan, December 17, 1965; Msgr. Joseph McCaffrey File, AANY. William F. Buckley's classic account of his candidacy in the 1965 New York City mayoral race is *The Unmaking of a Mayor* (New York: Viking, 1966).

67 "Msgr. McCaffrey, 'Bishop of Times Square,' Is Retiring," *New York Times*, June 29, 1968, 17.

68 "Pre-Civil War Church Is Being Redecorated," *New York Times*, August 16, 1960, 60.

69 For the New Right, see Bennett, *Party of Fear*, 332–408. From the perspective of the early twenty-first century, Bennett was overly sanguine when he argued in 1988 that the emergence of the New Right of the 1970s and 1980s showed that "antialien themes" would no longer be key to rightist movements in the United States. The classic analysis of white ethnics, including their Catholic-inflected consciousness, in the latter twentieth century is Michael Novak, *The Rise of the Unmeltable Ethnics* (New York: Macmillan, 1972). For the reaction of white ethnic Catholics against the Civil Rights Movement and integration in the urban North, see McGreevy, *Parish Boundaries*.

70 "R.G. Rappleyea, 66, Pastor Emeritus Dies," *New York Times*, August 11, 1991, 41. In 1991, a New Jersey priest, John Bambrick, accused Fr. Anthony Eremito, copastor of Holy Cross, of sexually abusing him when he was a teenager. Archdiocesan authorities removed Eremito from assignments in the New York Archdiocese, but he would serve as a priest in New Jersey and Texas before losing his priestly faculties in 2002. Eremito's extensive ministry as a priest in multiple dioceses after his removal from Holy Cross reveals the laxity with which church authorities treated allegations of abuse before the *Boston Globe* published a comprehensive investigation of clerical sexual abuse in 2002. "Priest Who Saw Abuse From Other Side Becomes Watchdog," *New York Times*, July 7, 2002. For Fr. Peter Colapietro, Holy Cross pastor from 1995 to 2013, see "Last Call for the Saloon Priest," *New York Times*, June 23, 2013.

EPILOGUE

1 "Longtime Peace Activist Jesuit Fr. Bill Bichsel Dies at Age 86," *National Catholic Reporter*, March 3, 2015. This paragraph includes reflection on my experience as the faculty advisor for the Radical Catholics for Justice and Peace from its founding in fall 1999 through my departure from the Evergreen State College in June 2006.

2 Patricia O'Connell Killen, "The Geography of a Minority Religion: Catholicism in the Pacific Northwest," *U.S. Catholic Historian* 18, no. 3 (2000): 51–57; *St. Michael's Parish, Olympia, Washington, 1875–1975: 100 Years in the Seattle Archdiocese* (Olympia, WA: Tumwater Printing and Graphic Arts, 1976).

3 The classic treatment of the tension between Catholicism and American culture in American Catholic identity is Jay P. Dolan, *In Search of an American Catholicism: A History of Religion and Culture in Tension* (New York: Oxford University Press, 2003). "The Bishops and Religious Liberty," *Commonweal*, May 30, 2012.

4 Barbara A. Perry, "Catholics and the Supreme Court: From the 'Catholic Seat' to the New Majority," in *Catholics and Politics: The Dynamic Tension Between State and Power*, ed. Kristin E. Heyer, Mark J. Rozell, and Michael A. Genovese (Washington, DC: Georgetown University Press, 2008), 155–74; "Why Do Catholics Hold a Strong Majority on the Supreme Court?," CNN, July 10, 2018, www.cnn.com. For Catholicism and American conservatism from the mid-twentieth through the early twenty-first centuries, see Betty Clermont, *The Neo-Catholics: Implementing Christian Nationalism in America* (Atlanta: Clarity Press, 2009).

5 John Tracy Ellis, *American Catholicism*, 2nd ed. (Chicago: University of Chicago Press, 1969); Pew Research Center, "How the Faithful Voted," November 10, 2008, www.pewforum.org; Pew Research Center, "How the Faithful Voted: 2012 Preliminary Analysis," November 7, 2012, www.pewforum.org; Pew Research Center, "How the Faithful Voted: A Preliminary 2016 Analysis," November 9, 2016, www.pewresearch.org; "New Data Suggest Clinton, Not Trump, Won Catholic Vote," *America: The Jesuit Review*, April 6, 2017, www.americamagazine.org; "As Trump Visits Iowa, He'll Find Dramatically Altered Dubuque County Political Land-

scape," *Des Moines Register*, July 25, 2018; "Your Rabbi? Probably a Democrat. Your Baptist Pastor? Probably a Republican. Your Priest. Who Knows," *New York Times*, June 12, 2017. Mark Silk and Andrew Walsh noted a rise in evangelical Protestants in Wisconsin to 24 percent in 2010, with Catholics at 29 percent and mainline Protestants at 24 percent, helping to explain the rightward shift of the Badger State's politics in the early twenty-first century even as white Catholics swung between Democrats and Republicans. Mark Silk and Andrew Walsh, eds., *One Nation, Divisible: How Regional Religious Differences Shape American Politics* (Lanham, MD: Rowman & Littlefield, 2008), 228.

6 "Catholic Priest Says He Denied Joe Biden Communion at Mass in South Carolina Because of Abortion Views," *USA Today*, October 29, 2019; "Looking Past Roe, Can 'Pro-Life' Democrats Still Find Home in Party?," *Christian Science Monitor*, February 4, 2020.

7 "Poll Finds Many U.S. Catholics Breaking with Church over Contraception, Abortion and L.G.B.T. Rights," *America: The Jesuit Review*, September 28, 2016, www.americamagazine.org; Pew Research Center, "In U.S., Decline of Christianity Continues at Rapid Pace," October 17, 2019, www.pewforum.org.

8 Timothy Matovina, *Latino Catholicism: Transformations in America's Largest Church* (Princeton, NJ: Princeton University Press, 2011), 30–31; David W. Machawek, "New Players and New Patterns," in *Religion and Public Life in the Pacific Region: Fluid Identities*, ed. Wade Clark Roof and Mark Silk (Walnut Creek, CA: AltaMira Press, 2005), 92; Carl Bankston III, "Vietnamese-American Catholicism: Transplanted and Flourishing," *U.S. Catholic Historian* 18, no. 1 (2000): 36–53.

9 Paul Gifford, "Some Recent Developments in African Christianity," *African Affairs* 93, no. 373 (1994): 513–34.

10 Jaime R. Vidal, "The American Church and the Puerto Rican People," *U.S. Catholic Historian* 9 (Winter–Spring 1990): 129–35.

11 James M. O'Toole, *The Faithful* (Cambridge, MA: Harvard University Press, 2008), 94–144; Matovina, *Latino Catholicism*, 54.

INDEX

Alemany, Joseph Sadoc, 104–105
Alito, Samuel, 167
Alvarado, Maria Ignacia, 99
Alvarado, Xavier, 94
Amat, Taddeus, 105–107, 210n24
American annexation: of California, 7, 92, 100
Americanization model of US Catholic history, 8, 177–178n1, 206n3
anticlericalism, 3, 22, 39, 78, 82–83, 85–86, 109–110
anti-Catholicism: in academia, 11; in American public culture, 152–156, 222n49; in the American South, 156; in colonial America, 132–134; and nativism, 66, 136
anticommunism, 33, 77–78, 90, 157–160
Arzube, Juan, 123
Asare-Dankwah, John, 54
Assumption, Feast of the, 61, 77, 82, 101–102
Assumption Parish, Manhattan, 149
Avella, Steven, 82

Bambrick, John, 225n70
Bardstown, Kentucky, 133
Barlow, Philip, 192n3
Baudier, Roger, 41
Begue de Packman, Ana, 108, 211n27
Behrman, Martin, 31–33, 36
Benedict XVI, 165, 169
Benedictine monks, 74
Benoit, Jill, 56, 58
Bezou, Henry, 32, 37, 39, 45–46, 49

Bichsel, Bill, 165
Bieber, Elizabeth, 89
Bismarck, Otto von, 73
Blackbourn, David, 83
Blenk, James Hubert Herbert, 28–29, 32, 35
Blessing of the Animals (*Benedicion de los Animales*) ritual, 116–117, 213n53
Blessed Sacrament Parish, New Orleans, 29, 184n32, 190n98
Bobrow, Robert, 120
Boucree, Harold and Olympia, 43, 48, 56–58
Brise, Adèle, 6, 77, 79–81, 83–91, 200n7, 203n32
Brise, Lambert, 80–81
Brise, Marie, 81
Brophy, Martin J., 220n31
Brown Scare, 111–112
Brown v. Board of Education, 44
Buckley, William F., 162
Busch, Joseph, 74
Bush, George W., 168
Bushnell, Alexander, 65

Caballeria, Juan, 110–111
Cabeza de Vaca, Álvar Núñez, 96
Cahensly, Peter Paul, 197n32
Caillouet, Louis Philip, 41
Caillouet, Lucien Joseph, 41–42, 45–47, 59
Calvert, Cecil, 132
Capuchins, 21, 23, 134
Cárdenas, Lázaro 39
Carrillo, Leo, 213n53

Protestantism (*cont.*)
in Louisiana, 13, 16, 21, 60; in the
Lower Midwestern U.S., 61, 192n3,
196n26; and Mexican Americans,
106, 111–112; in the Pacific Northwest,
165–166; and the second Ku Klux
Klan, 153; and the social gospel, 146; in
Southern California, 7, 92–93, 102; and
support for Senator Joseph McCarthy's
anticommunism, 160; in the Upper
Midwestern U.S., 192n3, 225–226n5
Province of the Sisters of Charity, 15

Race: and Catholic slaveholding in
Maryland, 133; and Mexicans in Los
Angeles, 103–104, 108, 110–111, 113–119,
125–126, 170–171, 210n24, 215n75; and
white Catholics and African Americans in New Orleans, 3–5, 13–60, 151,
170–171, 184n33, 187n60, 191n110; and
white Catholics and African Ameri-
cans and Latinx in New York City, 131,
134, 142–144, 149–151, 156, 161–163, 167,
170–171
Radical Catholics for Justice and Peace,
165–166
Raho, Bernardo, 104–105
Ramirez, Francisco P., 102, 106
Ramírez, José Antonio, 95
religious sisters, 10–11, 13, 15, 21–22, 28–29,
33, 41, 46, 50–51, 58, 69, 72, 77, 84, 86,
136, 172, 184n33, 210n24
Rerum Novarum (1891), 149
Rice, Martin, 71
Ricken, David, 6, 77, 79, 85–88, 203n32
Rivas y Damas, Arturo, 125
Roberts, John, 167
Roe v. Wade (1973), 166
Romero, Oscar, 124–125
Roosevelt, Franklin D., 38, 156–157
Rosati, Joseph, 139
Ryan, John, 155
Rubio, Gonzales, 104

Ruiz, Antonio, 105
Rummel, Joseph F., 38, 41–42, 44–45

Sacred Heart of Jesus devotion, 65, 142
Sacred Heart Parish, Manhattan, 149,
220n31
Sampson, William, 135
Sanctuary Movement, 7, 126, 128
San Fernando Cathedral, San Antonio,
Texas, 205–206n2
San Gabriel Mission, 93–95, 97, 127
Sarría, Vicente, 94
Satolli, Francesco, 9, 148–149
St. Anthony Church, Florence, South
Carolina, 169
St. Anthony's Church, Davenport, 65
St. Anthony Claret, 111
St. Augustine, Florida, 95
St. Augustine Parish, New Orleans, 22,
24, 55
St. Basil's Catholic Church, Los Angeles,
123
St. Benedict the Moor Parish, Manhat-
tan, 150
St. Brigid's Parish, Manhattan, 140
St. Clare's Parish, Manhattan, 151
St. Clemens Mary Parish, Manhattan, 151
St. Elizabeth Ann Seton, 135–136
St. Francis of Assisi Parish, Manhattan,
149
St. Francis of Assisi Parish, New Orleans,
38
St. Francis Xavier Church, Iowa City,
68–71
St. Henry Parish, New Orleans, 55,
190n98
St. Joan of Arc (St. Dominic) Parish, New
Orleans, 29, 190n98
St. John the Baptist Parish, Manhattan,
140, 149, 163
St. John the Baptish Parish, Waunakee,
Wisconsin, 74
St. Joseph's Parish, Gretna, Louisiana, 38

ABOUT THE AUTHOR

Michael J. Pfeifer is Professor of History at John Jay College of Criminal Justice and the CUNY Graduate Center. A native of Middleton, Wisconsin, he is the author or editor of six books and numerous articles that explore the regional and transnational contexts of American social history.

Some primary
focus on parish
Synthetic –
teaching book –
diversity of church historically : too simple
    to pit libs vs conservs.
Succinct, richly drawn
immigrant church
institutions, Clergy – little on laity.
    broad overview leaves no space for individs

define 'transnatl' ?

transnatl : devotion to Lourdes, Eur priests early
segregation to integration 1960s –
bl maj c 1970, 1st bl priest 1975 → African liturgies
African priest, Nigerian runs Ghanaian, Tanzanian
closed 2006 – merged –
primary, secondary